PRAISE FOR "ROADMAP TO EXPORT SUCCESS"

Over his decades in trade and exporting, Maurice Kogon has been doing anything but sitting still. This guide does a great job of distilling some of the key lessons Maurice has not only developed but has put into practice to guide companies into becoming successful exporters.

— *Kevin Klowden, Executive Director, Milken Institute Center for Regional Economics and California Center*

* * *

This is one of the very best business-oriented guides to exporting I have seen. Maurice clearly understands the subject matter, and his book guides the reader through the export process explaining step-by-step what it takes to succeed as an exporter. I highly recommend it.

— *Robert Erwin, Director, Export-U.com*

* * *

Written in a very practical, effective and interactive manner, this book is a must read for entrepreneurs, SMEs and business consultants contemplating or involved in international expansion via exporting.

— *Anatoly Zhuplev, Professor, International Business & Entrepreneurship & Chair, Department of Management, Loyola Marymount University, Los Angeles*

The amount of intricate knowledge that Maurice casually imparts on anyone he works with is invaluable to their success. Maurice's ability to dissect and solve issues facing exporters is a testament to his lifetime dedication to international trade. His inclusion of this knowledge in a practical and useful book as *Roadmap to Export Success* will move you past the obstacles of exporting and into the export process. This book has offered me both the courage and the tools to venture into international markets.

— Simona Racek, International Expansion Advisor, Los Angeles SBDC and California International Trade Center; President, Women In International Trade, Orange County Chapter

* * *

I am impressed with the scope and the depth of *Roadmap to Export Success*, which serves as a practical guide to a small company seeking to sell in overseas markets. The book follows a logical progression of topics that leads a company through the important stages to launch an export initiative without the jargon, acronyms, and academic theory that characterizes so many of these export guides. I highly recommend this book for serious practitioners—both new and existing exporters.

— Martin Brill, Program Manager, International Trade, Kutztown University SBDC

ROADMAP TO EXPORT SUCCESS

TAKE YOUR COMPANY FROM LOCAL TO GLOBAL

MAURICE KOGON

www.tradecomplianceinstitute.org

Printed in USA

ISBN Paperback 978-0-578-85186-0

ISBN Ebook 978-0-578-85187-7

CONTENTS

APPENDICES

ABOUT THE AUTHOR

Maurice Kogon, founder of Kogon Trade Consulting (KTC), has spent nearly 60 years in the international business field as a U.S. Government official, business executive, educator, and consultant. Currently, as KTC President, Maurice devotes most of his time to pro-bono export mentoring, guest-lecturing, serving on the NASBITE International and other advisory boards, and maintaining the Trade Information Database[1], an extensive free database of international trade information and tools on his International Trade Compliance Institute Website[2]. In

2017, Maurice teamed up with the Milken Institute to direct New-to-Export (NTE) 101-LA[3], a step-by-step program to enable non-exporting manufacturers to start and expand exports.

Maurice's U.S. government career spanned over 33 years (1961-94) with the U.S. Department of Commerce (USDOC) in Washington, DC, where he oversaw many of the agency's strategic planning, trade information, and export assistance services. While at USDOC, Maurice was also tapped to develop and manage the Worldwide Information & Trade System (WITS), an early precursor of today's Trade.gov. In 2001, Maurice moved to Torrance, California to direct the El Camino College Center for International Trade Development (2001-13).

Throughout his career, Maurice has written and lectured extensively on international trade and has developed numerous Web-based export tools, including this guide and **Exporting Basics**[4], **Export FAQs**[5], and **Export Readiness Assessment System**[6]. He has a BA and MA in Foreign Affairs from George Washington University. He has taught international business courses at Cal State University Northridge, George Washington University, and Virginia Tech, and continues to guest-lecture at local universities and for Port of Los Angeles trade training programs. He has consulted for U.S. and international clients, including the Egyptian Government and the UN's International Trade Centre in Geneva.

Maurice is a past President of NASBITE (2008-09), has served for many years as a NASBITE Board member, and helped to develop NASBITE's Certified Global Business Professional (CGBP) credential and national exam. He was honored in 2013 as the recipient of NASBITE's John Otis Lifetime Achievement Award.

INTRODUCTION

When I first got into the export assistance field nearly 60 years ago, I was struck by a truly puzzling phenomenon. Over 75% of American manufacturers did not export, even though the U.S. had the world's largest economy and was by far the world's largest manufacturer and exporter. Sadly, in the more than half-century since, we have the same 75% ratio of non-exporting manufacturers. Not all, but many of these 75% non-exporting manufacturers have the potential to export, especially those with already strong domestic track records. If they have survived and succeeded in the world's most competitive market, our own, essentially against the same competition they would face as exporters, they should be able to compete anywhere.

As noted in my 2011 testimony before the House Committee on Small Business[1], this is our national export paradox—"We are a very large exporting nation, but not a nation of exporters." Why is it that so many U.S. manufacturers sell solely to the U.S. market, with less than 5% of the world's population, when they potentially could make much more money by also exporting to the nearly 200 countries outside the U.S., with 95% of the world's population? To try to encourage more non-exporters to overcome their resistance and give exporting a try, I decided to write this guide as a companion to my Exporting Basics[2],

Export FAQs[3], and Export Readiness Assessment System[4]. While this guide focuses initially on start-up exporters, it also addresses needs of both new-and existing exporters to diversify and expand their export markets

Chapter 1—Is Exporting for Me?, is for new-to-export (NTE) firms thinking about exporting as a new revenue stream, but aren't sure if it's for them. It deals with why exporting might make sense in their situation; how exporting is both similar to and different from selling domestically; and the benefits, costs and risks of exporting. This chapter also addresses the myths and excuses that deter more companies from exporting at all or to their full potential.

Chapter 2—Five Stages of Export Development, is for NTEs willing to give exporting a try, but want to know what lies ahead if they take the plunge. It lays out five sequential stages they'll need to advance through to get from their start point of not exporting to the end point of successful exporting, and what they'll need to know and be able to do at each stage.

Chapter 3—Special Needs of New Exporters, is for NTEs who now understand the stages that lie ahead as they start their export developmental process, but don't yet know what specific help they'll likely need at each stage. It lays out 27 such needs that uniquely confront NTEs, and identifies the types and sources of help that address each need.

Chapter 4—Build Export Capacity, is for NTEs ready to start Stage 1 of the process—develop a capacity to export they don't yet have. It covers how to assess the export potential of their products and the export readiness of their company; and where they can get the help they'll need along the way—especially free-or low-cost export advice, training and assistance.

Chapter 5—Find and Enter Best Export Markets, is for newly-ready exporters looking for their first target markets, as well as existing exporters looking for additional promising markets. It covers how to differentiate better from lesser markets; and how best to distribute, price, promote, and adapt to each promising new market (market entry strategy).

Chapter 6—Make Export Sales and Get Paid, is for new and existing exporters beginning to attract foreign inquiries and orders in target markets and need to know how best to convert them into actual export sales. It covers how to respond to inquiries; quote prices; vet potential buyers and distributors; negotiate the terms of sale (price, credit, delivery); select payment options; and protect against buyer default.

Chapter 7—Comply with Regulatory and Documentary Requirements, is for new and existing exporters that have closed the deal and now need to assure compliance with any applicable trade regulations or documentary requirements. It covers U.S. requirements to export the product (e.g., U.S. export controls for national security or health and safety purposes); as well as foreign tariff and non-tariff barriers to import the product. It also covers the host of shipping and other documents commonly required at both ends.

Chapter 8—Prepare Goods for Delivery, is for new and existing exporters that have the regulatory approvals and documents needed at both ends, and are ready to prepare the goods for delivery. It describes how the goods need to be packaged, marked and labeled to protect them from damage in transit and to assure that the packaging materials themselves are not contaminated (e.g., pests) and will not harm the environment.

Chapter 9—Deliver the Export Goods, is for new and existing exporters that are now ready for the final step to get the goods from here to there. It covers how to insure the cargo against damage or loss in transit and the transport modes available to transport the goods to their final destination.

This Guide has links to many external Web resources—e.g., names of organizations and programs, laws and regulations, terminology, etc. —to amplify points made. They are marked with superscripts in numerical order on their respective pages and consolidated with url addresses in the Index to Linked Resources at the end of this book. Because links can change or go bad over time, try looking for a replacement link on the site or for comparable information. In any case, please feel free to contact me at mkogon@socal.rr.com for an updated link (or for anything else about exporting).

For more information and trade resources, please visit www. tradecomplianceinstitute.org.

CHAPTER 1

IS EXPORTING FOR ME?

1A. What Is Exporting?

An export, for our purposes in this book, occurs when you sell a product or service to a buyer in another country (e.g., from the U.S. to Mexico). Let's say, for example, the U.S. product is lipstick or the service is Web design. It counts as an export as soon as it's sold to the buyer in Mexico (or to any other country). It doesn't matter if you are the original producer or a middleman making the sale, it's still an export.

* * *

1B. A Huge World Market Awaits Exporters

Did you know that the U.S. is a world leader in manufacturing and exporting, but that only 1% of all U.S. businesses export, and only 25% of all U.S. manufacturers export? Not only that. Over half of the 25% of the exporting manufacturers sell only to two countries—Canada and Mexico—not to any of the nearly 200 other countries in the world. This abysmally low ratio of U.S. non-exporters to exporters is hard to fathom, given that the U.S. has only 5% of the world's consumers and only 15% of the world's purchasing power. That's right. The rest of the world has 95% of the world's consumers and 85% of the world's purchasing power. Let's assume you are mainly in business to make more money. If so, does it make sense to limit your sales to only 5% of your potential customers, when you could be selling to 95% more potential customers in 190+ other countries? Why forfeit that huge potential to increase your sales and profits? Put another way, "What are you thinking?"

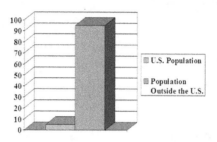

There's no doubt that many more of the non-exporters have the potential to export, especially those with already strong domestic track records and nationwide distribution. If they've survived and succeeded in the U.S., the world's most competitive market—against the same competition they would face as exporters—they could likely compete anywhere. They just haven't tried, or perhaps they tried but gave up too soon.

* * *

1C. Myths About Exporting

Many prior studies have examined why so few U.S. manufacturers export, the factors responsible, and the needs that must be met to increase exporter involvement. These studies have generally found that the non-exporters lack motivation, interest or confidence, stemming from:

- Misconceptions—I'm too small, can't afford it, can't compete, too complicated, too risky.
- Fear—of the unknown, of regulations, of not getting paid, of IPR risks, of legal liability.
- Ignorance—of their export potential, of the benefits, of the steps and procedures.

Let's take a deeper look at the reasons given for not exporting—or more accurately, the excuses—causing so many to miss out on huge opportunities to increase sales and profits.

"I'm too small to export; only large firms with name recognition, ample resources, and export departments can export successfully."

False! Smallness of the company is not the barrier to exporting, any more than it's a barrier to selling in the U.S. In fact, over 95% of the U.S. firms that do export are small businesses. Many have fewer than 20 employees and annual sales in the $1-10 million range. It's true that large firms typically account for far more total exports by value (over 85% in the U.S.), but small firms dominate the exporting population in the U.S. and most other countries. The real issue here is not the size of the company, but whether its product has export potential. Does the company (of whatever size) have a **product** that someone overseas may want? If enough buyers in the U.S. want it, you can be sure that enough buyers in the much larger world market will also want it.

"I can't afford to export; I don't have the money to hire people, market myself abroad, or expand production if I get new export business."

Not true! There are low-cost ways to market and promote abroad and finance new export orders. These don't require hiring new staff or setting up an export department. The Internet and Social Media offer low-cost ways to reach potential customers worldwide, as well as to conduct international market research. At little or no cost, for example, you can pull up relevant trade statistics; assess potential best markets; promote your company and products worldwide; and find specific leads to buy or distribute your products. Free-or low-cost personalized help is also available from federal, state and local trade assistance organizations. They typically offer one-on-one export counseling, export workshops, and market research and matchmaking services. If you need financing for export purposes, the U.S. Small Business Administration (SBA)[1] or the U.S. Export-Import Bank (Exim)[2] can help with loan guarantees.

"I can't compete overseas; my products are unknown, and my prices are probably too high for foreign markets."

Not likely. You may not realize it, but when you sell in the domestic U.S. market, you're already competing against the very same foreign competitors you'll face in foreign markets. Why? Because the U.S is a huge importer, and much of your competition in the U.S. is probably from imports. If you can compete successfully against them here with your current pricing, you can likely compete against them anywhere. The world is large, with varied needs and interests. If your product is bought domestically, it might well be wanted and affordable somewhere else in the world. What makes your product sell in the home market can help it sell abroad. Price is important, but it's not the only selling point. Other competitive factors are need for the product, utility, quality, service, credit, consumer taste—these may override price. In any case, don't automatically assume your price is uncompetitive. Your products could still be a bargain in strong-currency countries, even after adding overseas delivery costs and import duties.

"Exporting is too risky; I might not get paid. My intellectual property might get ripped off. I might break a law I didn't know about."

Not necessarily! Selling anywhere has risks, even here at home, but they can be reduced with common-sense due diligence. If your major fear is not getting paid, you can protect against foreign-buyer default in several ways. One is to use a bank-backed Letter of Credit (L/C) as the method of payment. Another is to purchase very low-cost export credit insurance that guarantees payment should the buyer default (see

4

Chapter 6D on payment methods and **6E** on protections against default). To avoid possible scams, check references through the Internet, your bank, or an international credit reporting agency. If you have a patent, trademark or copyright, there are ways to protect it overseas as you do here. While trade laws vary by country, most are straightforward and non-threatening (see **Chapter 7B** on foreign regulatory compliance). For advice and help with contracts, protecting intellectual property, etc., consult a lawyer specializing in international trade.

"Exporting is too complicated; I don't know how."

Complexities, yes, but you don't need to be the one to demystify them. You can use outside experts to deal with the complications, including freight forwarders, commercial banks, and overseas agents and distributors. Between them, they can represent you, find overseas customers, present you with sales orders, handle all the export paperwork, assure you get paid, and deliver the goods. You fill the orders and get paid for the sale. If export business warrants, hire your own expert. Or, become more knowledgeable yourself. Personalized "how-to" counseling is available at no cost from many local trade assistance organizations. Export workshops and online export tutorials are other ways to learn at modest cost. Once you learn more and gain confidence, you can better decide how much to do yourself and how much to rely on export support services.

"I'm too busy with the domestic market to think about exporting."

That may appear understandable, given the seemingly large U.S. market, but it's a very shortsighted view generally and a nonsensical view in a recessed economy. What if you have a seasonal product (e.g., ski equipment)? When the U.S. winter season ends, winter is just starting in other countries. If your high tech product becomes obsolete in the U.S., you modernize here, but the older technology will still have demand in many less-developed countries. If a U.S. recession cuts domestic demand for your product, other countries might still be booming. Rather than idle your capacity or lay off workers, look for export opportunities in these other countries. The "too busy" claim is basically saying, "I don't have time for and am not interested in the additional sales that exports could bring." Let's put that to the test. If a new sales order came from another State, say from Pennsylvania instead of Mexico, would you also say "No, I'm too busy for the new Pennsylvania customer?" Not likely. More likely, the "too busy" retort masks the other fear-and-ignorance excuses for not exporting.

* * *

1D. Exporting Compared with Domestic Marketing

Many non-exporters falsely assume that exporting is so much different from domestic selling that they couldn't possibly adjust. Actually, domestic selling and exporting are alike in many ways. If you simply apply to exporting what you're already familiar with domestically, you can then learn to deal with the differences and do well as an exporter.

Similarities of Exporting to Domestic Selling. Exporting, like domestic selling, is basic marketing first and foremost.

- If the product or service for export is the same that you sell domestically, you already know what's good about it and would tout it similarly to a foreign audience.
- If you sell domestically to a particular racial, religious, cultural, ethnic, or linguistic niche, you will find a comparable niche in any number of other countries.
- If your domestic product is seasonal, you can sell it to countries with coinciding seasons or, better yet, whose seasons start when yours ends.
- If you already conduct market research domestically, you could apply the same familiar techniques to size-up and assess potential foreign markets.
- The strategies and techniques you use to distribute, price, and promote your products domestically, including social media promotion and eCommerce sales, will likely make sense in export markets, or could be readily adapted as needed.

6

- You could respond to inquiries and RFQs from foreign customers in the same way as domestically, adjusting as needed for translation and added transportation costs.
- The price, credit-and delivery terms you negotiate with domestic customers could also apply to export customers, although you would use more due diligence and an export payment method that assures you get paid.
- If your product is already compliant with any domestic health, safety or other regulations, it would likely also satisfy comparable foreign regulations, making it easier to obtain any needed permits or certifications.
- If you ship to your domestic customers by truck, rail, air or vessel, these are the same methods you would use to ship to some or most foreign countries.

Dissimilarities of Exporting to Domestic Selling. Despite the many similarities to help ease the transition to exporting, there are also important differences. You'll need to take them into account, but don't worry, help is available from many sources to facilitate the adjustment (see **Chapter 4D** for sources of help). Here are the main dissimilarities:

Exports are still traditionally channeled through agents or distributors, notwithstanding the steady increase in direct eCommerce sales to end-users. Consider these intermediaries as assets for you, not extra layers. They know the market and have contacts with the end-users. As your representatives in the market, they develop and send you sales orders, arrange for payment, prepare required import documents, and clear the delivered goods through customs. Many are equipped to stock, install and service the goods. The end-users know and prefer to deal with them, rather than buy direct from you or other foreign suppliers. See **Chapter 5G** for more on finding qualified agents or distributors to represent you abroad.

Exports involve an exchange of foreign currency into your preferred currency. For example, a Mexican importer has pesos, but you want to be paid in U.S. dollars. Assuming you quote your purchase price in U.S. dollars, the importer would put up the peso equivalent at the then prevailing exchange rate. A foreign exchange bank would convert the pesos into the U.S. dollar amount you quoted. You would get paid that amount in U.S. dollars, not the pesos. Experienced exporters might use hedging techniques to protect against exchange rate fluctuations, but if you just want the dollar amount you specified, simply quote your selling price in U.S. dollars and let the importer deal with any exchange rate fluctuations.

Export sales use different payment methods. Except for smaller purchases, exporters rarely get paid up front. Rather, importers mostly want to pay either when the goods arrive or at some agreed time thereafter (e.g., 30-60 days). Payment on arrival (cash on delivery in effect) is typically processed through banks, using Letters of Credit (L/Cs) or Documentary Collections (D/Cs). Through a bank-to-bank "confirmation" process, L/Cs virtually guarantee payment by the exporter's own bank; D/Cs at least assure that buyers cannot get the goods on arrival until they pay. Allowing buyers to pay later, after getting the goods, is riskier, but you can guarantee payment even in these situations with export credit insurance. See **Chapter 6D** and **6E** for more on export payment methods and protecting against buyer default.

Exporting involves more and different paperwork. Exports are subject to a host of documentary requirements at both ends. Because even trivial mistakes can be costly, most exporters use freight forwarders to tell them not only which documents are needed, but also to fill them out and submit them. The modest freight forwarding fees are routinely factored into the export price quote. Unless you have an experienced, in-house logistics department, you should not attempt to handle your own export documentation. For more on documentation and freight forwarders, see **Chapter 7C**.

Exporting typically incurs added transportation and insurance costs to deliver the goods. If the importer asks for a CIF price quote—the International Commercial Term (INCOTERM) for cost, insurance and freight—the exporter must determine and include all costs from the factory to the end foreign destination. The freight forwarder will not only calculate these costs for you, but will also obtain the cargo insurance and book the cargo. If the importer asks instead for a price quote just from your factory (EXW), or from the departure port or airport (FAS or FOB), you would not be responsible for the transportation or insurance beyond those points. For more on INCOTERMS, and who pays for insurance and transportation, see **Chapter 6C** and **Appendix G8**.

Exports are subject to import duties and taxes in the importing countries. Import duties range from zero to prohibitive, depending on the country and product. The importer pays the duties and taxes. If the levies are too high, as in some protectionist countries, you would not have a market. However, duties are no longer a barrier in most countries and, in the 20+ countries with which the U.S. has Free Trade Agreements (FTAs), you would pay zero or very low duties. Freight forwarders can advise on the current import duties in any country.

Other countries have widely differing laws and business practices that could affect what you need to do to gain access to the market. Although some pose obstacles and risks for exporters, many are business friendly and relatively easy to comply with. It's best to research potential regulatory constraints in each country and seek counsel from your freight forwarder or an international law firm if needed. For more on trade regulations, see **Chapter 7**.

Linguistic, demographic and environmental variations are more pronounced abroad. These differences can make or break your export sales. Take care not to offend your foreign customers in the words, symbols and body language you use in your promotional material and business negotiations. In addition, your products must "fit" the market environment—the climate, terrain, sizes of people and things, consumer tastes and preferences, etc. The Internet is a great, free source of cultural, economic and demographic information. Your local Commerce Department field office also has relevant information on each country and can refer you to "localization" specialists to help you adapt your product or approach as needed.

* * *

1E. Benefits of Exporting

Exporting benefits both the nation and the exporting firms. The nation benefits as exports create more jobs, spur economic growth, increase tax revenues, and reduce trade deficits. For the exporters, the big benefit is more money. Exporting enables you to increase your sales, diversify your markets, offset lags in domestic demand, extend product life cycles, use idle capacity, and reduce unit costs through economies of scale. Exports also help sharpen competitiveness, broaden contacts, and enhance understanding of global markets and cultures.

Exports increase sales and income. Selling more is the surest way to make more money. Foreign markets offer greatly increased sales opportunities. If you don't export, you're competing only for a larger slice of the domestic pie. With exporting, you expand the pie—the entire world is your market. The U.S., for example, is the world's largest market. Yet, as earlier noted, over 95% of the world's population and two-thirds of its purchasing power lie outside the U.S. To illustrate hypothetically, say you currently export only within California. Assume it's worth $1 million overall, and you have a 5% share ($50,000 sales). If you branch out to the $10 million Western regional market, you can double your sales with only a 1% market share. At a 5% share, your sales would increase ten-fold. Next, you expand to the nationwide $100 million market, with the same multiplier effect. Most successful firms do just that. They start locally, expand regionally, and then grow nationally, increasing sales at each stage. But too many of them stop there, as if the world market didn't exist. Why stop at the border? There's no sales barrier that automatically begins where your border ends.

Exports diversify market risk; offset lags in domestic demand. The world market offers new sales options when domestic business slows down. Exports can help offset slow-downs during recessions and seasonal changes. When the domestic economy stagnates, the economy in other countries may be growing. As their production and consumption increase, their import demand rises. In your slow periods, rather than accumulate inventory, idle more capacity, or lay off people, explore export opportunities in growth economies. Similarly, when it's summer or winter domestically, it's just the reverse in many other parts of the world. When your season ends, these countries are looking for the seasonal products you just stopped selling at home.

Exports extend product life cycles. As technology advances and tastes change, many products become obsolete or lose their appeal, particularly in highly industrialized markets. But these products may still be valued elsewhere. Over half the world's economies are less developed. They may not need or can't afford your latest model. They may even prefer less costly, earlier versions or used or reconditioned products. Pursue exports in markets that still value goods no longer in demand in the domestic market.

Exports use idle capacity; reduce unit costs. Increased exports put idle production capacity to work, often with the same equipment, staff and capital investment. With increased export production and sales, you can achieve economies of scale and spread costs over a larger volume of revenue. You reduce average unit costs and increase overall profitability and competitiveness.

* * *

1F. Costs of Exporting

Export costs can be kept low, but can't be avoided altogether. If you're just starting, you'll have the usual start-up costs for an office, equipment, and supplies. As a new exporter, you'll incur some initial research costs to identify your best markets. To enter these markets, you'll have costs to gain exposure, set up sales and distribution networks, and attract customers. As your exports grow, you might translate your sales literature, travel overseas, advertise more, and participate in trade shows abroad. In some countries, you may have to redesign or modify your product to meet local requirements or customer preferences. Generally, the more you spend to prepare, promote, and adapt for export, the greater the return. But don't be deterred by limited funds. You can start even on a small budget. You can also borrow at reasonable rates to help with higher export start-up and operating expenses. Sources include home-equity loans, loans from family, and government export financing programs of the U.S. Small Business Administration[3] or the U.S. Export-Import Bank[4].

Examples of Exporting Costs

Premises. If you already have a production site, or use a contract manufacturer to produce to your specifications, you're already equipped to start exporting. If not, you'll need to set up space for an office and production facility or find a contract manufacturer. For your own premises, look particularly for leased space in enterprise zones or industrial parks that may offer location incentives. If you're an intermediary, such as an Export Management Company (EMC), you'll need an office, either in your home or in leased space. Check with a realtor on costs for renting office space and with an accountant on home-office tax deductions. If you're home-based, consider a mailing address that sounds more professional, such as a suite number in executive premises with mail drop and conference room services.

Personnel. You may not need additional personnel if you're an EMC. One experienced person can handle the work for several exporter clients—gather market research, seek overseas customers, respond to inquiries, prepare export paperwork, and arrange for delivery of the goods. You might want a back-up in case you're sick, on vacation, or traveling.

If you're already producing a product or service, you can export through an EMC without adding or training your own company staff. EMCs already have relationships abroad and will incur some or all of the initial costs to find you customers and generate orders. You pay only if and when they produce export results, usually a commission based on a percentage of the sale. Export Trading Companies (ETCs) and some EMCs also buy goods outright from domestic producers for resale (export) abroad. You, as the supplier, would get paid right away and would also benefit from exposure of your product abroad. See **Appendix F3** for a sample representative agreement with an EMC.

If you intend to handle some or all of the export work in-house, you should hire an export manager or train someone on staff. The training should focus on market research and analysis, market entry planning, intercultural communication, market promotion, export financing, handling of export inquiries and orders, regulatory and documentary compliance, and export shipping. This export guide can be used for staff training, along with other Internet export guides[5] and many webinar and videos[6]. You can also attend free-or low-cost workshops offered by local export assistance organizations. See **Chapter 4D** for sources of export help.

Equipment & supplies. You'll need the usual office furnishings, computer and software, telephone and FAX, and office supplies, including letterhead stationery and writing materials. For a home office, your telephone should be for business only, not the family phone. You'll need a new line installed for that.

Communications. A successful exporter constantly communicates— most cost-effectively by e-mail and phone, including face-to-face by Zoom or Skype at little or no cost.

Market research & planning. The Web is a great free source for much of the export information you'll need, including the latest U.S. and international trade statistics; detailed country commercial guides; in-depth industry and country market surveys; and specific overseas trade opportunities and business contacts. The best Web sources, such as the Trade Information Database[7] and the Commerce Department's Trade.gov[8] have aggregated much of this information in one-stop portals for easy access.

Advertising & sales promotion. If you're a new or infrequent exporter, you're probably not known outside your country. You'll need to promote yourself to get overseas exposure and attract inquiries and orders. A company website with an appealing "About Us" page and descriptions of your products and services, can be your first window to the world. A web designer can create an attractive site for you, or you can do it yourself with inexpensive Web design software. You can register your dot.com domain for a small fee. Because your individual site may be difficult to find on the very crowded Web, you should also take steps to elevate your site in searches, known as "search engine optimization" (SEO)[9], and make use of all appropriate social media (e.g., Google, Facebook, Linked-In, YouTube) to market your company and products to a worldwide audience. Whenever possible, list your product for export in Internet export directories (e.g., Export Yellow Pages[10]), and place free press releases in industry journals with international circulation. Higher-cost options include paid telemarketing, media ads, and participation in overseas trade shows. For more on marketing and promotion, see **Chapter 5E**.

* * *

1G. Risks of Exporting

Self-inflicted risks. For newer exporters, don't try to run before you crawl. Crawling is safer until you gain more experience. This applies both to do-it-yourself (direct) exporters, as well as intermediaries (EMCs/ETCs). The risks are different for each group, but potentially costly for both without common-sense precautions. Do the homework to master the fundamentals, seek advice from export experts (often free), attend "how-to" export seminars and webinars, and use specialists to handle the banking, regulatory and logistics details.

If you already make and sell your product successfully in the domestic market, don't assume that exporting is just an extension of what you've been doing. There are differences, and you can make mistakes in the transition. Before you take the plunge, take care to avoid these common mistakes:

- Don't pursue too many export markets at once, or the wrong markets.
- Don't use sales literature that unwittingly offends.
- Don't apply domestic marketing methods in countries with different business practices.

- Don't appoint incompetent overseas representatives that can't be terminated.
- Don't fail to protect your intellectual property if vulnerable to copying.
- Don't agree to payment methods or terms that leave you at undue risk.
- Don't try to handle all the shipping and documentation yourself.

Financial risks. Your main concern is non-payment after you've shipped the goods, either because the importer can't or won't pay. You can largely avoid default by selling on a Letter of Credit[11] (L/C) basis or with export credit insurance[12]. Irrevocable, confirmed L/Cs virtually assure payment, because the buyer must deposit the money in advance at his bank, and a correspondent bank in your country then takes on the obligation to pay you. However, many foreign buyers want delayed payments: e.g., on open account within 30-120 days after the goods arrive. These terms are customary when you trust the buyer. You might also extend credit if your competitors are offering these terms. Doing so increases your risk, particularly if, by payment time, the buyer's local purchase costs have increased due to depreciation against your currency. See **Chapters 6D** and **6E** for more on methods of payment, including L/Cs, and protecting against buyer default.

If buyers won't pay, it's usually for one of two reasons: you haven't complied with the terms of sale in their view, they're dishonest, or they can no longer afford the payment. You must comply with the terms specified in the L/C and the shipping documents. With reasonable precautions, you can recognize dishonest buyers. You can obtain company profiles and credit reports on many foreign companies from banks and credit-reporting firms. Government export assistance agencies in some countries offer a similar service. In the U.S., for example, the Commerce Department's International Company Profile (ICP)[13] service provides detailed financial and commercial information on the foreign companies you specify, including an opinion on whether the firm would be a suitable partner for U.S. firms.

Business risks. Beware of deals "too good to be true." Take elementary precautions to learn about potential business partners. Graft and corruption are common in many countries. The line between what's customary and tolerable, and what's excessive or illegal, is not always clear. Seek advice from a lawyer or a country specialist in a trade assistance organization. Watch out for potential customers that might pirate you patent, trademark or copyright. Take special care to appoint suitable overseas agents and distributors. Some may already represent your competitors, or be so busy they can't do justice for your products. They may not have the qualifications or capabilities they claimed, such as the ability to stock, install and service your goods. In some countries, once you sign an agent/distributor agreement, it's almost impossible to terminate.

Legal risks. What you don't know can hurt you. Every country has its own business laws and regulations, and you're presumed to know them. Many are similar to U.S. laws or follow international standards. Some vary widely by country, affecting import procedures, agent/distributor agreements, treatment of intellectual property, rights to own businesses or land, tax liability, currency trading, health and technical standards, and even what is allowable to eat, drink or wear. Failure to comply could trigger fines or worse. See also Foreign Trade Laws & Regulations[14] in the ITCI's Trade Information Database[15]. Take the time to do market research and seek legal advice as needed.

Political risks. You're not in America now. Political upheavals in other countries can cause dramatic changes, including shifts in economic policy, nationalization, expropriations, loss of personal rights, and physical danger. Political strife can prompt foreign reactions in the form of economic sanctions, boycotts, and embargoes. Be alert to what's happening in the world. Most common are the shifts to the economic right or left that often come with elections. Some shifts can favor exporters. For example, shifts toward privatization and trade liberalization can open new opportunities for exporters.

Particular risks for export intermediaries. If you're a start-up Export Management Company, you can be overwhelmed if you try to find immediate "matches" for trade leads you've uncovered. Don't assume that every supplier would welcome an export opportunity, or would want you to represent them just because you found a lead. Even if they might, they'll want more details about the buyer, the market, and you. You'll need to convince them the lead is viable, the market warrants attention, you understand their product, and you can handle their export business. You'll need knowledge of the market and experience in export fundamentals and procedures. If you're just starting out, you might face rejection or make mistakes that could harm you or your clients.

If you do find willing suppliers, you should cement the relationship with an Export Representation Agreement that authorizes you to represent them for export. See a sample agreement in **Appendix F4**. That agreement should have a "non-circumvention" clause to protect you from possible attempts by the supplier to bypass you and deal directly with foreign buyers you brought to their attention. Inexperienced EMCs often make the mistake of disclosing the name of the buyer, or vice versa, before they have the non-circumvention protection. Once you have that protection, if either party bypasses you anyway, you can legally claim the commission you would have gotten from the sale.

CHAPTER 2

FIVE STAGES OF EXPORT DEVELOPMENT

Successful exporters typically transition through five sequential stages, starting from not exporting at all to the final stage where exports are an ongoing and important part of the business.

- **Stage 1**: Build Export Capacity
- **Stage 2:** Find and Enter Best Export Markets
- **Stage 3:** Make Export Sales and Get Paid
- **Stage 4:** Comply with Regulatory and Documentary Requirements
- **Stage 5:** Deliver the Goods

* * *

2A. Stage 1: Build Export Capacity

At this initial stage, a company is thinking about exporting and starts the process to:

- Assess the likely export potential and competitiveness of its products;

- Assess whether it has the commitment and capacity to sustain an export effort;
- Acquire a basic understanding of the how-to's of exporting; and
- Identify the sources of export advice, information, and assistance they'll need once they start.

Here are typical Stage 1 to-do's:

- **Conduct a pre-export SWOT analysis** to assess the company's underlying strengths, weaknesses, opportunities and threats as it currently operates. Consider actions to improve domestic productivity and competitiveness if needed (e.g., lean manufacturing techniques).
- **Take Maurice Kogon's free, 23-question Export Readiness Assessment[1] diagnostic.** Consider any recommended actions to overcome weaknesses as a potential exporter.
- **Read any or many of the free export guides[2]** available on the Web, to get a better understanding of export fundamentals.
- **Learn to use free, web-based portals** offering one-stop access to extensive information on all aspects of exporting. Examples include Maurice Kogon's Trade Information Database[3]; the Commerce Department's Trade.Gov[4]; and Michigan State University's globalEDGE[5].
- **Look for free or low-cost export training opportunities**, such as export workshops and webinars typically offered at local Small Business Development Centers (SBDCs). See also the many export videos and tutorials freely available on the Web.
- **Identify nearby sources of export help and support**, such as for start-up advice and training, market research, distributor searches, export promotion and finance, regulatory compliance, freight forwarding, and networking. See **Chapter 4D** for organizations that offer such export help and would welcome your call.

* * *

2B. Stage 2: Find & Enter Best Export Markets

At this second stage, the company has reasonable confidence in its export competitiveness, potential, and readiness, has identified its export support network, and now needs to:

- Determine how many and which markets to focus on for export sales. One option is to "go-global" at the outset; another is to target on some initial "best" markets.
- Set payment policy and price points for each export product.
- Establish an export budget and assure that financing is available to cover the budgeted costs.
- If opting for a "go-global" (all markets) approach, assure that your Web-and social media capabilities are optimized and globalized to service all comers. Build in eCommerce (B2C or B2B) functionality to accept payments and deliver the goods.
- If opting instead for a "best-market" approach, develop tailored, affordable, and actionable market entry plans (EMP) for each target market. The EMPs should cover four key elements of market entry strategy—distribution, pricing, promotion, and adaptation to local conditions. Set time frames and take the recommended actions to implement the target-market EMPs.

Here are typical Stage 2 to-do's (addressed in more detail in **Chapter 5**):

- **Use U.S. export-and foreign import statistics** as a first clue to gauge exportability of your product and your most promising markets. For example, U.S. export statistics can pinpoint the largest and fastest growing export destinations for products like yours, and UN import statistics can show which countries are the largest and fastest growing importers of those same products. Official statistics on U.S. exports and foreign imports by country are freely available at USITC Dataweb[6] and the United Nations Intracen[7], respectively.

- **Pull up free market research reports** that identify and assess best foreign markets for products in your industry. Two good starting sources are the Commerce Department's Country Commercial Guides[8] and Top Market Series[9]. They address issues important to market entry strategy—e.g., demand trends business customs and practices, competition, market access, etc.).
- **Use available free templates to draft an Export Market Plan (EMP)** for each target market. The EMP should include country-specific strategies, actions, and budgets for distribution, pricing, promotion and adaptation. See a suggested EMP template (**Appendix E1**) and a sample of a completed EMP (**Appendix E2**), based on that template.
- **Implement the promotional steps recommended in the "go-global" plan or country-specific EMPs** to increase overseas market exposure and attract inquiries, leads and purchase orders. Such steps could include optimizing and globalizing your website; using social media with global outreach (e.g., Google, Facebook, Linked-In, YouTube); listing your product in electronic directories (e.g., Export Yellow Pages[10] and ThinkGlobal/ExportUSA[11]); and exhibiting at foreign and domestic trade shows that attract foreign buyers.
- **Contact the nearest U.S. Export Assistance Center**[12] (USEAC) for possible use of Commerce services to promote your product and find qualified, interested and reputable distributors in a target market.

* * *

2C. Stage 3: Make Export Sales and Get Paid

In this third stage, the company has already promoted itself globally or in target markets; has appointed distributors where needed; is beginning to receive expressions of interest from potential buyers; and now needs to:

- Respond promptly to inquiries and leads, including requests for quote;
- Negotiate price/credit/delivery terms and close deals with the interested buyers; and
- Secure any needed export financing and credit insurance for each transaction.

Here are typical Stage 3 to-do's (addressed in more detail in **Chapter 6):**

- **Create a kit of inquiry-response forms** for fast response to foreign requests for information about the company, the product, price quotes, and invoices. See sample response forms in **Appendices G1** and **G2**.
- **Determine negotiating options in advance** if the buyer resists your first offer—e.g., your tolerable margin to reduce the price, or to allow more time to pay, and/or to expedite delivery, if these will make a difference.
- **Establish a relationship with a preferred commercial bank** for any needed export financing, such as for pre-export working capital or transactions to be paid for by Letter of Credit (L/C) or Documentary Collections.
- **Establish a relationship with the U.S. Export-Import Bank**[13] for export credit insurance to protect against buyer default on open account terms.

* * *

2D. Stage 4: Comply with Regulatory and Documentary Requirements

In this fourth stage, the company already has a purchase order, selected the payment method, secured any needed financing, and now must:

- Comply with any applicable U.S. regulations to export the product;
- Comply with any applicable target-country import regulations;
- Comply with any applicable documentary requirement at both ends.

Here are typical Stage 4 to-do's (addressed in more detail in **Chapter 7**):

- **Establish a relationship with a freight forwarder** experienced in your type of product and/or target countries. The freight forwarder can advise you of applicable U.S. and foreign trade regulations and prepare all required shipping documents.
- **Establish a relationship with an international attorney** to further assure compliance with relevant international trade laws and regulations beyond the freight forwarder's purview, such as contracts and agreements, intellectual property protection, taxation, and anti-bribery laws.

2E. Stage 5: Deliver the Goods

In this fifth stage, the company has already obtained all necessary permissions (e.g., certificates, licenses, etc.) and documents (e.g., commercial invoice, bill of lading, etc.) at both ends and now must:

- Determine the date for delivery to the buyer.
- Determine where to deliver the goods by that date and

whether you or the buyer should insure the goods against any damage in transit. This is the function of Incoterms.

- Determine the mode of transportation for delivery to the specified destination (e.g., by truck, rail, ship, air).
- Mark, label, package and otherwise prepare the goods for delivery.
- Obtain any needed cargo insurance.
- Arrange to transportation the goods to the agreed destination.

Here are typical Stage 5 to-do's—addressed in more detail in **Chapters 8 and 9**):

- **Become familiar with Incoterms 2020**[14]. These terms specify where the buyer wants you to deliver the goods for pickup (e.g., at your factory, at the port of export, at the port of import) and which party has liability for the goods in transit.
- **Arrange for your freight forwarder to pick up the goods,** palletize or containerize them, and transport them to the specified destination, unless the Incoterms call for the buyer to pick up the goods at your place.
- **Buy cargo insurance** if you are responsible to protect against damage to the goods in transit.

* * *

2F. 122 Questions Exporters Should Consider Asking

As companies advance through the five export stages, they will likely have many questions about how to do this or that or what to do next. Quite often, new or newer exporters often don't yet know enough to ask the right questions. Although this book attempts to anticipate and respond to asked as well as unasked questions, it does not presume to address every possible question. To help fill voids and especially to trigger thinking, here are 122 specific questions exporters might want to find answers to, organized under 15 broad topics. Start by asking your export counselor. You can also search the Web, using these questions as keywords to narrow the search. You will find web sources in the form of free videos and other tutorial resources to answer all of these questions.

I. Why Export—Benefits and Risks

- How can I benefit from exporting as a producer of a good or service?
- What are the risks of exporting, and how can I avoid them?

II. Direct vs. Indirect Exporting—Do It Yourself, or Through an Intermediary

- If exporting makes sense for me, should I do it myself or use a domestic intermediary?
- If I want to export through a domestic intermediary, where can I find one?

III. Export Start-Up—As Producers or Intermediaries

- Do I need any special legal structure or permit to operate an export business?
- Do I need a DUNS # as an exporter, and how can I get one if needed?
- How do I start exporting as a producer, and what is involved?
- How do I start exporting as an intermediary, and what is involved?
- How and where can I find sources of export start-up capital?

IV. Get Help from Export Experts

- Who can I turn to for export advice and assistance?
- Where can I learn more about how to export and learn the basic steps and procedures?
- If my product is a "service," can I export it, and who can help?
- How can SBDCs and SCORE help me start and manage an export business?

- How can the U.S. Commercial Service (USCS) help me export non-agricultural products?
- How can the Foreign Agricultural Service (FAS) help me export agricultural products?
- How can the SBA and Export-Import Bank help me finance and insure my export sales?
- How can commercial banks help me finance my export operations?
- How can a freight forwarder help with my export documentation and logistics?

V. Build Export Capacity—Prepare for Export

- Am I export-ready, and do I have what it takes to export?
- How can I assess/strengthen my company's export competitiveness?
- How can I determine if my product has export potential?
- How do I develop a plan to start or expand my export activity?
- How do I develop a budget for new or expanded export activity?
- How can I globalize my website for export audiences?
- How can I develop global eCommerce, social media, and digital marketing capabilities?
- How can business information systems help me better manage my export operations?
- How and where can I find contract manufacturers to private-label my export products?
- How should I price my products for export markets?

VI. Classify Products for Export—Commodity Coding Systems

- What are the relevant coding systems to classify my export products?
- How do I find the HS code or Schedule B number for my export products?

- How do I find the Export Control Classification Number (ECCN) for my export products?

VII. Find Best Export Markets

- How can I find the best export markets for my products?
- What statistical and research tools can help me identify best export markets?

VIII. Develop Target-Market Entry Strategy

A. Market Entry Planning

- How do I develop and adapt entry plans for my target markets?

B. Cultural and Regulatory Adaptation Strategy

- How does culture impact how I should conduct my export operations?
- How does culture impact how I should interact and communicate with export customers?
- What changes in my product or marketing might I need for cultural or regulatory reasons?

C. Distribution Strategy

- What are the options to sell and distribute my products in target markets?
- For market distribution, should I look for an agent or distributor, and what's the difference?
- How can I find potential foreign buyers or agents/distributors for my product?
- How can I verify the bona fides of potential foreign partners?
- Do I need a written agreement with my foreign partner, and what should it include?

D. Pricing Strategy

- How should I determine the price for my products in target markets?

E. Promotion Strategy

- What marketing methods and media are mainly used to promote export products?
- How can I use or enhance my website to reach global customers?
- How can I use eCommerce, social media, and digital marketing to attract foreign buyers?
- How can I use trade shows and trade missions to attract foreign buyers?
- How can I avoid paying import duties for trade show goods I plan to bring back?
- If a promotional sales trip to the market makes sense, how should I prepare for it?
- What financing is available to defray my costs for export marketing and promotion?

IX. Make Export Sales

- What are Proforma and Commercial Invoices, and how are they used to bill export customers?
- What are Incoterms, and how are they used to specify price, delivery points, and liability en route?
- How can I use Incoterms to manage shipping costs and risks?
- How and where can I get working capital to promote sales and fill large orders?
- How can I protect against adverse changes in exchange rates?
- How can a small business like mine sell to foreign governments?
- When and how can the U. S. support my bid for a foreign government procurement?

X. Get Paid for Export Sales

- How do I get paid for traditional export sales?
- How can I get paid for my eCommerce export sales?
- What are Letters of Credit, and how do they work as an export payment method?
- What are Documentary Collections, and how do they work as an export payment method?
- What is Open Account, and how does it work as an export payment method?
- What are the risks of non-payment by my foreign buyer?
- What are the risks of non-payment by my foreign buyer, including commercial, economic, and political factors?
- What is factoring, and how does it assure that I get paid for export sales?
- How can Exim protect against buyer default on open account sales (30-120 days)?
- How can Exim protect against buyer default for medium-term sales of capital goods (5-7 yrs)?
- Can anyone help me apply for Exim export credit insurance at no charge?
- If Exim won't insure me as a new exporter, who else can provide it?
- If my foreign buyers need financing to buy my product, where can they get it?

XI. Protect International Legal Interests

- How can I protect against foreign theft of my intellectual property?
- How can I protect other legal interests in foreign markets?
- How should I handle a demand for a bribe to secure a sale or a needed approval?
- What foreign bribes are prohibited under the U.S. Foreign Corrupt Practices Act?

- What should I do if told I can only export to my target country if I boycott another country?
- What methods are available to resolve international commercial disputes?

XII. Comply with U.S. and International Regulatory Requirements

A. U.S. National Security Export Controls (EAR, ITAR, OFAC)

- Which U.S. agencies have primary responsibility for national security export controls?
- What basic export controls are enforced by these agencies?
- What are BIS Export Administration Regulations (EAR), and how do I comply?
- What is the BIS Commerce Control List (CCL)?
- What are Export Control Classification Numbers (ECCNs)?
- How do I use the CCL/ECCNs to classify products for EAR purposes?
- When are products considered "deemed exports" under the EAR?
- How do I know if a foreign buyer is a "denied" party under the EAR?
- How do I determine if I need an export license for EAR compliance?
- How do I know if my product is eligible for an EAR license exception?
- How do I apply for an EAR export license?
- How do I set up an EAR compliance program in my company?
- What are DDTC International Traffic in Arms Regulations (ITAR), and how do I comply?
- If I sell my product in the U.S. for a military purpose, must I still register under ITAR?
- How do I register my company under ITAR if required?
- How do I set up an ITAR compliance program in my company?
- What are Office of Foreign Assets Control (OFAC) regulations (FACR), and how do I comply?

- How do I know which countries are sanctioned under FACR?
- How do I set up an OFAC compliance program in my company?

B. U.S. Health/Safety Export Regulations

- What certificates might I need to export products under FDA jurisdiction?
- How do I apply for FDA export certificates?
- What U.S. certificates might I need to export products under USDA jurisdiction?
- What U.S. certificates might I need to export products under TTB jurisdiction?
- Are any special U.S. permits needed to export "dangerous" or "hazardous" goods?

C. Foreign Tariff & Non-Tariff Barriers

- What are tariff barriers to trade (import duties/taxes), and how are they calculated?
- How do I determine the import duty for my product in target markets?
- Which countries might be duty free for my products under U.S. FTAs?
- How can I benefit from zero-or low tariffs under the United States-Mexico-Canada Agreement (USMCA)?
- How do I determine country of origin of my products for preferential duty treatment?
- What are non-tariff trade barriers (NTBs)?
- How do I determine if my product is subject to any non-tariff barriers in target markets?

D. International Standards

- What international standards might I want to certify for or comply with?

XIII. Comply with U.S. & International Documentary Requirements

A. U.S. Documentary Requirements

- What is the Automated Commercial Environment (ACE) for export documentation?
- How do I register and set up an account in ACE?
- What export documents must be filed under ACE, and how do I file them?
- What are the Automated Export System (AES) and Electronic Export Information (EEI)?
- What EEI documents must be filed in the AES, and how do I file them?

B. International Documentary Requirements

- What are the most commonly needed export shipping documents?
- What do I do if asked for a Consular Invoice?
- What protection do Bills of Lading (B/Ls) offer in the export transaction?

XIV. Prepare Goods for Export Shipment (Marking, Labeling, Packaging)

- How are export goods typically marked and labeled?
- How can I safely package my goods for export shipment?
- How must hazardous materials in particular be marked, labeled and packaged?

XV. Deliver Goods to Export Destinations

- Who can help with my export logistics?
- What software tools are available to help with export logistics?
- How do I insure my goods against damage in transit?
- Why do I need a "General Average" clause in my cargo insurance policy?
- How can I transport my goods to foreign markets?

CHAPTER 3

SPECIAL NEEDS OF NEW EXPORTERS

New exporters (NTEs) have not previously exported for the many reasons already covered in **Chapter 1**. Even if open to exporting, NTEs often don't know what questions to ask or how much and what kinds of help they'll need along the way. To make matters worse, most export assistance organizations do not accept NTEs as clients—"newbies" are too hard. They instead favor "export-ready" firms that can make more immediate use of their advice and programs. Still another hurdle for all exporters, including NTEs, is that no one organization can help with all export needs. Some organizations can do "this," but not "that." NTEs invariably need a lot of both, so they must first search, often vainly, for start-up help, and then navigate through the maze of other organizations that can help with their next set of needs.

The list below addresses 27 special needs of NTEs from start-up through the 5 stages of export development discussed in **Chapter 2**. Of these 27 needs, 11 are at the capacity-building stage prior to export (Stage I). The 16 additional needs arise at different points during Stages II-V, after the NTEs become export-ready. The list further identifies organizations, programs, data sources, and/or sections of this book that can help with each of the 27 needs.

3A. 11 NTE Needs at Pre-Export (Start-Up) Stage

Stage 1: Help with legal/technical/entrepreneurial matters for pre-export manufacturers

- SBA/SBDCs[1] and SCORE[2]—some have free legal counselors
- NIST/MEPs[3]—some conduct-free competitive assessments for manufacturers

Stage I: Help with start-up business plans for exporting

- SBA/SBDCs and SCORE—free counseling and Business Plan templates[4]

Stage I: Help with budgeting for a new export operation

- SBDCs—free counseling
- SCORE—free counseling

Stage I: Help to find contract manufacturers that can private-label products for export

- SCORE—free counseling
- NIST/MEPs—Product Design and Development[5]

Stage I: Help to get seed capital for manufacturers starting a new export activity

- SBA investment loans[6]
- Bank loans[7], microloans[8], Crowdfunding[9], etc.
- Angel investors[10] and venture capital (VC)[11]

Stage I: Help to assess the export competitiveness of a manufacturing operation

- NIST / MEPs—some regional MEPs offer free manufacturing assessments

Stage I: Help to assess a product's export potential and a company's readiness to export

- Maurice Kogon's Export Readiness Assessment System[12]
- DOC/Exporter Assessments[13]
- This book—**Chapters 4A** and **4B**

Stage I: Help to find experts for export advice

- DOC / USEACs[14]—all have free export counselors
- SBDCs—many have free export counselors
- DECs[15]—all have volunteer experts in many aspects of exporting
- State Trade Development Offices[16]—all have free export counselors

Stage I: Help to find local export support services

- Freight forwarders[17]
- U.S. Commercial Banks[18]
- U.S. international trade lawyers[19]
- This book—**Chapter 4D**

Stage I: Help to learn how-to-export (online sources, export workshops/courses)

- Web-based free export guides[20]
- Web-based export tutorials[21]
- Upcoming DOC Webinars[22]
- This book—**Chapter 4C**

Stage I: Help to develop global website/social media/eCommerce capabilities

- SBDC and SCORE Webinars—check Monthly Calendars for closest branches
- DOC/eCommerce Innovation Lab[23]
- Getting to Global/Global eCommerce 101[24]
- SBA/State Trade Expansion Program (STEP)[25] grants
- This book—**Chapter 5E**

* * *

3B. 16 Needs as NTEs Become Export-Ready

Stage II: Help to identify best export markets for a product

- USEAC and SBDC export counselors
- U.S. export statistics by product and country (Dataweb[26]; Trade Stats Express[27])
- Intracen/Foreign import statistics by product and country[28]
- DOC/Top Market Series[29], by industry; Google Market Finder[30]
- This book—**Chapter 5B**

Stage II: Help to develop country-specific market entry strategies and plans

- USEAC and SBDC export counselors
- Export Market Plan template DOC/Sample Export Plan[31]
- SBA/**Export Business Planner**
- DOC/Country Commercial Guides[32] and Top Market Series
- NIST/MEP/ExporTech Program[33]
- This book—**Chapter 5D**

Stage II: Help with marketing and promotion in target markets

- DOC/Search Trade Events[34]
- DOC/Trade Shows and Trade Missions Programs[35]
- SBA/State Trade Expansion Program (STEP) grants)
- Getting to Global[36]
- This book—**Chapter 5E**

Stage II: Help to price products for export

- USEAC and SBDC export counselors
- Guide to Export Pricing[37]
- This book—**Chapter 5D**

Stage II: Help to find and vet potential foreign buyers and/or distributors

- DOC/IPS[38], Gold Key Service[39], and ICP[40] programs
- International Credit Reports (Coface, D&B, etc.)
- This book—**Chapter 5F**

Stage II: Help with terms of agent/distributor agreements

- DOC/International Partner Agreements[41]
- Exporting Basics Sample Agent/Distributor Agreement —**Appendix F4**

Stage III: Help to respond to RFQs

- DOC/Pricing considerations[42]
- Incoterms 2020[43]
- This book—**Chapter 6C** and Export Quotation Worksheet (**Appendix G7**)

Stage III: Help to negotiate and close deals with foreign buyers

- This book—**Chapter 6C**

Stage III: Help to access pre-export working capital for large orders

- SBA/Export Working Capital Guaranty Program[44]
- Exim/Export Working Capital Guaranty Program[45]
- This book—**Chapter 4D**

Stage III: Help with methods of payment for export sales

- International commercial banks (e.g., Citibank, Chase)
- DOC/Trade Finance Guide[46]
- This book—**Chapter 6D**

Stage III: Help to protect against foreign buyer default

- Exim/Export Credit Insurance[47]
- Commercial—Meridian Finance Group[48], Brett Tarnet Insurance Services[49]
- This book—**Chapter 6E**

Stage III: Help to protect intellectual property rights (IPR) in target markets

- DOC/Protect Your Intellectual Property[50]
- IPR attorneys

Stage III: Help to comply with applicable U.S. or foreign trade regulations

- Freight forwarders
- DOC/BIS Export Administration Regulations (EAR)[51]
- DOS/DDTC/International Traffic in Arms Regulations (ITAR)[52]

- This book—**Chapter 7A** and **7B**

Stage IV: Help to comply with applicable U.S. or foreign documentary requirements

- Freight forwarders
- This book—**Chapter 7C**

Stage V: Help with packaging for in-transit protection and regulatory compliance

- Freight forwarders
- Exporting Basics Cargo Insurance—**Chapter 9A**
- This book—**Chapter 8A** and **8B**

Stage V: Help with transporting goods from the factory to the specified destinations

- Freight forwarders
- This book—**Chapter 9B**

Key to Acronyms

BIS: Bureau of Industry & Security
DDTC: Directorate of Defense Trade Controls
DOC: Department of Commerce
Exim: Export-Import Bank
ICC: International Chamber of Commerce
ICP: International Company Profile
IPS: International Partner Search
MEPs: Manufacturing Extension Partnerships
NACBFF: National Association of Customs Brokers/Freight Forwarders
NIST: National Institute of Standards
SCORE: Service Corps of Retired Executives
USEACs: U.S. Export Assistance Centers

CHAPTER 4

BUILD EXPORT CAPACITY

You don't need to be an expert to export, but you will need an exportable product, adequate start-up resources, sound domestic marketing methods, and a committed management. Prospective exporters rarely start with all the attributes that assure export success. However, with reasonable effort and guidance, you can begin to fill the gaps and reach a point where exporting becomes viable. If you have not exported before, don't assume the worst. You lack the experience, but not necessarily the potential to export. Every experienced exporter was at one time a non-exporter.

If you believe exporting might be a possibility, given the benefits, costs and risks, your next step is to assess your chances for success. For a detailed, customized assessment, you can take Maurice Kogon's free, on-line Export Readiness Assessment[1]. After answering 23 questions from the options given, you get immediate feedback about the likely export potential of your product and the strengths and weaknesses of your company as a potential exporter.

4A. Assess Your Product's Export Potential

Products won't sell anywhere, let alone have export potential, if there is no demand for them or they can't compete. To have export potential,

43

your product must find a need or want in at least in one foreign market, and it must be able to meet the competition from other suppliers. To compete, your product must match or exceed the appeal of others—in meeting needs, in price, in quality, etc. Equally important, you must be open to the customary ways that exporting is conducted and that your buyers will expect. Here is a quick overview of **export potential positives and negatives.**

Export Potential Positives

- You are already selling nationwide. Exporting is a logical next step.
- Your domestic sales are stable or growing. That shows you have kept pace with your competition, including against imports from the same competitors you will face abroad.
- You are price-competitive domestically. Your prices should also be tolerable abroad.
- Your product is "superior" in some key way—unique or different, more versatile, more advanced technology, more durable. That also gives you an edge abroad.
- If necessary to make the export sale, you would be flexible on pricing and/or payment terms.
- If necessary to comply with local regulatory requirements and cultures, you would consider reasonable modifications of your product's design, ingredients, shape or color.
- If necessary to market more effectively and avoid cultural blunders, you would be open to globalizing your website, utilizing local social media, and adapting your sales literature.

Export Potential Negatives

- Your product could not be made competitive beyond the domestic market, no matter how willing you might be to try.
- You would not be open to any modifications in product or practices needed to make an export sale.

- Your product would cost too much to transport, compared with competitors from nearer countries.
- Your product would require face-to-face training (installation, after-sales service) too costly to be competitive.

These indicators of foreign demand and competitiveness can help you assess the likely export potential of your products.

Indicators of foreign demand

Products just like yours are already exported in significant amounts and/or are growing rapidly, as reflected in official export statistics. If your competitors are already exporting similar products, a demand clearly exists that you may also be able to tap. You can find the latest U.S. export statistics for your product, by its Schedule B[2] or Harmonized System (HS)[3] code number, at USITC Trade DataWeb[4].

Products just like yours are already being heavily imported by other countries and/or are growing rapidly, as reflected in official world import statistics. If other countries are importing large and fast-growing amounts of products like yours, particularly if a good share of those imports are coming from your country, it means there is potential for your product as well. You can find the latest foreign import statistics for your product, by HS code, at the UN/International Trade Centre Website[5].

Foreign companies have expressed interest in your company or product. Unsolicited foreign inquiries by Email or through your Website are a strong indicator of potential demand. They offer tangible proof that you've been discovered abroad. You may not know how or why, but count it as a plus that someone overseas has taken the initiative to search you out. Many companies say they first started exporting only after and because they received unsolicited foreign inquiries. If you haven't been approached yet, don't be discouraged. A likely reason is not lack of interest or demand, but lack of awareness. Your company and product probably just aren't known abroad, either favorably or unfavorably. You need exposure abroad to pique interest and demand. See **Chapter 5E** for tips on export marketing and promotion.

Indicators of foreign competitiveness

Your product is already selling reasonably well in the domestic market. A strong domestic sales performance is a good indicator of export competitiveness. If domestic sales are increasing, or have at least kept pace with competitors, you could well be competitive abroad. You've already shown strength in the domestic market against the same domestic and imported products you'd likely face in export markets. The overseas playing field will be different. You may need to adjust your pricing somewhat to compete in specific markets. You may have to absorb added marketing and shipping costs to remain price competitive. You may have to offer credit terms and wait longer for payment to match competitors. You may need to adapt your product to comply with local standards and tastes. Are you prepared to do what it takes to compete? If not, you won't succeed as an exporter. Even if you have weak domestic sales, don't necessarily assume you're uncompetitive for export. In fact, if your sluggish sales are due mainly to a domestic economic slowdown, or to product obsolescence, exporting may offer a promising outlet. When the domestic economy stagnates, other countries may be booming. As their production and consumption increase, their demand for imports also rises, including possibly for yours.

You have a relatively strong share of the domestic market. Market share is a key indicator of product competitiveness, whether you're selling locally, regionally or nationally. If your share of that market is already high or growing, or at least holding steady, your product likely has fundamental competitive strengths; e.g., attractive pricing, uniqueness, high quality, strong service and customer support, or other. These competitive assets are as appealing to foreign buyers as domestic. A low or declining market share reflects competitive weaknesses. Because competition is even more intense overseas, the chances are that you would do no better overseas, and probably worse. However, this could depend on the reasons for your low domestic market share.

For example, if product obsolescence is the reason, exporting may offer an opportunity. Other countries, particularly lower income or less developed countries, may not need the latest technology and may value yours for its presumably lower cost.

Your product is price-competitive in the domestic market. Domestic price-competitiveness is a big plus in exporting. Competition abroad is usually stiffer than at home, and price is often a decisive competitive factor. A competitive price is a must for products that are otherwise indistinguishable, such as basic commodities. Even for performance-based products, price often becomes decisive at some point. Unless your product is indisputably superior to the others, or is indispensable, the buyer may ultimately let price be the final determinant. If your prices are competitive domestically, you're in a strong position to offer very attractive export pricing as well. While you may need to add some export delivery costs to your prices (e.g., freight, insurance, etc.), so too will most of your exporting competitors. You can thus retain your relative price advantage in many export markets. On the other hand, if you have little or no price advantage domestically, and have no offsetting product strengths (superior quality, uniqueness), exporting may not be a viable option. Given the importance of competitive pricing, you should try to obtain comparative price information before you enter a target market. If necessary, strongly consider adjusting your prices to meet the competition.

Your product compares favorably with domestic competitors in features and benefits. It helps to be "superior" in some key way, particularly when you're higher priced than your competition. Foreign buyers look at product performance, not just cost, when they make procurement decisions (e.g., dependability, versatility, durability, repair frequency, productivity, labor-saving etc.). They will often pay more to get more or better. If your product fits a niche in the domestic market, or has some advantage over competing products, you have strong export potential. If you have no particular qualitative advantages, you may still have export potential. Many of the most heavily exported products are virtually indistinguishable (e.g., agricultural products, raw materials and semi-manufactures). You and your competitors alike must use price and credit as your main selling points. If you do have a distinguishable product, but it's comparatively "inferior," consider markets that are less selective. Buyers in many less-developed, cost-conscious, labor-intensive countries may not need or want the "best" or "latest." They'll often take a lesser product to pay less (e.g., manually-operated vs. automated equipment, yesterday's technology, no frills models).

* * *

4B. Assess Your Company's Export Readiness

An "export-ready" company has five basic attributes:

1. Its top management is willing to give exporting a good try;
2. It has adequate finances for at least a small export budget;
3. It has in-house staff with some export knowledge, or would acquire it (train or hire);
4. Its organizational structure could absorb the additional workload as exports develop; and
5. It uses sound business practices domestically that also make sense for exporting.

Maurice Kogon's free, online Export Readiness Assessment[6] diagnostic addresses these export prerequisites, tells you how you rate in each area, and suggests steps and actions you can take to become more export ready.

Indicators of export readiness

Your top management is committed to exporting as a new or expanded area of activity. Exporting should not be pursued opportunistically or for the "wrong" reasons—e.g., to make a quick buck, only to shut it off abruptly if not enough happens soon enough. Management should see the "right" reasons for exporting—as a contribution to sound, specific company goals and a significant new facet of its business—and be willing to wait the 2-4 times longer it may take to gain traction, compared with domestic selling. "Where there's a will, there's a way." If the management will exists, ways can be found to make a product more salable; overcome or adjust to tight budgets; or to better market a product. Reluctant, indifferent, or impatient top management won't make that happen. If you're not sure, you might try low-risk, go-slow approaches to test the waters and build more confidence in your export potential.

Your company has adequate finances for a first-year export budget. If you're already established domestically, you might incur incremental export costs for market research to identify best markets and entry strategies, although much of this is freely available from the Web and local federal and state export assistance centers. To gain market exposure abroad, you'll need funds to market and promote yourself, such as by enhancing your website and marketing materials or by exhibiting at foreign and domestic trade shows that attract foreign buyers. As export orders come in, you may need more working capital to fill them if beyond the stock you have in inventory. If your customers want delayed payment terms, you'll need to cover the cash flow while awaiting payment. You can minimize these and other incremental costs, but you can't eliminate them entirely.

Your domestic marketing practices are also conducive to exporting. Sound methodology is as critical in exporting as in domestic selling. If you've been successful at home, the chances are that you base your decisions on market research and analysis, have a strong sales and distribution network, effectively promote your company and products, and give priority to customer service. Exporting requires the same sound methodology, but may also need to be adapted for countries with different marketing and distribution practices. How you enter and develop a foreign market is important. Marketing and distribution practices vary by country and are often dictated by law, custom, or necessity. Some countries may require or prefer certain marketing or distribution methods, such as use of local representatives. Some countries have excellent mass media and high receptivity to advertising, trade shows, mail order, etc. Others shun these approaches or do not have or use the available social media and other communication technologies to support them. Are you prepared to adapt your marketing methods? If not, you'll need to limit yourself to markets more like your own.

You could promptly fill new export orders from present inventory or other sources. Exporters should be able to respond promptly to any new foreign orders. Foreign buyers typically can buy from other sources, and if you can't fill the order when they want it, they'll usually find someone else who can. Don't start or impair a relationship with delays and apologies. If you have idle plant capacity, you're probably in a good position to fill any new orders. You may already have inventory on hand, or you could increase production fairly quickly without needing more workers, materials or equipment. With that flexibility, you can go after new export business as aggressively as you wish.

* * *

4C. Learn the Fundamentals of Exporting

If you are established domestically, you already know how to run a business, just not yet for export. You probably routinely conduct research, plan, budget, finance, market, manage a sales network, fill orders, control inventory, service customers, comply with regulations, and package and ship goods. These basic practices also apply to exporting, so you're able to start with the needed knowledge and skills you already have. As a new exporter, what more will you need to know and be able to do? In essence, you'll need to learn how to adapt to selling to a "foreign," not domestic market—to customers with often different languages, cultural idiosyncrasies, and physical characteristics, and to countries with often different regulations, business practices, and environmental conditions. You'll also need to learn to adapt to some of the procedural differences, such as different payment methods and added transportation costs. You can acquire this additional learning in many no-or low-cost ways. First, read the how-to-export literature widely available, such as this book and others. Look for training opportunities, such as export workshops and Web-based export webinars and videos. The topics range from start-up (e.g., is exporting for me?) to cross-cultural communication and negotiation, legal do's and don'ts, exporting to particular countries, and the functional how-to's of market research, target-marketing, market entry planning, international matchmaking, export finance and insurance, regulatory and documentary compliance, and transportation and logistics.

* * *

4D. Know Where to Go for Export Help

No company can know everything or do everything alone, especially in exporting. Those who don't know when they need export help, or don't seek it when they need it, or don't use it when they get it, will not last long. At some point, you'll typically need help with start-up export advice and training; information on how-to export and for market research and planning; assistance with international matchmaking and promotion; legal assistance to protect interests and comply with regulations; and help to finance, insure, and move the goods. Make a list of local sources you can turn to when you'll need their help.

U.S. sources of export advice and assistance

Many local, state, and federal organizations offer export advice and assistance. Unfortunately, they prefer to work mostly with "export-ready" firms, not new exporters (harder to work with). No one organization can meet all export needs, but if you know who can do what, you can find some organizations or programs that can meet one or more of these basic needs—access to capital for export operations, export-readiness assessment, export counseling and training, best-market identification and entry planning, traditional and digital marketing and sales promotion, B2C and B2B eCommerce sales, matchmaking, financing, risk-mitigation, regulatory compliance, and supply chain management. These agencies all have web sites that explain their services and how to contact them. In most cases, simply call for a free appointment and meet directly with an export counselor.

Local export organizations and services. Local-level initiatives come mainly from county/city economic development agencies[7], NGOs such as World Trade Centers (WTCs)[8] and chambers of commerce[9], and universities and community colleges that host international trade assistance centers. They typically focus on early-stage export development—export counseling, export workshops and webinars, and networking events. Some of the larger chambers also issue Certificates of Origin and Certificates of Free Sale.

State-level export organizations and services. Most States have Trade Development Offices[10] with experienced export counselors. They offer counseling and training comparable to Commerce Department U.S. Export Assistance Centers (USEACs) and SBA Small Business Development Centers (SBDCs)—see Federal below). Some States have regional branch offices, as well as their own overseas offices to support home-State companies. The States are also the primary conduit for State Trade Expansion Program (STEP)[11] grants (e.g., up to $5,000 per company). These grants can be used to cover planned costs for export market development and trade promotion activities, such as for website globalization and translations and fees for matchmaking and trade promotion programs.

Federal export organizations and services

The U.S. has two primary export assistance organizations that offer a wide range of export assistance services—The International Trade Administration (ITA)[12] of the U.S. Department of Commerce (USDOC) and the Foreign Agricultural Service (FAS)[13] of the U.S. Department of Agriculture (USDA). Three other organizations provide more specialized export assistance—the U.S. Small Business Administration (SBA)[14], the U.S. Export-Import Bank (Exim)[15], and the U.S. Trade and Development Agency (TDA)[16].

ITA is the lead assistance agency for exporters of manufactured products and services. ITA's domestic arm—the U.S. Commercial Service (USCS)[17]—oversees a large staff of trade specialists at U.S. Export Assistance Centers (USEACs)[18] in over 100 U.S. cities. USEAC staff can counsel and assist U.S. firms in all aspects of exporting, including with market research and matchmaking and promotion programs (e.g., trade missions[19], trade shows[20], two rep-find services (International Partner Search[21] and Gold Key Matching Service[22]), and a rep-vetting service (International Company Profile[23]). USCS also maintains Trade.gov (formerly Export.gov), a Web portal with extensive, free trade information. ITA's overseas arm—the Foreign Commercial Service (FCS)[24]—manages a nearly worldwide commercial staff at U.S. embassies and consulates in more than 75 countries, including American Senior Commercial Officers (SCOs) and Commercial Attachés, along with more permanently-stationed Foreign Service Nationals (FSNs). They counsel visiting U.S. companies, conduct country-specific market research, carry out the USCS trade assistance programs in their countries, advocate for U.S. companies competing against foreign bidders for major contracts, and help resolve commercial disputes. All such trade specialists are listed in the Directory of U.S. Offices[25] and Directory of Overseas Offices[26] and can be contacted directly for free appointments.

USDA/FAS has a large network of agricultural counselors, attachés and trade officers at U.S. embassies in many countries. The FAS Web portal[27] has extensive country-and-product-specific market research[28]. FAS also has several cost-share programs to assist exporters of food and agricultural products. The Agricultural Trade Promotion Program (ATP)[29] helps exporters develop new markets and mitigate adverse effects of foreign tariff and non-tariff barriers. The Emerging Markets Program (EMP)[30] provides funding for technical assistance, such as for feasibility studies, market research, sectorial assessments, orientation visits, specialized training and business workshops. The Export Credit Guarantee Program (GSM-102)[31] provides credit guarantees to encourage exports to buyers in mostly developing countries that have sufficient foreign exchange available to make scheduled payments. Under the Foreign Market Development (FMD) Program[32], also known as the Cooperator Program, FAS partners with cooperating U.S. non-profit commodity or trade associations to promote U.S. commodities overseas.

SBA, while not primarily an export assistance agency, has an Office of International Trade (OIT)[33] and a nationwide network of Small Business Development Centers (SBDCs)[34] and SCORE[35] offices. SBDCs and SCORE chapters offer free export counseling and regularly host workshops and webinars on export –related topics.

TDA can help exporters in two ways. The Project Preparation Assistance Program[36] finances feasibility studies to help U.S. firms compete for foreign projects and by encouraging the foreign project managers to incorporate U.S.-oriented procurement specs in their RFQs. TDA's Reverse Trade Mission[37] program pays for trips to the U.S. by foreign buyer delegations to observe the design, manufacture and operation of U.S. products and services.

U.S. and international sources of trade information

The Web is an information goldmine for exporters. "Googling" is the usual search method, but can meander through many paths and still not find all the most fruitful nuggets. Alternatively, you can search a few specialized Web "portals" that have aggregated the most useful trade information into one place. Four such portals provide the most extensive, one-stop coverage—ITCI's Trade Information Database[38]; USDOC/ITA's Trade.gov[39] (formerly Export.gov); the USDA's FAS.gov[40]; and Michigan State University's globalEDGE[41]. From one or more of these entirely free U.S. sources, exporters can find valuable how-to-export guides and tutorials; trade, economic and demographic statistics; country-and industry-specific market research; intercultural tips; regulatory and documentary requirements; and databases of potential suppliers, importers and distributors.

ITCI's Export Start-Up Kit[42] exclusively has Maurice Kogon's Export Readiness Assessment System (ERAS), a diagnostic test that provides detailed immediate feedback on the test-taker's export potential and readiness. ITCI's Trade Information Database[43] (TID) links not only to most of the international trade resources in the other three portals, but also to many more U.S. and international sources they do not include. That gives you the option to stay within ITCI to access what you would otherwise need to pull separately from each of the other portals or spend hours Googling. ITCI/TID's nearly 1,000 links[44] are organized into 12 broad categories and 74 subcategories.

ITCI/TID Categories and Subjects Covered	
TID Categories	**Subjects Covered**
Trade Readiness Tools	Information and tools to prepare and train for exporting
Trade Reference Tools	Look-ups to commodity codes, trade terms and conversions
Trade & Economic Data	Worldwide trade, demographic and economic data
Foreign Market Research	Reports on countries, industries, and culture for market planning
Trade Contacts & Leads	Trade directories and specific trade lead for exporters
Trade/Investment Regulations	U.S. and foreign regulations affecting market access
Trade Documentation	U.S. & foreign requirements/forms for documentary compliance
Trade Promotion	Programs to promote exports and find international partners
Trade Finance & Insurance	Guides and programs to finance and insure exports
Trade Transport & Logistics	Requirements and tools to manage logistics and deliver the goods
International Trade News	Export-related news feeds, Blogs, periodicals, and publications
Trade Resources Directory	Federal, State, international, commercial, and academic resources

Trade.gov covers the export guides, tutorials, country-and product-specific market research, and programs and services offered by Commerce's International Trade Administration (ITA). Since Trade.gov is mostly limited to ITA resources, it does not include useful trade information of sister USDOC agencies, such as trade statistics (Census Bureau) or export control requirements (Bureau of Industry and Security). Trade.gov also does not include any of the extensive trade information produced by other government agencies, such as Customs & Border Protection (CBP) and the Departments of State, Energy, and Transportation. You would need to go to the databases of each of those agencies, or to the ITCI site.

FAS.gov is a comprehensive one-stop source of food and agriculture trade information, with separate categories for Commodities and Products[45], Countries and Regions[46], Data and Analysis[47], and Trade Programs[48].

GlobalEDGE[49] contains a wealth of global resources[50], export tutorials[51], diagnostic tools[52], and industry and country information[53].

International sources of relevant data are also available, particularly from the many UN-and related agencies, including the UN Regional Commissions[54]; UNCTAD/ITC's COMTRADE[55] import and export statistics by country and product; and the World Bank[56] and International Monetary Fund (IMF)[57], with in depth country reports and economic and financial data.

Prominent commercial sources include Euromonitor[58] (industry reports); Internet World Stats[59], Kompass[60] and D&B Hoovers[61] (databases of U.S. and foreign manufacturers); and PIERS[62], Datamyne[63] and Panjiva[64] databases of U.S. and foreign exporters and importers, based on Bills of Lading.

U.S. sources of export finance

The U.S. Government has several loan programs to help exporters finance exports and/or export activities, including the U.S. Export Import Bank (Exim)[65], the U.S. Small Business Administration (SBA)[66] and the U.S. Department of Agriculture's Foreign Agricultural Service (FAS). Most U.S. States also offer small grants under their respective State Trade Expansion Programs (STEP)[67] to cover planned export development and promotion expenses.

The U.S. Export Import Bank (Exim) is the U.S Government's official export credit agency. It has three major programs to finance U.S. exports—Export Working Capital Guaranty Program (EWCGP)[68]; Medium–and Long-Term financing for foreign buyers[69]; and Export Credit Insurance[70]. Exim's EWCGP is for companies that need pre-export working capital to fill orders beyond existing inventory. Say, for example, a foreign buyer wants 1,000 units of your product and is willing to guarantee the payment under a Letter of Credit (L/C). However, you only have 500 units in stock, and it will cost you

$250,000 to get more labor, materials or equipment to fill the rest of the order. You need a "bridge" loan, in effect, that will be repaid from the L/C-guaranteed proceeds of the export sale. Banks are the customary source for such loans, but they traditionally look to your assets as the basis for lending, not eventual export proceeds even if guaranteed by an L/C. That's where Exim's EWCGP comes in. It reassures the bank that, if anything goes wrong, Exim itself will guarantee repayment of the $250,000 loan. Exim can also make direct loans to foreign buyers of U.S. goods to make purchase more affordable. Exim's Medium-and Long-Term financing applies to fairly large orders of U.S. capital goods and related services that foreign buyers would be unable to pay for in the short term. The foreign buyer makes a cash payment of at least 15% and then has up to 5 years (medium term) or over 7 years (long term) to repay. Exim Export Credit Insurance protects U.S. exporters against default by their foreign buyers. The default risk is greatest when foreign buyers insist on "open account" terms; i.e., deferring payment until sometime after they get the goods. If that is the only way you'll get the export sale, you can buy Exim export credit insurance at very low cost. The policy guarantees payment by Exim if for any reason the buyer fails to pay when due. See Exim's Video Gallery[71] and Webinars[72] for more details on Exim export finance programs.

SBA offers several export loan guaranty programs administered by Senior International Credit Officers co-located at USEACs. SBA's Export Working Capital Guaranty Program (EWCGP)[73] is very similar to the Exim EWCGP discussed above, but a bit more tailored for small businesses. SBA's Export Express[74] program can fund of up to $500,000 (term loan or revolving line of credit). It can help small businesses defray costs of overseas promotion, including costs to participate in foreign trade shows, conduct market research, translate their product brochures or catalogues. SBA also administers State Trade Expansion Program (STEP)[75] grants channeled through the individual States. Some States offer STEP grants up to $5,000 per company to cover planned export development costs, such as for website development and globalization, translations of export marketing materials, and participation in foreign trade shows and missions.

USDA/FAS offers several financing programs specifically for agricultural exports. The Export Credit Guarantee Program[76] guarantees repayment when U.S. banks extend credit to foreign banks to finance sales of U.S. agricultural products. The Facility Guarantee Program provides credit guarantees to support infrastructure improvements in countries where demand for U.S. agricultural products may be limited by lack of adequate facilities. USDA/FAS also has a Foreign Market Development (FMD) Program[77], also known as the Cooperator Program, works through regional agricultural trade associations to offset exporter costs for a wide range of export marketing activities. For example, the Western U.S. Trade Association (WUSATA)[78] and the Southern U.S. Trade Association (SUSTA)[79] both provide 50% cost reimbursement for up to $300,000 of eligible international marketing expenses under their respective FundMatch[80] and 50% CostShare[81] programs.

U.S. sources of export banking, logistics, and legal services

Once you know which organizations, services, and resources can best help you in your pre-export capacity-building stage, you should also begin to identify the more "transactional" help you'll need as export inquiries and orders start to come in. In particular, you'll at least need an international commercial bank to handle export payments; an international freight forwarder to handle export documentation and logistics; and, depending on complexity, an international attorney to handle export contracts and agreements, regulatory compliance, and to protect any at-risk intellectual property or other legal interests. It's important to line these players up in advance, not wait until their services are needed

International commercial banks are not the thousands of nationwide community banks that just handle your checking/savings accounts or make car, real estate, and small business loans. The far fewer international commercial banks may also offer these services, but have departments that specialize in international trade transactions. They handle all the ways to get paid for your export sales, including by wire transfers, Documentary Collections, and Letters of Credit (see more on these methods of payment in **Chapter 6D**). These banks have familiar names—Bank of America, Chase, Citibank, etc.). They all have correspondent relationships with comparable foreign banks. Speakers from these banks typically make presentations at export workshops, so you can make a connection there. Here also is a directory of the largest international commercial banks in the U.S.[82]

International freight forwarders specialize in the documentation, logistics and physical transportation of export cargo, whether by truck, rail, ship, or air. They facilitate the entire trip, including calculating point-to-point costs for quoting prices, preparing all necessary documents, picking up the goods from the factory, loading them on pallets or in containers, and booking and tracking the cargo. Most freight forwarders are generalists, but some specialize by transportation mode (sea or air), industry/product, destination country/region, or special needs (e.g., refrigeration, hazardous materials). As with the bankers, freight forwarders also typically speak at export workshops. Otherwise, to find the best freight forwarders for your needs, check with the National Customs Brokers & Freight Forwarders Association (NCB-FAA)[83] for a referral.

International attorneys can help protect your legal interests and assure that you comply with any applicable foreign laws and regulation. You can avert trouble on your own up to a point with basic due diligence and free advice from export counselors and freight forwarders. However, you may eventually need an international attorney to make sure you do certain things right. Attorney can draw up contracts of sale and representation agreements. They can file for foreign patents, trademarks or copyrights if you have vulnerable intellectual property. Try for a free consultation before committing. Local bar associations can generally give referrals. Another source is the District Export Council (DEC)[84] in your region. DECs are advisory bodies whose members are appointed by the Secretary of Commerce. Many DEC members are international attorneys and are generally open to volunteering at least some initial legal advice.

CHAPTER 5

FIND AND ENTER BEST EXPORT MARKETS

5A. Develop an Overall Export Market Plan

Systematic market planning is essential to exporting and can help avoid costly mistakes. As the old adage goes, unsuccessful companies don't "plan to fail, they fail to plan." What might work domestically may not work overseas. Depending on the country, exporters could face different income levels and demand cycles; different languages, cultures and environments; different laws and regulations; different ways of doing business; and different risks. An Export Market Plan (EMP) should provide a structure and step-by-step roadmap for your export activities in each target country. It should set goals, strategies, and timetables that take account of the differences among countries. Above all, the EMP must be realistic, manageable, and achievable within your resources. In its simplest form, it addresses three basic questions:

- Which markets are best to pursue?
- What's the best entry strategy for each target market?
- What specific actions need to be taken to implement the recommended strategy?

For guidance in developing an EMP, see **Appendix E1** (Export Market Plan Template) and **Appendix E2** (Sample Export Market Plan) based on the template. The ITCI Trade Information Database[1] has much of the information you'll need to develop the EMP, including U.S. and foreign trade and demographic statistics; country and industry-specific market surveys; intercultural research; and U.S. and foreign trade laws and regulations.

* * *

5B. Identify Best Markets for Export

This section does not apply to you if your export strategy is to sell to any and all markets off a shopping cart, either on your own website or an Amazon-type platform. With that "go-global" approach, you are opening yourself to the world, not looking for any particular "best" market. This eCommerce approach, essentially inviting all comers, has benefits as well as risks. See **Chapter 5E** for more on eCommerce pros, cons, and best practices.

As a new exporter, you may not want to spread yourself that broadly or pursue markets that aren't right for you. It may be more manageable and still effective to aim for a first cut of 1 to 3 target markets. The "best" target markets offer a combination of high comfort for your company and high potential for your products. High-comfort markets are those you're close to in some way—you may speak the language, know the culture; or have relatives or other trusted contacts there. However, high comfort markets may not offer the highest potential for your products. You ultimately want to be in high-potential markets— those with large, emerging or fast-growing imports of products like yours, limited local or foreign competition; and no barriers to market entry. If you can find high potential markets that are also high in comfort, better yet.

Here are 5 Q&As that apply to any product or industry and can help identify your "best" markets, particularly when comparatively displayed in the Export Potential Matrix shown below. The Web has most of the information you'll need to answer the questions (see quick links under each question and additional Web sources in **Chapter 5C** below).

1. **Where are products like mine mostly exported?** Look for the largest and fastest growing export destinations for comparable products. USITC DataWeb[2] and USDOC's Trade Stats Express[3] are free sources of official U.S. export statistics by product and country.

2. **Which countries are mostly importing products like mine?** Look for countries with the largest and fastest growing imports of comparable product. UN COMTRADE[4] and International Trade Centre Trade Map[5] are free sources of official foreign import statistics by product and country.

3. **In which countries would products like mine be most competitive?** Look for countries with limited competition from local producers and where the U.S. also competes well against other foreign suppliers (e.g., U.S. market share of 15% or more). UN COMTRADE shows imports by product from each supplier country. Commerce Department Country Commercial Guides[6] and Top Market Series[7] both have sections that address industry-specific local and foreign competition.

4. **Where are products like mine most welcome and easiest to sell?** Look for countries with high receptivity to comparable product and no significant import barriers. Country Commercial Guides and Top Market Series both have sections on market accessibility and import regulations.

5. **Which markets do the experts consider most promising for products like mine?** Look for countries recommended as "Best-Prospect" markets for comparable products. Sources: Country Commercial Guides and Top Market Series.

Export Market Potential Matrix: Selection Criteria

The matrix technique shown below can help you compare market potentials for your products for any number of countries. The illustrative matrix shows how well 5 hypothetical countries met the 11 illustrative criteria drawn from the 5 preceding questions. A double "XX" in a column indicates the country significantly met the criterion; a single "X" signifies minimally met; and a "blank" means the country didn't meet the criterion. The more promising markets are those with XX or X across the most number of columns. In this case, Countries 3 and 1 appear far more promising than the others. See **Appendix D1 (Market Potential Matrix)** and **Appendix D2 (Trade Statistics Worksheets 1-6)** to help you fill out your own matrix.

Export Market Potential Matrix: Selection Criteria

	1	2	3	4	5	6	7	8	9	10	11
Country 1	X	XX	X	XX	X	X	XX	X	XX	XX	XX
Country 2		X			XX			X		X	X
Country 3	XX	X	XX	XX	XX	XX	XX	X	XX	XX	XX
Country 4			X	X					X	X	
Country 5		X			X						
Country 6+											

Key: Columns/Criteria

1. Largest export markets, latest year
2. Fastest growing export markets, past 3 yrs.
3. Fastest growing export markets, latest year
4. Largest importing countries, latest year
5. Fastest growing importing countries, past 3 yrs.
6. Fastest growing importing countries, latest year
7. Strong share of import market, latest year
8. Limited competition from local producers
9. High receptivity to products from your country
10. No significant market barriers
11. Recommended as a "best" export market

It's conceivable that better markets could be found with criteria more specific to a product's application or target audience, such as the indicators below. More likely, these will reaffirm the Matrix findings, not find different markets.

To get supporting data for these additional indicators, see the World Economic and Demographic Data[8] section of the ITCI Trade Information Database.

- **Economic indicators**—for luxury and other high-end products, or products more affordable for target users, look for countries with high-or low per capita incomes as appropriate.
- **Demographic indicators**—for products aimed at a particular age range, sex, race, religion, profession, medical condition, etc., look for countries with the largest and fastest-growing populations within that target audience.
- **Sectoral indicators**—for products aimed at particular industry sectors, such as manufacturing, health care, construction, banking, utilities, etc., look for countries with the largest and fastest-growing number of entities in those sectors.
- **Infrastructure indicators**—for products that use or require technology or physical infrastructure, such as telecommunications, power, transportation, ports, etc., look for countries with the basic facilities needed.

* * *

5C. Sources of Market Potential Data

Most or all of the data needed to identify your target markets can be found on the ITCI Trade Information Database[9], including trade, economic and demographic statistics and international market research covering virtually all countries in the world.

U.S. trade statistics[10] compiled by the U.S. Census Bureau provide the data needed for Matrix columns 1-3 (Best sources: USITC DataWeb[11] or USDOC's Trade Stats Express[12]). The Commodity-by-Country series shows U.S. exports of a specified product to all destination countries. The Country-by-Commodity series shows all U.S. products exported to a specified country. With these statistics, you can spot the largest and fastest growing export markets for products like yours; or identify the largest and fastest growing U.S. exports to a particular country. Individual tables can be downloaded to a spreadsheet. Once in the spreadsheet, you can do whatever calculations and sorting you wish (e.g., growth rates, rank ordering, projections, etc.). See **Appendix D2 (Worksheets 1-6)** for sample Commodity-by-Country U.S. export statistics

Foreign trade statistics[13] (Matrix columns 4-7) help "size up" markets of interest, identify the major supplier countries, and compare competitor country market shares. (Best sources: UN COMTRADE[14] and International Trade Centre[15].) Each country compiles and publishes its own import statistics. The United Nations also consolidates and publishes the data, but in broader product categories and on a less current basis.

Foreign Market Research (Matrix columns 8-11) can provide more detailed assessments of market potentials for your products in promising countries. Chapter IV of Commerce Department Country Commercial Guides[16] identifies the industries offering the best prospects for U.S. exports in the target country over the coming two years. These can be considered "recommended" industries for Matrix column 11. International market surveys and reports are available by product and/or country from DOC/ITA (manufactures and services research[17]) and USDA/FAS (commodities and products research). These comprehensive reports typically cover overall demand trends; best sales prospects within the subsector; key end-user segments; major competitors; customary business practices, market barriers, and useful government and industry contacts. They offer corroborating information for columns 8-11 in the Matrix. DOC/ITA also offers a Customized Market Research[18] service tailored to a company's specific product. A customized survey is conducted in the selected market to assess sales prospects, identify competitors, compare prices, recommend marketing and distribution channels, and identify potentially interested buyers and distributors.

* * *

5D. Develop Market-Specific Entry Plans

Each target market needs its own market entry strategy. Foreign markets can differ in many ways—in income levels, technical standards, climates, sizes of people and space, language, religion, cultural preferences and taboos, business practices, etc. These differences often dictate whether your products could freely access the market, could be afforded, could tolerate the local physical environment, would "fit" or operate efficiently, or would appeal to or offend potential buyers. Without a market-conducive entry strategy, you will not maximize your market potential; or worse, you could make costly mistakes. The biggest mistake is to assume that all markets can be approached in the same way, or the way you operate domestically. In its simplest form, a market entry plan should address 4 key points—distribution, pricing, promotion, and adaptation/localization.

Distribution strategy. Distribution options include selling through local agents or distributors; selling directly to buyers; hiring overseas sales staff; or setting up overseas sales offices, joint ventures or subsidiaries. The right approach largely depends on how much control you want over the process, the expected volume of sales, the openness of the market, and what is customary in each market. For guidance on which approach is best in any given market, see Country Commercial Guides (CCGs) and industry-specific Top Market Series[19]. CCGs cover distribution options in **Chapter 3**, "Marketing U.S. Products and Services in (country)." The Top Market reports discuss customary and recommended distribution channels for specific products in each recommended country.

Selling through local agents or distributors is the norm in most markets. As market "insiders," they speak the language, understand how business is done, know who and where the customers are, and are conveniently nearby for after-sale service. They can also support you in ways that you can't as well from afar. For example, they can develop and send you sales orders, arrange payment, prepare required import documents, and clear the goods through customs. If they function in an **agent** capacity, you pay them a commission per sale. As **distribu-**

tors, they generally purchase the goods and resell them at a markup, while still representing you. Many distributors are equipped to stock, install and service the goods. In larger, developed markets, agents and distributors often specialize by industry. In smaller, less developed markets, they're more likely to carry many different lines. If you opt for this distribution method, it's critical to find the "right" agent or distributor for your product and support needs. See **Chapter 5G** for tips on finding and vetting agents and distributors.

Selling direct to end users. Direct selling avoids intermediary costs and offers more control over price, service, and level of effort. Direct sales could be a good option for products needed by finite groups of end-users (e.g., utilities, hospitals, or other discrete sectors). In most countries, you could probably identify and contact them yourself. Another direct selling method is **online**—through an eCommerce shopping cart. Here you would sell directly to anyone who finds you on the web and places an order. This method has limitations. It could work well for exports of consumer goods—typically purchased in smaller amounts by credit card—but not as well for industrial goods. These are mostly purchased in much larger amounts and paid by traditional Letters of Credit or Documentary Collections, not off shopping carts by credit card.

Pricing strategy. You should have your global pricing strategy in place before you solicit export sales, as potential buyers will invariably ask "what's the price." You basically have two pricing options—price to compete (at least above cost) or price as high as the market will bear. The optimum price will depend on the conditions in each country that affect ability or willingness to pay (e.g., affordability, available substitutes, competition). For this reason, your global pricing strategy should not be a "one price fits all" model. Moreover, even if research points to a reasonable price point for a country, buyers may still try to bargain for a lower price. If you have no margin for a price cut, you could try to justify the higher price by touting superior or cost-saving product attributes and/or by offering more generous payment terms.

Ideally, your export price should cover all costs, meet the competition, attract buyers, and still make a profit. That's a tall order, complicated by the fact that the "optimum" price in one market may not work in other markets. Your pricing strategy should generally start with your domestic price, since that price already factors in your desired profit margin above your production and overhead costs. If that will work in your target markets, leave it there. However, you may need to adjust down or up under certain circumstances.

Pricing down. You may need to cut prices if faced with strong competition or price resistance in target markets. If selling through local distributors, you'll need to factor in a distributor discount. The distributor determines any further price markup, usually in consultation with you.

Pricing up. The good reason for pricing up is that the market will bear it. That's usually a function of high market demand, lack of competing substitutes, and your product's particular attributes (new or unique, superior quality, brand recognition). More common are price hikes specific to exporting, such as to cover potential costs to adapt the product to meet foreign regulatory requirements or cultural preferences. You might also have pre-shipment costs to test and certify that the product meets specifications of the importer or importing country, or for stronger packaging to protect against damage to the goods in transit.

Your global pricing strategy should also include a "how-to-get-paid" element, as some payment methods can make the price more or less tolerable to the buyer. For example, if the buyer resists a proposed price, a requirement to pay in advance will reinforce the price resistance. On the other hand, by offering more time to pay (e.g., credit terms on open account), buyers may be more willing to pay the higher price. In this sense, a global pricing strategy should be seen more broadly as a global pricing-and payments strategy. Whether you can price up or must price down, flexibility is important if you really want the sale. As long as you can still make a reasonable profit, you might consider volume discounts, or low introductory pricing to gain a foothold in the market, or delayed payment terms to offset price resistance.

Several free resources can help you develop your pricing and payment strategy. All USDOC/ITA Country Commercial Guides (CCGs)[20] have a chapter on "Selling U.S. Products & Services in [select any country]" that covers "Selling Factors and Techniques," "Pricing," and "Methods of Payment." ITA industry-specific Top Market Series[21] can give you a feel for market demand, ability to pay, the extent of competition, and whether price and credit are key competitive factors in the market. Getting actual comparative prices takes more digging. You could ask a prospective overseas rep to check market prices, or pay for a customized market survey, such as Commerce's Customized Market Research[22].

Promotion strategy. You will need some promotion in target markets to make your presence known. Your promotion strategy should spell out the techniques to be used in each market; how much to spend; and who will do it—you and/or your overseas representatives. The promotion options for export are generally the same as domestically—your company website, social media, e-mail, press releases, paid ads, and trade events. Most countries can accommodate any of these methods. However, some techniques may work better than others in particular markets. Also, some cost more. You can promote effectively at low cost through your website, social media, and e-mail. Higher-cost promotions include overseas business trips and trade shows and missions (e.g., added costs for airfare, hotels, food, and event fees). If you opt for the higher, in-country promotions, your overseas rep may be able to handle these without you, or at least share in the costs. Techniques that work best in a given market are covered in Chapter 3 of Country Commercial Guides ("Marketing U.S. Products and Services in [Country]." See **5E** below for much more detail on marketing and promotion techniques.

Adaptation/localization strategy. You might need to make adaptations to your product to avoid offending the **cultures** of your customers or to comply with a country's **regulations** (e.g., local health, safety or technical standards). You might also need to adapt your marketing materials and negotiating style to avoid cultural offense, or to be better understood in translation.

Cultural adaptation. "Culture" encompasses a broad range of traits— values and beliefs, ethics, concepts of right and wrong, morality, humility, honor, fairness, religion, language, tastes, and business customs. Cultural traditions often determine whether foreign customers or counterparts will react favorably or negatively to your product, your marketing, or how you personally interact with your customers. A complicating factor is that cultures not only vary among countries, but also internally in countries with diverse ethnic, religious, and linguistic populations. Of all cultural factors, **religion, language, negotiating styles,** and **business customs** need special attention.

Religion. An estimated 80% of the world's population is religiously affiliated in some way, and every country has at least one dominant religion. Notwithstanding some basic commonalities, virtually all religions have "taboos" that can determine success or failure in a target country. Your **product** can offend if its shape or color is perceived as sacrilegious or triggers negative emotions (e.g., sadness, grief, death). The most common product taboos are food-related. For example, in Hindu India, cows are sacred and beef is prohibited. In countries with large Jewish or Muslim populations, many shoppers will only buy food with Kosher or Halal certifications. See Food and Drink Prohibitions[23] for more examples of food-related taboos. Your marketing can fail if it uses images, words, and shapes considered sacrilegious or that symbolize grief, bad luck, unhappiness, etc. Logos can create good or bad impressions in different countries, particularly if depicting animals or astrological symbols. Colors are also problematic, as they inspire positive emotions in some countries and negative in others. For example, yellow conveys happiness and warmth in most of North America, but death, sorrow and mourning in Latin America. Red represents happiness, joy and celebration in most Asian countries, but symbolizes caution, danger and evil in Middle Eastern countries. For more examples of how colors are perceived in different countries, see Colors Across Cultures[24]. This does not mean you must try to adapt your product or marketing to every existing religion. You could reasonably focus on large customer bases in one or more of the world's top five religions—Christianity, Islam, Hinduism, Judaism, and Buddhism.

Language differences must also be adapted to as needed. Every country has a primary language, and most also have other regional or indigenous languages. For example, India is largely Hindi-speaking, but also has 21 other major languages and over 720 different dialects. English is a fairly universal business language, but may not be understood at all or by large segments of a country's consuming public. You can address language differences by translating versions of your websites, marketing materials, and written communication into target-country languages. However, with 190+ countries and their many different languages, it makes no sense to translate into every possible language. Better to limit translations to one or more of the most widely spoken languages (e.g., Spanish, French, Chinese), unless your target is a single large market with only one major language (e.g., Germany or Japan). Although translations help bridge language divides, they can also have unexpected adverse consequences. Some words, idioms, or company slogans that resonate at home may translate into laughable or even morally offensive meanings elsewhere. For example, Kentucky Fried Chicken's "Finger-Lickin Good" slogan was interpreted as "Eat your fingers off" in China. PepsiCo's "Come Alive with Pepsi" ad translated as "Pepsi brings your ancestors back from the dead" in Taiwan. Vicks brand cough drops became "Ficks" in Germany (slang for sexual intercourse), because the Germans pronounce the letter "v" as "f." For more examples of translation blunders, see "20 Epic Fails in Global Branding."[25]

Negotiating styles. Each country has its own "business etiquette" that can promote deal-making if respected or break the deal if ignored. In this sense, doing it the "right" way may be more important than the deal itself. The 1958 book, "The Ugly American," depicted Americans as oblivious to local customs and generally obnoxious. Despite the passage of years, there is still a perception that Americans are impatient negotiators—let's "cut to the chase." That doesn't go over well in the many "high context"[26] countries in Asia, Latin America, and the Middle East. Their approach to a negotiation is to first take time to build a relationship—get to know you, your family, etc.—before ever "talking turkey" about a deal or contract. Your body language and gestures are key during this interaction with customers. For examples of how body language and gestures are perceived, see "Body Language And Gestures Across The World[27]".

Business customs. Most countries have their own ways of doing business—also known as "business etiquette." You should pay particular attention to and respect local customs for dress code, business cards, use of names and titles, punctuality, welcome and unwelcome topics of conversation, and gift-giving. This adaptation need is best capsulated in the expression, "When in Rome, do as the Romans do." One glaring exception to such blending in is how you handle customary corruption and bribery pressures in countries where "pay to play" is endemic. You probably can't avoid --"everybody does it"—the customary grease demands by petty bureaucrats to move paperwork. However, Americans must draw the line at bribing foreign **government** officials (e.g., to get a lucrative contract), even if others do it. Such bribes are strictly prohibited under the U.S. Foreign Corrupt Practices Act (FCPA)[28]. The FCPA does not technically prohibit bribes to **non-government** takers (an ethical judgment), although the country might itself prohibit such bribes.

Cultural missteps are preventable with advance research and planning. You should take time to research the cultures in each target country and factor any needed adaptations into the market plan. Here are a few of many free Web resources for this purpose:

- The intercultural research[29] area of the ITCI Trade Information Database[30].
- Commerce Department Top Market Series[31] and Country Commercial Guides[32] (see standard chapters on "Business Travel—"Business Customs" and "Trade Regulations."
- Kwintessential Global Guide to Etiquette, Customs & Protocol[33]
- Passport to Trade—Business Etiquette—31 Countries[34]
- Country Intercultural Insights[35]
- BSI Country Guides[36] and Keys to Success[37]

Regulatory adaptation. Your "as is" product won't be allowed entry in a market if it is incompatible with local health, safety or technical standards. All countries have such standards to protect the public or to assure technical compatibility with local systems (e.g., electrical). Before selecting any target market, you need to determine if your products are already compatible with the country's standards or could be cost-effectively adapted to meet them. These standards generally apply to domestic as well as imported products. They are administered by standards bodies in each country and cover a wide range of products. Required adaptations could take several forms, some potentially more costly than others. For example, you night need to convert measures from U.S. to metric; or electrical products from 60 to 50 cycles, or 110 to 220 volt. You might need to downsize appliances or other equipment to fit in smaller spaces. You might need to add or remove ingredients in medicinals or cosmetics, or list ingredients differently in your labels. Except for some standards broadly recognized through international consensus, each country's standards may well differ for the same product, forcing exporters to comply separately for each country. This usually involves getting some form of proof of compliance, such as a certification by an approved body, in some cases backed by mandatory testing. This process can range from nominal cost to very costly and time-consuming.

While all this may seem overwhelming for any exporter, let alone a new exporter, don't despair and, especially, don't give up. You don't have to be a lawyer, or hire one, to find out if any specific regulations in a country would require some form of adaptation of your product. You have three basic options for free or low cost advice—your local U.S. Export Assistance Center (USEAC); the foreign country's U.S.-based embassy or consulate; and your own freight forwarder. These sources can at least tell you what permissions you will need to comply. It's up to you to decide the cost/benefit of any needed adaptation. Of the three sources, the USEACs are your best bet. They have a primary motivation to help you export, and they have direct phone and Email access to their in-country counterparts in the target country who can get the answers, often including the actual specifications you would need to comply with.

You can also do your own research, at least to get the regulatory lay of the land in any country. Here are some free sources of country-specific regulatory information:

- National Trade Estimate Reports on Foreign Trade Barriers[38] (annually updated)
- USDOC Country Commercial Guides[39] (annually updated)
- USDOC Top Market Series[40] (industry-specific by country)
- Market Access Sectoral and Trade Barriers Database (EU)[41]

* * *

5E. Market & Promote in Best Markets

If you're not already known abroad, overseas promotion is a must. You won't sell much if the buyers don't know who you are. Generally, the more you promote, the greater the impact. You can best increase your overseas market exposure through a combination of broadcast and targeted techniques.

Broadcast promotion aims to reach the widest possible audience with your marketing message—to let customers anywhere in the world know who you are, what you do, and why they should want your particular offerings. With the Internet and the worldwide web, you can now do that at very low cost and cost per lead. Virtually anything you say on your company website and in social media can be instantly seen almost anywhere in the world, even if only intended for the domestic market. The potential drawback is that you might get more responses than you want, particularly from foreign firms merely fishing for product samples or proprietary or competitive information. If you're prepared for all comers, or can easily separate wheat from chaff, here are some broadcast options worth a try.

Website optimization. If you're a serious business, you already have company website. However, it may not yet be optimized. A website that **optimally** presents and promotes you would have a look and feel —all the bells and whistles—best able to impress viewers and ultimately lead to purchases. Among other attributes, your Home page would need to immediately grab and hold interest—attractive colors and symbols; informative, but not overly busy; and easy to navigate down logical paths (e.g., About Us, Products and Services, Contacts, etc.). As a selling tool, your website should serve as a virtual company brochure or catalog, with inspirational text and images, price sheets, order forms, etc. If your model is to sell directly online (eCommerce), you would also need a secure shopping cart, with order- confirmation- and fulfillment capabilities. Website optimization also has a dimension beyond just optimal appearance and functionality. With now millions of other sites on the worldwide web, your optimized website can easily get lost in the crowd. You need to take steps to elevate your ranking, so that your website comes up at or near the top when customers search, not so far down that they'll stop looking. That is the purpose of Search Engine Optimization (SEO)[42], a technique that loads the source code with all the keywords ("meta tags") that a searcher will most likely use to find companies and products like yours. If your existing website is not yet optimized in either respect, you will probably need a professional website designer and/or SEO specialist to get this done, at costs commensurate with the complexity. To cut costs, you might try a local college willing to assign your optimization project to a student team.

Website globalization. If you have not yet done any or much exporting, the chances are that you designed your website with just the domestic market in mind. Yet, your website can potentially be "seen" by anyone in the world at any given moment. So, if you want to start or expand exports, you need to ask if your existing website is okay as is. Even if it looks good and works effectively for the domestic market, will it come across as well in foreign markets? It may well not, due especially to the many cultural, language and religious differences around the world. There is no such thing as a website with universal appeal and efficacy for every user in 190+ different countries. Website globalization does not purport to do that. Rather, it aims to enhance the domestic website to also appeal to as many interested foreign users as possible. For example, if your existing site is entirely in English, the mostly non-English speaking countries in the world may miss the point. Since it's not feasible to translate for every country's language, you might consider translations for the languages shared by many countries in the world, such as Spanish, French, or Chinese. To reduce the risk of cultural offenses, you might add or change to words, colors, shapes and symbols generally considered positive in most world cultures. These enhancements just relate to the site's front-end look and feel. Some technical changes to the back end will also be needed. You will likely need a website globalization specialist[43] for this work, especially for back-end enhancements.

Website localization[44] goes a step beyond globalization. You would set up a subsidiary site in each target market—in effect, a "mirror" of the home site. Each such local site would have the domain name for that country (e.g., ABC.uk for the United Kingdom or ABC.ca for Canada). It would have an entirely local look and feel, in the local language and with relevant country-specific content. Given the cost to set up multiple local sites, you should probably reserve this option for just your highest potential markets where localized content would make a big difference.

Social media promotion is a low-cost way to get your message out to a large global audience. You're probably already familiar with four of the major platforms—Google, Facebook, LinkedIn, and YouTube. They and others have global reach. If you use these media for domestic marketing, you can apply the same basic mechanics for foreign markets. You may, however, need to adjust your messaging for markets with different languages and cultures. These adaptations for digital marketing are essentially the same as those discussed above for website globalization[45]. Each social media platform has its own tricks of the trade to maximize exposure.

Here are a few to consider:

Google is not just the world's leading search engine. It is also a powerful worldwide marketing medium. Google Ads[46] allow you to highlight in 3 sentences what might best excite customers almost anywhere in the world and draw them to your website (preferably globalized). You pay only for any resulting clicks to your website or calls to your business.

YouTube is the second most visited website after Google. Your YouTube videos should be "infomercials" that explain, inform, and ultimately generate interest and sales leads. YouTube Ads[47] enable potential customers to take action when they watch or search for videos. You pay only when they show interest. If you're not that skilled at video-making and uploading, consider using a professional video agency. For do-it-yourselfers, at least use a quality microphone and other recording equipment, and record your videos in HD.

Facebook, now including Instagram and Messenger, is also huge globally. Over 2 billion people worldwide use Facebook products every day. You can use either your Facebook business Page or Facebook Ads Manager to drive target customers to your website. Facebook Ads Manager[48] is the starting point to run ads on Facebook, as well as on Instagram, Messenger or Audience Network. It's an all-in-one tool to create ads, manage when and where they'll run, and track how well your campaigns are performing.

LinkedIn reaches over 675 million active professionals worldwide, targetable by job title, function, industry, country, and/or professional or personal interests. LinkedIn Leads[49] can help build your brand, generate leads, and drive traffic to your website.

Email campaigns are a very cost-effective way to promote to your client base. In addition to your own Email contacts, you can buy qualified mailing lists in your target field. Bear in mind, however, that recipients are often bombarded with unwanted messages and will not open every one. Try to craft messages that appear "must-read" at first glance. Also consider how often to send messages to the same targets —not so rarely that you're forgotten, but not so often that you're a nuisance and get "unsubscribed." Above all, you must not "spam[50]." That means keeping each message to a finite number of recipients and not mass-blasting to the point you could be sanctioned.

Export directories, unlike directories of manufacturers[51], only list companies actually engaged or interested in exporting. Since many manufacturers do not export, foreign buyers will more likely look in an export directory to find potential suppliers. It's to your advantage to be listed in export directories, particularly those with worldwide Internet outreach. There are two types of export directories—company-specific and product-specific. An export company directory essentially lists the companies by name and industry category, with fewer details about their specific export products (e.g., Export Yellow Pages[52]). An export product directory highlights the products for export, often with detailed descriptions and images. For example, ThinkGlobal's Expor-tUSA[53] promotes U.S. products and services worldwide through a magazine and a companion on-line service. Each listing provides brief product information and a photo, with links to the company's E-mail address and Web site. You should seek opportunities to list in both types of directories. However, since foreign buyers primarily look for products, not companies, you may get better promotional results from listings in export product directories.

Export "sell" offers. You can post your own "offers to sell" in a number of different electronic trade lead systems, such as Alibaba[54]. It's best to provide as much information as possible in your offer, to reassure potential respondents that you are a serious and reliable supplier. It's especially helpful to be specific in describing your export product (specifications, uses, benefits), quantity available, price and delivery options, your bona fides, and what you would like to know from respondents. See **Appendix G4** for suggested particulars to include in a sell offer. Also, use discretion in selecting trade lead systems. Most allow anyone to post an export offer and have no quality control.

Trade press ads. Many industry magazines published domestically are also circulated abroad. When you advertise or get a favorable review in these industry journals, you reach the same interest groups overseas as domestically—producers, buyers, distributors, and other procurement decision-makers. Nearly all industry magazines carry paid ads, and most have sections that announce or evaluate new products.

Targeted promotion is market-specific. It tailors your promotion just for the one or few markets you think are "best" for you. Since you're not trying to be everywhere at once, you can adapt your message to the particular circumstance in each market—the language, culture, demographics, regulations, etc.—and to the promotional media and methods with the highest return on investment, such as more costly trade missions and trade shows. The costs are higher, but so is the impact and potential rewards. If you have foreign representatives, they can do some or all of the promotion in their territories, usually on a cost-sharing basis. Consider these targeted promotion techniques:

Overseas Business Trips. Face-to-face promotion can be very persuasive. The key is to know whom to see before you get there. Don't waste precious time looking after you arrive. If you don't know anyone in particular, ask for help from a trade assistance organization with overseas representatives. For example, the U.S. Commerce Department can arrange advance appointments and make introductions for U.S. exporters, under its fee-based Gold Key[55] matching service. Other Gold Key options, if needed, include orientation briefings, market research, interpreter service for meetings, and assistance in developing a market strategy and effective follow-up. States can also provide some or all of these matchmaking services where they have overseas offices.

Overseas trade shows. They're more costly, but a trade show puts you face-to-face with many potential customers at once, all able to see you and your products first hand. You can talk face-to face, book orders, and perhaps even sell off the floor. Trade show opportunities exist all over the world. Every country has at least one major annual trade show. Many countries have shows throughout the year, often on specific industry themes. For names, dates and locations, check any one of several on line trade show directories, such as AUMA[56] or the U.S. Commerce Department's Trade Show[57] directory. It's not always easy to get into major overseas shows on your own. They're often booked years in advance. However, you can still participate if a trade assistance organization or industry association has already reserved a pavilion or booth space for eligible exporters. For example, DOC/ITA's Trade Event Partnership Program[58] places U.S. firms in pavilions at leading international trade shows, sometimes as late as six months before the start date, and provides services ranging from advance promotion to booth set-up help, "repfind" assistance, embassy briefings, and other on-site assistance for U.S. exhibitors.

Domestic trade shows. Some domestic trade shows attract large numbers of foreign buyers. They're serious buyers, because they've come a long way to see what's new. If you're an exhibitor, they can see you just as well there as at a foreign show. You get the best of both worlds—the domestic exposure you mainly want, plus spin-off exposure to foreign buyers. The U.S. Commerce Department provides matchmaking support at over 40 domestic trade shows annually under its Trade Event Partnership Program (formerly International Buyer Program) and makes vigorous efforts to attract foreign buyers to these shows. IBP-designated events can be found in the U.S. Commerce Department's Trade Events directory.

Catalog shows. In the U.S., your State may offer opportunities for companies to showcase their product catalogs abroad. These events do not require your physical presence and are much less costly than trade shows. Catalog shows are normally theme-specific and typically make stops in several selected countries. At each stop, foreign prospects can view the displayed catalogs, brochures, videos and other sales materials. You receive any resulting sales leads, along with a list of all foreign buyers attending the event. Check the Commerce Department's Trade Event Partnership Program for dates of upcoming Catalog Shows.

Overseas trade missions. Traveling with a group can add impact to your visit. A group, particularly an "official" delegation, has more prestige, gets more notice and opens more doors. Many state governments and industry associations organize such overseas trade missions. The U.S. Department of Commerce also organizes or certifies Trade Missions[59] specifically designed for matchmaking. Before the trip, Commerce trade specialists evaluate each company's export potential, find and screen contacts, handle the logistics, provide in-country business briefings, and arrange one-on-one meetings with prospective clients. Trade mission opportunities are usually announced well in advance, and your chances of getting on one are good if you apply early enough. Upcoming U.S. Trade Missions are listed in the U.S. Commerce Department's Trade Missions schedule.

* * *

5F. Find Foreign Buyers

You can't assume that the buyers will find you. Most likely, you'll need to find or attract them yourself. There are two basic sources of "buy" leads—the leads you or your reps develop first-hand; and the leads you can solicit or find on international trade lead systems, such as Ali Baba. Clearly, the best leads are the first-hand leads that respond to your promotions, that you uncover at trade shows, on overseas trade missions or business trips, or that your overseas reps find for you. While better, these leads are also more costly to develop. If you don't have overseas reps, or can't afford to promote or travel, try the "second-hand" leads from the online systems. Be sure to quickly follow up leads that look promising, since your competitors can also find these same leads. The ITCI Trade Information Database[60] provides access to Hot Trade Leads[61] that include specific overseas "buy" offers self-posted by individual importers. Whatever your source, use due diligence to assure that the buyers are reputable (see **Chapter 6B—Screen Potential Buyers**). Some of the best leads are for major construction and other development projects still in the planning stage. Many are well-financed by the foreign government or the World Bank and its network of regional development banks. These banks list proposed and pending projects and procurement opportunities on their respective websites, along with procedures for bidding. The initial bidders are invariably large "prime" contractors, but they turn to smaller subcontractors to actually supply the needed equipment, supplies and services.

For procurement leads, see:

- World Bank International Business Opportunities[62]
- African Development Bank Business Opportunities[63]
- Asian Development Bank Business Opportunities[64]
- European Bank's Procurement Opportunities[65]
- Inter-American Development Bank Projects[66]
- North American Development Bank Information[67]

- Trade Development Agency (TDA) Pipeline[68]
- Trade Development Agency (TDA) Feasibility Studies & Projects[69]

* * *

5G. Find Potential Agents/Distributors

If your entry strategy is to sell through agents or distributors, it's crucial to find the "right" one for each market. The "better" representatives have a good feel for the market—they know who's who in your industry, and they know the culture and regulations and how best to develop and sustain your export sales. "Poor" reps, on the other hand, could seriously hamper your export prospects. Among warning signs, they might be overloaded with other accounts; or already represent your competitors; or be unable to stock, install, or service your product if needed. The poor-rep problem is compounded if the country's laws make it difficult or costly to terminate the relationship. Therefore, you want to choose carefully. Finding good overseas reps is a four-step process: 1) identify prospects; 2) check their bona fides; 3) negotiate a representation agreement; and 4) support your reps over time.

Identify prospects. You can try to find prospects on your own or use a rep-find matchmaking service. Do-it-yourself searching can be frustrating and costly without solid leads or recommendations. You can look in directories of foreign manufacturers and importers[70] or purchase targeted mailing lists. However, the listed companies are just names, not necessarily interested or reputable. You could also seek referrals or recommendations from trade associations or from exporters with complementary product lines. Once you have name, you should follow up to solicit possible interest. See a sample **Agent/Distributor Search Letter (Appendix F1)**. A better and still affordable way might be to use a rep-find service... Some State export assistance agencies offer rep-find services to resident exporters. The U.S. Department of Commerce offers two, fee-based repfind services— International Partner Search[71] (IPS) and Gold Key Matching[72] service. In both cases, you would provide requested details about your export product and market objectives. With this information, a U.S. Embassy trade specialist will identify a number of qualified prospects that have expressed interest in representing you. With the IPS, the exporter can follow up with each prospect as desired **without traveling** to the target country. With the Gold Key, the exporter goes to the country for prearranged, face-to-face meetings with each prospect, accompanied by the Embassy trade specialist.

As of 2020, the fee for an IPS is $750 for small companies, $1,750 for medium companies, and $2,250 for large companies. The fee for an IPS Plus Virtual Introductions is $900 for small companies (+$30 per introduction beyond 5), $2,100 for medium companies (+$70 per introduction beyond 5) and $2,700 for large companies[3] (+$90 per introduction beyond 5).

Check bona fides. However you identify prospects, you should thoroughly screen each one before you make a selection. The first key to selection is to know what you want in a rep—then screen to see which ones have those required attributes. The requirements may vary by product, but five basic qualities are fundamental:

- **Experience**—has a solid track record as a rep; expertise in your product area; and strong connections in the user community;
- **Capability**—is not otherwise overloaded and, if needed, can effectively stock and promote your product, train users, and install and service equipment;
- **Motivation**—is enthusiastic about your product and able and willing to give it priority;
- **Loyalty**—does not represent a competitor and would not desert you for a competitor;
- **Honesty**—has a good reputation in the industry and good bank and trade references.

For each serious candidate, you should compile background information at least on the points below. See **Agent/Distributor Qualifications Checklist (Appendix F2)** for more detailed assessment criteria.

- Current status and history
- Principal officers and sales staff
- Warehouse and service facilities
- Sales territory covered
- Current sales volume
- Typical customer profiles
- Foreign firms currently represented
- Trade and bank references
- Capability to meet your requirements
- Opinion on the potential for your products

Don't hesitate to ask prospects for this information. They'll respond if they want your business. Of course, don't go by what they alone say, since they might give self-serving answers. You should also seek neutral sources for corroboration. Check bank references for one. Consider fee-based, company background reports, such as Commerce Department's International Company Profile (ICP)[73] service, or credit reports done by several international credit reporting agencies[74]. A direct meeting with top prospects is also wise at some point, preferably at their premises. Bear in mind, this is a two-way street. Your prospects will also want to know more about your bona fides—who you are and whether you would be a reliable and supportive supplier. First impressions count, so your initial interaction is very important. You should tell them more about your company and products and your market objectives, the qualifications you seek in a potential rep, and what the rep could expect from you (pricing, payment terms, delivery, promotional support, etc.). You should respond promptly to all serious responses, try to answer all questions as fully as possible, and provide standard product literature. Use discretion in sending costly samples, in case they could be easily copied. Samples should be reserved for the top prospects.

Negotiate representation agreements. Once you've found suitable matches, you should formally engage them under an agent/distributor agreement. These agreements spell out the terms of the relationship and the responsibilities of each party. See **Sample Foreign Representa-**

tion Agreement (Appendix F4) for illustrative provisions. These agreements usually cover the following points:

- Products covered
- Territory covered (e.g., country)
- Exclusive or non-exclusive
- Minimum sales/purchase obligations
- Non-circumvention
- Responsibility for marketing/promotion
- Responsibility for shipping
- Responsibility for user training
- Responsibility for technical support
- Allocation of expenses
- Terms of commission/payment
- Handling of complaints and disputes
- Conditions of termination

These points are negotiable. Aim for a mutually beneficial agreement that motivates the rep and protects your interests. The rep will seek your commitment to respond promptly to orders, deliver the product on time, provide any needed training or other specified support, and pay a fair share of any joint marketing and promotion expenses. These are reasonable conditions. In turn, you should seek the following commitments from the rep:

- To apply the utmost skill and ability to the sale of your products
- To effectively perform the marketing, promotion and support tasks you specify
- To meet any performance goals you specify (e.g., sales volume and growth)
- Not to handle competing lines
- Not to disclose confidential information about your company and products
- Not to bind you to agreements without your prior approval

It's also vital to have an escape clause in the agreement. You need the flexibility to make a safe, clean break if the rep doesn't perform as agreed. Most agreements have a duration date (e.g., one year), with automatic annual renewal unless either party opts to terminate. Advance notice is typically required for termination (e.g., 30, 60 or 90 days), and it usually must be for cause if before the normal term (e.g., failure to meet specified performance levels). However, some countries limit termination rights in order to protect local businesses. Without an enforceable termination clause, you might have to retain a poor performer longer than you want, or pay a high fee to sever the relationship. You should consult an internationally experienced attorney before drafting your own or signing any agent/distributor agreement. See here for more tips on negotiating international partner agreements[75].

Support your overseas reps. Good reps need your cooperation and support as much as you need theirs. Treat them as you would your domestic sales force. Your prices, terms and commissions should be reasonable. At the least, you should:

- Alert your reps to planned changes to the product line, pricing and delivery
- Respond promptly to their calls and correspondence
- Provide product training and customer support as needed
- Consider help with promotions, including cost sharing for trade shows and media ads
- Deliver the goods when and as promised

If volume warrants, make periodic visits to help motivate the reps and also get a better feel for what and how they're doing.

CHAPTER 6

MAKE EXPORT SALES AND GET PAID

An export sale usually starts with an inquiry. Someone overseas has heard of you and wants more information. The inquiry might be general (e.g., "Tell me more about your company and product") or specific (e.g., "What's the price?"). Inquiries are precious. Buyers typically have other options. You should respond quickly, fully and professionally. If prospects seem interested in what you tell them, they'll follow up with more specific requests for price, delivery and payment terms. As you provide requested information, you should also ask the prospects for information, such as who they are and what they do. Basically, you need to know if they are serious and reputable. If you're satisfied and want the business, be prepared to negotiate until you've mutually agreed on all the terms (e.g., price, payment, compliance, delivery).

* * *

6A. Respond to Export Inquiries

Follow these basic rules to respond to inquiries and requests for information (see **Sample Responses to Inquiries from Prospective Buyers**

(Appendix G1) and **Sample Responses to Inquiries from Prospective Agents/Distributors (Appendix G2).**

Reply quickly or not at all. Delay implies lack of interest or insensitivity to the inquirer's needs. Also, delays give competitors more time to win the business. Use E-mail, fax, or express delivery as appropriate.

Answer all questions. The inquirers may ask many questions, but should not have to ask the same questions twice. If one of your standard responses answers the questions, send it. If not, revise it to answer the questions.

Use a business-like tone. Impersonal form responses don't make a good impression. Print all responses on company letterhead. If not already embedded in the letterhead, add name, title, phone, fax, E-mail and Web address. If starting from a standard message, add customized touches to appear more directly responsive. Avoid slang or informal responses.

Reply in the language specified. Most inquiries are in English. Some are in the inquirer's language, but invite a reply in English. If the inquiry is not in English, have it translated so it's clear what the inquirer wants. Translate the response if requested. Commercial translators will do this for a fee. Some colleges and universities also offer translation services. For instant translations of uncomplicated messages, try Google's Language Tools.

Should you respond to every inquiry? No. You might disregard form letters or inquiries that are clearly unprofessional or poorly written. However, it's not always possible to distinguish serious from frivolous requests. Err on the side of responding to all or most inquiries. If in doubt, don't send samples or bulky product literature that costs more in postage.

6B. Screen Potential Buyers

Before committing to any sale, verify that the buyer can be trusted, especially to pay when due. Due diligence is critical. To assess ability to pay start by requesting bank and trade references. Ask these references about their experiences with the buyer. If still uncertain, use services that report on the credit worthiness and other bona fides of foreign companies. Company credit reports are available from international credit reporting agencies[1] in many countries. Credit reports focus on a company's "financials" (e.g., capitalization, creditworthiness, cash flow, ability to pay on time). Most agencies only report on domestic companies, but those below can produce credit reports on virtually any company in any country.

- Equifax International Credit Reports[2]
- Experian International Business Credit Reports[3]
- FCIB Worldwide Credit Reports[4]
- Coface Analyze my Customers and Prospects[5] and Debtor Risk Assessments[6]
- Dun & Bradstreet (D&B) Credit Evaluator Plus[7]
- Graydon's International Credit Reports[8]

In addition to these sources, the Commerce Department's International Company Profile (ICP)[9] goes beyond financials to also assess the foreign company's overall "suitability" as a potential partner (buyer or distributor). The ICP investigation is conducted by a commercial specialist at a U.S. embassy or Consulate who is most familiar with the industry. U.S. exporters can order ICPs from a local U.S. Export Assistance Center. A number of U.S. States have overseas trade offices that will compile foreign company information for State residents. As of 2020, the fee for a "full" ICP is $700 for small companies, $1,200 for medium companies, and $2,000 for large companies. The fee for a "partial" ICP is $150 for small companies, $350 for medium companies, and $450 for large companies.

* * *

6C. Negotiate Terms of the Export Sale

Your discussions with potential foreign buyers should hopefully lead to a negotiation on the terms of a sale. These negotiation typically deal with **price, payment** and **delivery** terms.

Price terms. The price discussion usually starts with the buyer's request for a quote (RFQ). Buyers will just ask for your factory price if they plan to pick up the goods there and pay all further delivery costs. Or, they might ask for the price delivered to their country, or to points in between (e.g., the port of exit). Each specified point is defined by a 3-letter acronym, known as an International Commercial Term (Incoterm)[10]. For example, an EXW (ExWorks) quote is the price for pick-up at your factory. An FAS or FOB quote is the price to deliver to the port of exit. A CIF (Cost, Insurance, & Freight) quote is the price for delivery to the foreign port of entry. You would know your EXW price, because that is essentially your domestic sales price. However, you might not know the additional fees and transportation and insurance costs to deliver beyond the factory, especially if by air or sea to the destination country. Your freight forwarder can provide all such added costs to include in your price quote. For help with price quotes by Incoterm, see **Template for Responding to a Foreign Request for Quote (Appendix G5), Sample Export Quotation (Appendix G6)**, and **Export Quotation Worksheet (Appendix G7)**. For a more detailed explanation of Incoterms 2020, see **Appendix G8**.

Unless your product is a "must have" with no other source, the buyer may well say your price is too high. Don't give up at that point. A deal might still be negotiable. You could consider reducing the price to a still profitable level. If you can't or don't want to do that, you can try non-price reasons to buy your product, if applicable, such as its superiority in some way over competitors—e.g., unique, unmatched functionality, greater durability, cost-saving, just-in-time (JIT) delivery, etc. If those don't work, and you can afford the cash flow hit, your most persuasive counter to price resistance would be to allow the buyer more time to pay (e.g., 30-90 days after delivery). Don't be deterred by fear of not getting paid. As discussed in detail in **Chapter**

6E, you can buy very low-cost credit insurance to protect against buyer default.

Payment terms. Another common negotiable issue is how-and when you will get paid. You, the exporter, might start with, "pay me all up front," while the buyer might start with, "I'll pay you 30-90 days after I get the goods." If both stick with their starting points, no deal will result. If the deal is otherwise too good to pass up, one or the other might concede or accept somewhere in between, such as pay 25% up front and the balance on delivery, or pay me later, but with a "guaranty" of payment. This gets to the related issue of the method of payment—some methods are more secure than others. For example, a secure wire transfer or a credit card would be the up-front payment method. A standard bank instrument (e.g., a Letter of Credit or a sight or time draft) could be the method for payment on- or after delivery. These methods are discussed in more detail in **Chapter 6D.**

Delivery terms. You and the buyer need to agree on these, but they are not normally contentious. The main issues are, how to deliver (e.g., air or sea), by when to deliver (estimated departure or arrival dates), whether any special packaging is needed (e.g., for refrigeration or for HAZMAT protection), and possibly how often to deliver recurring orders. These delivery issues are covered in more detail in **Chapters 8 and 9.** Your freight forwarder can advise and handle all these matters.

When you and the buyer have agreed on the final terms, you would typically confirm them in a Proforma Invoice[11]. Proforma invoices are not bills for payment, since a sale has not yet occurred. They're basically quotations in an invoice format. They require more detail than domestic quotations, because the customer may also need them to obtain an import license or open a Letter of Credit. Although formats can vary, Proforma invoices should be neatly typed on business letterhead and cover the following points:

- Date prepared
- Total cubic volume and dimensions
- Exporter's name, address, telephone/fax/
- Delivery point

- Buyer's name and address
- Terms of sale
- Buyer's reference number and date of inquiry
- Payment terms and method
- List and brief description of products
- Insurance and shipping costs—who will pay
- Price per item (e.g., in US$)
- Total charges to be paid by customer
- Trade discount, if applicable
- Shipping date from factory or exit port
- Country of origin of the goods
- Estimated date of shipment arrival
- Gross and net shipping weight
- An explicit expiration date for quotation

6D. Select Method of Export Payment

Export payment terms and methods—when and how to get paid—are negotiable between exporter and importer. Both parties have interests and risks at stake, and each approaches the payment issue from somewhat opposite ends. These differences must be mutually understood and accommodated in a successful negotiation.

For exporters, the key payment issues are:

- How soon can I get paid (before or after shipment)
- How will I get paid (currency and payment method and process)
- How do I protect against non-payment (risk mitigation)

For importers, the converse issues are:

- How soon do I have to pay (the more time the better)
- How will I make the payment (currency and payment method and process)
- How do I make certain I get what I paid for

Timing of payment. Advance payment is not the norm in exporting. Foreign buyers generally will only pay for smaller purchases up front. While eCommerce exports with up front credit card payment are increasing, this is still mostly for smaller, consumer goods purchases. The vast majority of industrial and agricultural exports are still shipped before payment, with banks at each end processing the payments.

Payment currency. New or less experienced exporters should require payment in a stable currency (e.g., U.S. dollars). Even if the buyer's currency depreciates, you are still owed the dollar amount specified. More experienced exporters might use hedging techniques to lock in future exchange rates.

Methods of payment. Assuming agreement on the price, exports can be paid for in several different ways. The most common payment methods, from least risk to most risk for the exporters are:

- **100% cash in advance,** by wire transfer, credit card, or by discounting (factoring) the receivable.
- **Partial payment up front (e.g., 25-50%), the balance on delivery** (e.g., by L/C or D/P/Sight Draft as below).
- **Irrevocable, confirmed Letter of Credit** (L/C)—payment guaranteed by the exporter's bank, typically on delivery.
- **Documents Against Payment** (D/P), also known as a Sight Draft, paid on delivery.
- **Documents Against Acceptance** (D/A), also known as a Time Draft, paid at a specified date after delivery.

Cash in advance[12] is best for exporters, particularly by wire transfer, because there is no cash-flow burden and no risk of buyer default. Advance payment by credit card offers the same benefit, but could run the risk of credit card fraud. For foreign buyers, however, advance payment is the worst option. It not only shifts the cash-flow burden to them, but forces them to pay before they can even see what they are getting. Also, they know they can usually find a competing supplier willing to offer better terms. Therefore, unless this is a "must" buy with no other source, the buyer will likely say no to cash in advance. If faced with this resistance, try for an up-front installment payment, say 25-50%, with the balance paid on delivery or at a specified later time. If the buyer still says no, consider other payment options that also greatly reduce the payment risk, such as Letters of Credit, documentary collections, and even open account backed by export credit insurance. Alternatively, if the exporter is unwilling to sell without advance payment, another possible option is to discount or "factor" the receivable. Factoring[13] companies will buy the export receivable for a fee. After paying the exporter up front, the Factor takes on the risk of collecting from the importer. Factors logically charge a relatively high premium for this service, but it's a risk-free, up-front payment for exporters if they can afford it.

Letters of Credit (L/Cs)[14] are the most secure payment method after cash in advance and more acceptable to foreign buyers. The buyer starts at his bank by opening an L/C in the exporter's favor for the full amount of the sale. The L/C guarantees that the exporter will be paid by the buyer's bank (e.g., Bank of Mexico), not by the buyer. An L/C can be at sight (immediate payment upon presentation of documents), or it can be a time or date L/C (payment to be made at a specified future date). In return for the buyer's bank taking on the obligation to pay, the buyer agrees to repay the bank at some future date. That's between the two of them, not the exporter's concern. For even greater protection, the exporter's own bank can take on the payment obligation from the foreign bank. This is done through a routine, inter-bank "confirmation" process. The resulting payment instrument is known as an "Irrevocable, Confirmed L/C."

L/Cs are designed to protect both the exporter and the buyer. The exporter gets a guarantee of payment by a reputable bank; the buyer gets a guarantee that the exporter will deliver exactly what was ordered and by when, as specified in the L/C. To assure this mutual benefit, the L/C terms must be identical to terms in the purchase order and all related shipping documents. If there are any "discrepancies" among the documents, or the goods are not exactly as ordered or delivered on time, the buyer is not obliged to pay, and the bank is not obliged to release the payment. Thus, compliance with all L/C terms is crucial. The exporter's bank and freight forwarder can help make sure that the price and terms are reconciled in all the documents. Should an unexpected problem arise with the documents or the shipment, it can often be resolved amicably. Contact the buyer immediately and ask for an amendment to the L/C to correct the problem.

Here's a typical L/C scenario:

- The exporter and the buyer agree on the terms of a sale.
- The buyer applies for the L/C for the amount due from a local commercial bank (see a sample L/C **in Appendix H1**). The L/C is normally "irrevocable" (no changes permitted without the consent of both the buyer and the seller). The bank typically requires the buyer to put up collateral to cover the L/C amount. At this point, the buyer's bank takes on the obligation to pay the exporter.
- The buyer's bank prepares the irrevocable L/C and all L/C Instructions (**Appendix H2**).
- The buyer's bank sends the irrevocable L/C to its correspondent bank in the exporter's country, requesting "confirmation." At this point, the confirming bank (typically, the exporter's own bank) accepts the obligation to pay the exporter.
- The confirming bank sends the exporter a letter of confirmation along with the "confirmed, irrevocable" L/C.
- The exporter reviews and accepts all conditions in the L/C.
- The exporter's freight forwarder delivers the goods to the named exit port or airport.

- When the goods are loaded, the forwarder completes the necessary documents.
- The exporter or the forwarder present documents to the confirming bank showing full compliance with all product and delivery terms and conditions specified in the L/C.
- The confirming bank checks that documents are in order and sends them to the buyer's bank for review.
- The buyer gets the documents from his bank and uses them to claim the goods.
- The confirming bank pays the exporter at the time specified.

Compliance with all L/C terms is crucial. You should carefully review the L/C and make sure the price and terms are the same as agreed to in price quotes and other documents. If the L/C terms are not precisely met, the bank might not pay. Also, the bank will only pay the amount in the L/C, even if higher charges for shipping, insurance or other factors are documented. If the L/C terms can't be met, or it has errors or even misspellings, you should contact the buyer immediately and ask for an amendment to the L/C to correct the problem. To get paid, you must provide documentation showing that the goods were shipped by the date specified. The freight forwarder can advise about any unusual conditions that might delay shipment. You must also present the documents by the date specified. The bankers can advise whether there's enough time to meet a presentation deadline. You should always request that the L/C specify that partial shipments and transshipment will be allowed. This will avoid unforeseen problems at the last minute. Despite their fairly wide use and mutual benefit, L/Cs cost both parties more in bank fees than other methods. Moreover, the buyer must repay his bank for the L/C amount covered, at high interest rates in some countries. For these reasons, the parties may prefer other, less costly payment methods that still offer reasonable protection against buyer default, such as "Documentary Collections."

Documentary Collections[15] basically equate to cash on delivery (COD) or cash at a mutually agreed later date. They are relatively safe and are routinely handled by banks without the L/C-like fees. In the COD version, also known as **Documents Against Payment** (D/P)[16] or

"Sight Draft, the bank in the importing country receives title to the goods (in the form of the Bill of Lading accompanying the shipment). The buyer must pay the bank the full amount owed to get title (access) to the goods. If the buyer for some reason decides not to pay (a potential risk), the exporter can bring the goods back or sell to someone else, but not lose the goods. In the mutually-agreed delayed payment version, also known as **Documents Against Acceptance** (D/A)[17] or Time Draft, the goods are released to the buyer with a specified time to repay. This is open account in effect, more risky, but the exporter can virtually eliminate the risk by purchasing export credit insurance[18] from the U.S. Export-Import Bank. If the buyer later defaults for any reason, the insurance policy will cover nearly all the loss.

Open account[19] is the payment method most favored by the buyers, because they do not have to pay until some agreed upon time after they get the goods (typically 30-120 days). Inexperienced exporters generally avoid open account and lose many deals for fear that they will not get paid in the end. However, savvy exporters know how to protect against buyer default, even for open account sales. They also know that they can be much more competitive if willing to sell on open account, especially if their prices are higher than other suppliers. The risk can be mitigated almost entirely with an **export credit insurance policy**[20] from the U.S. Export-Import Bank (Exim). Under these very inexpensive policies, the exporter is guaranteed nearly full payment if the buyer later defaults. Without export insurance for open account terms, the exporter should be especially vigilant in due diligence or reserve this option only for buyers that are well established, have solid payment records, or have been thoroughly checked for creditworthiness.

Assuming agreement on the price, a typical compromise on payment and delivery that reasonably protects both parties might be a) payment on arrival, b) in USD, and c) by L/C or D/P. If price is a sticking point for the buyer, the seller could fall back to payment 30-90 days **after** delivery on open account, backed by Exim's export credit insurance.

* * *

6E. Protect Against Buyer Default

To some extent, sellers are always at risk of buyer default, even with domestic sales. Due diligence is the first line of defense. It's important to check out the reputability and credit worthiness of any potential buyer, unless they are already well-known to you or are well known in the industry. Learn what you can from the company's website, seek bank references, and consider credit and background checks from organizations providing these services (see **Chapter 6B, Screen Potential Buyers**). For unknown or uncertain buyers, try first for low risk, L/C or D/P terms, if not payment in advance. If the buyer insists on payment after delivery (time draft or open account), and you don't want to lose the sale, you still have a great, low-risk option. You can purchase **Export Credit Insurance** from the U.S. Export-Import Bank (Ex-Im). The insurance costs very little, guarantees nearly full payment if the buyer defaults for any commercial or political reason, and is a powerful tool to keep you in the mix if the buyer won't accept other terms you might prefer.

CHAPTER 7

COMPLY WITH REGULATORY & DOCUMENTARY REQUIREMENTS

All countries takes steps to control imports, mostly to protect domestic industries or to protect the public from potentially harmful goods (unsafe, unhealthy, immoral, technically incompatible, etc.). Import controls can take many forms—e.g., tariffs and non-tariff barriers such as quotas, exchange controls, health, safety and technical standards, buy-local procurement requirement). More surprising, perhaps, are the controls that many countries also impose on their own exports, especially including the U.S. The main instrument of control at both ends is a documentary requirement of some kind—e.g., a. license, certificate, or other form of permission.

* * *

7A. Comply with U.S. Export Regulations

The U.S. is especially concerned about exports that could endanger national security—in effect, that could "aid an enemy," but also exports that could injure, sicken or otherwise harm foreign consumers. The U.S. also controls exports for other reasons—e.g., to prevent depletion of products in short-supply, attest to the quality of potentially harmful products, and prevent anti-competitive practices.

U.S. national security export controls. The U.S. takes great care to prevent its exports from getting into the hands of foreign adversaries. Violations of national security export controls carry very severe penalties, even if unwitting. The relevant U.S. export controls apply in three specific ways—to the export **product**, to the foreign **end user**, and/or to the destination **country**. It's important to understand that **all** U.S. exports are **subject to** these national security controls and **may** require advance approval and a license to export. The onus is on you, the exporter, to determine in advance if any such export controls apply in your situation. If so, you'll need an export license, unless you qualify for a license exception. A product's Export Control Classification Number (ECCN)[1] determines whether and what type of license, if any, is required for a specified product, end-user, and/or destination. If in doubt, U.S. exporters may ask the Commerce Department's Bureau of Industry and Security[2] (BIS) for an "Advisory Opinion."

Product controls—could the product itself be used against the U.S. in foreign hands? If yes, the exporter would need to apply for and obtain an export license. Product-specific controls are administered by two U.S. agencies. The State Department's Directorate of Defense Trade Controls (DDTC)[3] controls purely military items under the International Traffic in Arms Regulations (ITAR)[4]. All the controlled military items are shown on the Munitions List[5]. The Commerce Department's BIS controls non-military (civilian) items, as well as items that could also have a "dual use" (civilian as well as military). For example, night vision goggles could have a dual use—one to hunt game at night (okay); the other to kill people at night (not okay). Under BIS' Export Administration Regulations (EAR)[6], all the controlled civilian and dual-use items are identified on the Commerce Control List[7] by their ECCN number. A freight forwarder can assist in flagging a license requirement, but the exporter has ultimate responsibility to determine if the export product appears on either list. If so, the exporter must apply for an export license from BIS. The fact that a product is controlled, however, does not mean it can't be exported. The license may well be granted. The good news is that over 90% of U.S. products exported are neither military nor dual use and therefore won't require an export license. For exports not requiring a license, simply specify "NLR" (no license required) on the Automated Export System (AES)[8] filing.

End-user controls—is the foreign intermediary or end user of the product considered dangerous? If so, they are "denied" for export of any product, even if a benign product. BIS maintains a Denied Persons List[9] and a Denied Entities List[10] of all blacklisted foreign individuals or organizations for this purpose. Exporters, with customary help from their freight forwarder, need to make sure they are not exporting to a denied party or entity.

Country controls—is the importing country a national security risk to the U.S? If so, any export or transfer of assets to that "sanctioned" country would require a license. BIS implements U.S. Government sanctions against Cuba, Iran, North Korea, Sudan, and Syria, either unilaterally or to implement United Nations Security Council Resolutions. The license requirements, license exceptions, and licensing policy vary, depending on the particular sanctioned country. In addition to BIS sanctions, the Department of the Treasury's Office of Foreign Assets Control (OFAC)[11] also implements certain sanctions against Cuba, Iran, North Korea, Sudan, and Syria under the Foreign Assets Control Regulations (FACR)[12]. Exporters and re-exporters are responsible for complying with all applicable regulatory requirements.

U.S. health, safety and sanitary export controls. These types of controls mainly assure that the exported goods meet the importing country's health, safety and/or quality standards. The controls mostly apply to food and agriculture items, biotechnology products, medical devices, cosmetics, and pharmaceuticals. To satisfy the requirement, exporters will usually need a "certificate" from the enforcing agency or, in many cases, from a chamber of commerce. For example, a Phytosanitary Certificate[13] attests that a shipment of grain is free from pathogens or pests. Food & Drug Administration (FDA) Export Certificates[14] may be needed to export animals, food, food ingredients, medical devices, pharmaceuticals, and cosmetics. These Certificates attest that the animal and food-related products are grown, produced, processed, packaged and labeled to the importing country's standards; and that the medical devices, pharmaceuticals and cosmetics are "of no lesser quality" than those sold in the U.S. market. See **Appendix I** for the products affected by these regulations and the agencies that enforce them.

U.S. product-specific export controls. Several U.S. agencies regulate exports of products that pose safety or health risks unrelated to national security, including hazardous materials, animal, food and agricultural products, medical devices, drugs and pharmaceuticals, and cosmetics. Much of the needed compliance information is freely available on the websites of the responsible enforcement agencies.

Hazardous materials controls: The Transportation Department's Pipeline and Hazardous Materials Safety Administration (PHMSA)[15] regulates international trade in hazardous materials (HAZMAT) through a permitting process under the Hazardous Materials Regulations (HMR)[16]. Exporters and importers of certain quantities and types of hazardous materials, including hazardous wastes, must file an annual registration statement with PHMSA and pay a fee.

Food and agricultural product controls: The Department of Agriculture has several units that regulate exports of agricultural products, mainly through inspections and certifications attesting to quality. USDA's Animal and Plant Health Inspection Service (APHIS)[17] issues Phytosanitary certificates[18] for exported and imported grains (free of pests and diseases). The Federal Grain Inspection Service (FGIS)[19] certifies to the quality of plants and plant products (e.g. bulbs, seeds, grain, fruits and vegetables, cut flowers). The Food Safety Inspection Service (FSIS)[20] similarly regulates exports of meat, poultry processed egg products and other food and agricultural products. The Food & Drug Administration (FDA)[21] Compliance and Enforcement[22] protects consumers from unsafe imported foods by monitoring foreign firms exporting to the U.S. and inspecting the goods on arrival.

Health-related product controls: FDA regulates exports of medical devices[23], radiation-emitting products[24], drugs[25], vaccines, blood & biologics[26], and cosmetics[27], primarily through Certificates of Free Sale[28] issued by FDA or by a State or Chamber of Commerce in behalf of FDA. These Certificates are also known by other names, such as

Health Certificate, Export Certificate, and Sanitary Certificates. They attest that the particular export product is U.S. made, is the same as that sold in the U.S., and that the manufacturer has no unresolved enforcement actions pending before the FDA or the State. Most foreign countries require such Certificates to assure that the product is not of lesser quality than that sold in the U.S.

U.S. anti-competitiveness trade controls: The U.S. protects against anti-competitiveness practices under the Foreign Corrupt Practices Act (FCPA)[29] and Anti-Boycott Regulations[30]. The FCPA, enforced by the Justice Department Fraud Section, prohibits U.S. firms from bribing foreign government officials "to assist in obtaining or retaining business," such as a bribe to win very large export deals. FCPA does not apply to bribes of non-government officials or to low-level "grease" payments often demanded by petty bureaucrats to expedite paperwork. U.S. Anti-Boycott Regulations, enforced by BIS' Office of Anti-Boycott Compliance (OAC)[31], prohibit U.S. firms from acceding to foreign demands to boycott another country as a condition for doing business. U.S. firms faced with such boycott demands can fend off the pressure by saying they cannot comply under U.S. law.

Advisory sources for U.S. export controls: The best sources for advice are internal legal staff or, if none, international attorneys and freight forwarders[32]. Other advisory sources are trade specialists at U.S. Export Assistance Centers[33] and enforcement staff at the regulatory agencies. Beyond expert advice, much of the needed information can be found here:

- U.S. National Security Export Controls (EAR, ITAR, FACR)[34]
- Other U.S. Export Laws & Regulations[35]

And on the websites of the relevant enforcement agencies listed in **Appendix I**.

$$* * *$$

7B. Comply with Foreign Import Regulations

All countries regulate imports to a greater or lesser extent, primarily through a combination of tariff and non-tariff barriers (NTBs). These measures can either encourage or discourage imports. For example, countries like Hong Kong and Singapore are open markets with mostly zero import duties and few other restrictions. Most industrialized countries also have relatively open markets. Less developed countries still tend to have higher, protectionist tariffs and NTBs. Tariffs, also known as import duties, are direct taxes on imported products. NTBs cover a broad spectrum of laws, regulations, and business practices that restrict imports for some policy purpose. Most NTBs are reasonable and tolerable –e.g., to protect public health and safety—others are more clearly to protect domestic industries from import competition. Whatever the reason, high tariffs and NTBs invariably increase the foreign buyer's import costs. To compensate, if easier markets can't be found, exporters may need to make costly product adaptations to comply with health, safety and technical standards, or make price concessions to remain competitive.

Tariffs[36]. Nearly all countries impose tariffs on at least some products, ranging from low rates to generate revenue to high rates to protect domestic industries. Tariffs are based on the product's Harmonized System (HS) code[37]. Most rates are assessed "ad valorem, as a percent (e.g., 25%) of the product's declared import value. Duties can also be "specific"—i.e., at a fixed amount per unit (e.g., $2 per pound). In some cases, duties may be a combination of ad valorem and specific. If you're faced with a prohibitive tariff, you probably cannot lower your prices enough to compete with domestic competitors. You might be better off avoiding high-tariff markets and look instead at zero-or low-duty markets, such as the 21 markets with which the U.S. has Free Trade Agreements[38]. If a high-duty market is too promising to pass up, you might consider local production within the country through a licensing agreement, joint venture, or subsidiary.

However, if you still want to export directly to the high-duty country, you might consider tariff engineering[39], a duty-reduction technique that can take two possible forms. One is to call your product by another (similar) name that has a lower duty. The new name would need to be comparable enough to pass muster. For example, calling an "apple" an "orange" would obviously not qualify, but calling a "doll" a "toy" did work in a classic U.S. court case. In that case, a U.S. company successfully argued that its action figure should be classified as a "toy" (at a lower duty rate), not as a "doll" (at a higher duty). The second method is to actually modify the character or design of the product just enough to qualify it under a different tariff code at a lower duty rate. As a hypothetical, for example, a 26.9% import duty on a woman's blouse with 50% cotton-50% polyester could be reduced to just 15.4% by slightly increasing the cotton content to 51%. The redesign method would not make sense if the savings from a lower duty were less than the cost to modify the product. Be aware also that Customs authorities tend to view tariff engineering suspiciously as potential duty evasion, not legitimate tax avoidance.

Duty and tax rates are published by the Customs agency in each country. You can also find import duties by country and product at these sources:

- WTO Tariff Schedules[40]
- WTO Tariff Analysis Online[41]
- FTA Tariff Search Tool by Country[42]
- Japan Import Tariffs[43]
- Canadian Customs Tariff[44]
- EU Tariff Lookup[45]

Non-tariff barriers (NTBs) broadly comprise all methods except tariffs to restrict imports. They take many forms that in one way or other aim at either protecting the country's domestic industries; economy and technical infrastructure; public health and safety; and/or business and cultural norms. Here are some of the more prevalent and impactful NTBs.

- **Quantitative restrictions** (QRs) are essentially quotas that limit how much of the product can be imported (by value or quantity) during a specified time period (e.g., quarterly or annually). QRs are mostly confined to labor-intensive industries heavily impacted by imports (e.g., textiles and apparel). The most extreme form of a QR, an outright import ban, is usually not for industry protection, but more to protect a religious or moral value (e.g., prohibited foods or items considered blasphemous).

- **Safety and technical standards** protect against products that could cause injury to the public (e.g., hazardous materials, unsafe toys) or would not be compatible with the country's industrial technology (e.g., electrical standards). These standards are administered by standards bodies in each country and generally apply to domestic as well as imported products. Except for some U.S. standards broadly recognized through international consensus (e.g., UL standards[46]), each country may have different standards for the same product, forcing companies to comply separately for each country. This usually involves getting some form of proof of compliance, such as a certification by an approved body, in some cases backed by mandatory testing. This process can be very costly and time-consuming.

The European Union has particularly rigorous product standards across many industries, most notably the CE (Conformité Européenne) Mark[47]. The mark consists of the CE logo and, if applicable, the four digit identification number of the Notified Body involved in the conformity assessment. The CE mark is the manufacturer's declaration that the product meets the prescribed health, safety, and environmental protection standards in the applicable EC directives[48]. Depending on the level of product risk, the CE mark is affixed to a product by the manufacturer or authorized representative charged with ensuring that the product meets all the CE marking requirements. In some cases, if a product has minimal risk, a manufacturer can self-certify with a declaration of conformity and affix the CE mark to its own product.

Sanitary and phytosanitary measures protect human and animal life from pests or unsafe additives, contaminants, toxins or disease-causing organisms in food. The protective measures can take many forms, depending on the country, such as proof that the food came from a disease-free area, requiring pre-shipment inspections or specific treatment or processing methods; setting maximum allowable levels of pesticide residues; or permitting only certain additives in food.

Import permits. Some countries, mostly developing, list products that can only be imported with permission from a designated authority. Importers apply to receive permission, usually in the form of a license to import. A "general" license permits imports of the listed product for a specified limited time. A "one-time" license allows import of a listed product at a specified quantity, price, and country of origin.

Foreign exchange controls. Certain "transitional economies" with foreign exchange shortages ("Article 14" countries), are allowed to limit the amount of hard currency (e.g., US$) that local companies can obtain for import transactions. Currently, 31 countries[49] still qualify to apply these controls.

Promotional restrictions. Many countries restrict or regulate how certain products can be advertised and promoted, mostly to protect against health risks, immorality, and scams. The most commonly regulated are alcohol and tobacco products, ethical drugs, contraceptives, personal hygiene products, undergarments, and films and books. The restrictions could include outright promotional bans, limits on the media used (e.g., not on TV) or time of day (e.g., late night only), limits on use of samples, or other. The relevant regulations are typically issued by agencies equivalent to the U.S. Food & Drug Administration (FDA) and Federal Trade Commission (FTC).

Distributor requirements. While most countries do not restrict the use of distributors, some have requirements on the terms of engagement. For example, in some countries, a local distributor is a requirement, not an option. Some countries make it difficult and costly to terminate a distributorship, even for cause. Distributors of movie and TV content may have to pay screening fees in some countries.

Corruption. Most developed countries have well enforced anti-corruption laws and regulations. In many developing countries, however, corruption is endemic—from low-level "grease" payments to move paperwork to high-level bribes to secure major contracts. The 2018 Corruption Perceptions Index[50] measures the perceived levels of public sector corruption in 180 countries and territories. Foreign companies seeking business in these countries need to factor into their marketing plan where to draw the line between what is customary and expected to get along versus what is illegal and to be avoided, even if customary. U.S. companies, in particular, are subject to the Foreign Corrupt Practices Act (FCPA)[51] that makes it illegal to bribe foreign government officials anywhere in the world as a means to "assist in obtaining or retaining businesss."

Country-specific NTBs are extensively covered in:

- **Country Commercial Guide (CCG)**[52] chapters on "Trade Regulations and Standards" and "Investment Climate" examine each country's trade and investment regulations.
- **National Trade Estimate Reports on Foreign Trade Barriers**[53] (all countries) are annually updated reports on trade barriers by country.
- **Market Access Sectoral and Trade Barriers Database (EU)**[54] can be searched by country, industry or barrier type to find barriers that apply to specific products in specific countries.
- **International Legal Resources**[55] provides links to web sites that specialize in international trade laws and regulations by topic and country.

* * *

7C. Comply with Documentary Requirements

Exporting involves a lot of paperwork—documents for regulatory compliance at both ends and shipping documents for transport purposes. All required documents must be fully and precisely completed. Even slight discrepancies or omissions could nullify a transaction. For smaller exporters, this might seem intimidating, but the good news is that your freight forwarder can do all the heavy lifting. Unless you're large enough to have your own freight department, find a good freight forwarder to handle your documentation. They know what documents are needed and routinely fill them out and submit them to the proper authorities.

Documents for U.S. regulatory compliance. The relevant U.S. regulations were covered in **7A** above. The documents needed to comply with these regulations can mostly be filed electronically through three primary U.S. export compliance systems—the **Automated Commercial Environment (ACE)**, the **Automated Export System (AES)**, and the **Simplified Network Application Process Redesign (SNAP)**.

- **ACE**[56] is the U.S. system for reporting all imports and exports. See the Customs & Border Protection (CBP) "Getting Started"[57] page for basic information about ACE and how to establish an ACE account and begin interacting with ACE.
- **AESDirect**[58] is the primary filing tool to submit Electronic Export Information (EEI)[59]. The EEI replaced the Shipper's Export Declaration and is a required U.S. Government filing for all exports valued at $2,500 or more, or $500 or more if shipped by mail. AES Direct is a free service from Census and Customs. AES will process the information and, if accepted, respond with an Internal Transaction Number (ITN). The application is hosted on the ACE portal. For more details. see AES User Guide[60] and EEI filing instructions[61] and videos, including Registering for AESDirect[62], Filing a Shipment in AESDirect[63], Response Messages from AES[64], Proof of Filing Citations[65], AESDirect—The Shipment Manager[66], and Elimination of the SSN in the AES[67].
- **Simplified Network Application Process Redesign** (SNAP-R)[68] is a free tool to electronically submit export license applications, commodity classification requests, and AGR notifications. SNAP-R applicants must register with BIS online to receive a Company Identification Number (CIN).

Documents for foreign regulatory compliance. The relevant foreign regulations were covered in **7B** above. A documentary requirement is the primary means of enforcement. Unless the exporter or importer submits the required document(s), the goods will likely not be released from customs. Here are commonly required documents for compliance purposes:

- **Consular Invoice**[69]. A few countries still require this document to assure that accurate values are declared for the export goods, all the shipping documents are in order, and the goods would not be subject to any trade restrictions in the importing country or violate any of its trade regulations. A Consular Invoice must be purchased from a consulate representing the importing country.
- **Sanitary or health certificates** are generally required to import non-processed plant products, such as grains, that could be harmed by pests, diseases, chemical treatments and weeds. These generic certificates may also have different names for different products (e.g., Phytosanitary Certificates[70] specifically for products susceptible to insect infestation), but all essentially confirm that the goods are free from disease or pests, and that the products have been prepared in accordance with prescribed standards. Normally, these certificates are issued by the Department of Agriculture of the exporter´s country.
- **Certificate of Free Sale**[71]: Many countries require a Certificate of Free Sale to import certain products for health related reasons, notably medical devices, cosmetics, pharmaceuticals, and processed foods. For U.S. exporters, the Certificate basically attests that the product is of no lesser quality than that produced and freely marketed and sold in the U.S., and that the manufacturer has no unresolved enforcement actions before either the Food & Drug Administration (FDA) or State. This Certificate is also known by other names, such as Health Certificate, Export Certificate, Sanitary Certificate, and Certificate of Sanitation. It can be obtained from FDA, an authorized State agency, and in most cases as well from a local chamber of commerce.

- **Pre-Shipment Inspection (PSI) Certificate**[72]: A pre-shipment inspection may be required by an importer or the importing country to assure that the goods are not defective or different from what was ordered. If required, the exporter must arrange for a physical inspection by an approved PSI organization in the exporting country. The findings are documented in a PSI inspection certificate. If defects or discrepancies are found, the exporter must take immediate steps to rectify any problems.

- **Certificate of Origin**[73]. Many countries grant trade preferences or restrict imports based on the country where a product originated. A Certificate of Origin identifies the country where the export product was originally manufactured in whole or in part. If the product contains material manufactured, produced, or grown in more than one country, the product belongs to the country where it last went through a substantial transformation. Generally, to qualify, at least 51% of the product's labor and materials must come from the claimed country of origin. The exporter can use company letterhead if allowed or a Certificate of Origin form to declare the percentage of original content). This document must then be "certified" or notarized, typically by a local chamber of commerce. The chamber will also want a copy of the commercial invoice to verify the claimed origin. For some countries, however, a local chamber certification is not acceptable. Exporters can use company letterhead if allowed or a Certificate of Origin form[74] to declare the percentage of original content. This document must then be "certified" or notarized. In the U.S. this is typically done by a local chamber of commerce. The chamber will want a copy of the commercial invoice to verify the claimed origin. For some countries, however, a local chamber certification is not acceptable. Many Middle Eastern countries, in particular, require certification by specific organizations, such as the U.S.-Arab Chamber of Commerce[75] (for Kuwait, Lebanon, Oman, Qatar, Sudan, Syria, Tunisia, United Arab Emirates, and Yemen); American Egyptian Cooperation Foundation[76] (for

Egypt); and the U.S.-Saudi Business Council[77] (for Saudi Arabia).

- **USMCA Certificate of Origin. The** United States-Mexico-Canada Agreement (USMCA), formerly NAFTA, grants zero or preferential duty status to U.S., Canadian, and Mexican products traded within the region. U.S. exporters wishing to export "originating goods" duty free into Canada or Mexico must have a valid certificate of origin, completed by either the exporter or the producer. Exporters must also be able to provide evidence proving "originating goods" status that formed the basis of their certification. Penalties/fines can be issued by Customs authorities for failure to comply with these requirements. Although USMCA has no official government-issued or government-approved USMCA Certificate of Origin form, all certifications must contain a set of "minimum data elements." For a sample of the interim form and guidance on what such "minimum data elements" might be, see USMCA Certificate of Origin[78].

- **Special Certificates of Origin under other U.S. Free Trade Agreements.** These Special Certificates of Origin may be required to qualify for preferences in these 18 countries plus USMCA with which the U.S. has **free trade agreements** (FTAs)[79].

- Australia
- Bahrain
- Chile
- Colombia
- Costa Rica
- Dom. Republic
- El Salvador
- Guatemala
- Honduras
- Israel
- Jordan
- Korea

- Morocco
- Nicaragua
- Oman
- Panama
- Peru
- Singapore
- USMCA

Commonly required shipping documents. These documents provide details about the products being shipped (what they are, quantity, value, destination, etc.). They are filed with the bank and the carrier.

Proforma invoices[80] are your first response to a foreign buyer's request for an informal or formal price quote. They are not true invoices, as is a Commercial Invoice, because the buyer has not yet agreed to the terms. If and when the buyer accepts the terms, you will follow with a Commercial Invoice that contains much of the same itemized information, but has all the final particulars. Proforma invoices should have a time limit, as the original manufacturing and transportation costs built into your price quote could increase over time. The Proforma invoice form typically asks for:

- Seller's/buyer's names and addresses
- Validity period for quotation
- Buyer's reference #s and inquiry date
- Total charges to be paid by customer
- List and brief description of products
- Delivery point
- Price of each item (in U.S. dollars
- Terms of sale
- Terms of payment
- Estimated shipping date
- Insurance and shipping costs
- Currency of sale

Commercial Invoices[81] are bills for the goods from the seller to the buyer. The buyer needs the Commercial Invoice to prove ownership and to arrange payment. Some governments use it to assess customs duties. It describes all aspects of the transaction—from who shipped what to whom, on what sales and payment terms, and at what prices. It shows the shipping date, the buyer's purchase order number, the tariff classification used by the buyer's country, and other relevant details between exporter and importer. It is also the primary document used by Customs in all countries for commodity control and valuation. Here are the fields and instructions for a U.S. exporter filling out a Commercial Invoice:

- **Seller** – Name and address of principal party responsible for effecting export from the Unites States. The Exporter as named on the exporter license (if applicable).
- **Sold to** – The name and address of the person/company to whom the goods are shipped to for the designated end use, or to the party so designated on the export license.
- **Ship to** (If different than "Sold to") - The intermediate consignee—that is the name and address of the party who effects delivery of the merchandise to the ultimate consignee, or the party so named on the export license of the forwarding agent. The name and address of the duly authorized forwarder acting as agent for the exporter.
- **Invoice number** – Invoice number assigned by the exporter.
- **Customer reference number** – Foreign customer's reference number.
- **Terms of sale** – Delivery and terms of sale agreement.
- **Terms of payment** – Terms, conditions, and currency of settlement as agreed upon by the vendor and purchaser per the pro forma invoice, customer purchase order and/or the letter of credit.
- **Currency of settlement** – Currency agreed upon between seller and buyer as payment.
- **Mode of shipment** – Indicate air, ocean, and/or surface.
- **Quantity** – Total number of units per the description line.
- **Description** – Provide full description of items shipped, the type of container, (carton, box, etc.), the gross weight per

container, and the quantity and unit of measure of the merchandise.

- **Unit of measure** – Record total net weight and total gross weight in kilograms (1 kilogram = 2.2 pounds) per description line.
- **Unit price** - Record the unit price of the merchandise per unit of measure.
- **Total price** – Calculate the extended value of the line.
- **Total commercial value** – Total value of the invoice.
- **Package marks** – Record in this field and on each package number (for example, "1 of 7,""3 of 7") shippers company name, country of origin (e.g., Made in USA), destination port of entry, package weight in kilograms, package size (length x width x height) and shipper's control number (optional).
- **Miscellaneous charges** – Charges (packing, insurance, etc. Record any miscellaneous charges that are to be paid by customer, such as export transportation, insurance, export packaging inland freight to peer, etc.).
- **Certifications** – Any certifications or declarations required of the shipper regarding any information recorded on the commercial invoice.

Export Packing Lists[82] are more detailed than a standard domestic packing list. They itemize the material in each individual package and indicate the type of package—box, crate, drum, carton, etc. They also show the individual net, legal, tare, and gross weights and measurements for each package (in both U.S. and metric systems). Package markings should be shown along with the shipper's and buyer's references. The packing list should be attached to the outside of a package in a waterproof envelope marked "Packing List Enclosed." The shipper or forwarding agent will use it to determine total weight and volume and whether the correct cargo is being shipped. Also, customs officials (both U.S. and foreign) may use the list to check the cargo. See sample Export Packing List[83].

Dock Receipts are issued by a direct ocean freight carrier to acknowledge receipt of an ocean shipment at the carrier's pier or shipping terminal. The Dock Receipt is surrendered to the shipping terminal when the delivery is completed. See sample Dock Receipt[84].

Bills of Lading (B/Ls)[85] are contracts between the owner of the goods and the carrier. An **Ocean Bill of Lading**[86] is negotiable and holds title to the goods, the key to getting paid at the other end. See sample **Ocean B/L**[87]. It goes to a designated bank in the importing country. The bank will not release the goods until the buyer pays or promises to pay at a mutually agreed date. A **Straight B/L**[88] is non-negotiable. It essentially consigns the shipment directly to the named consignee and no other party and is mainly used for open account or cash in advance transactions. The consignee can obtain possession of the goods after arrival upon presentation of a signed original bill of lading to the carrier.

Air Waybills (AWBs)[89] cover shipments by air from airport to airport. See sample Air Waybill[90]. Unlike Ocean B/Ls, AWBs are non-negotiable. They describe the goods and conditions of carriage, but do not specify the flight or when it will arrive. AWBs specify conditions, limitations of liability, shipping instructions, description of commodity, and applicable transportation charges.

Inspection Certificates are required by some purchasers and countries to attest to the specifications of the goods shipped. The inspection is usually performed by a third party, often an independent testing organization.

Dangerous Goods Forms are for products considered "dangerous" by the International Air Transport Association (IATA)[91] or the International Maritime Organization (IMO)[92]. The IATA form—the Shipper's Declaration for Dangerous Goods—is required for air shipments. A different version of the form is used for ocean shipments.

CHAPTER 8

PREPARE GOODS FOR DELIVERY

8A. Export Packaging

To move goods overseas, you'll need to pack and label them, mainly to protect the goods from damage or theft in transit. Beyond basic precautions, some steps are also legally required by the exporting or importing country. In these cases, the requirements are usually very specific and must be precisely followed. Packaging, marking and labeling advice can be obtained from freight forwarders[1], carriers and marine insurance companies. If you're not equipped to pack the goods yourself, use a professional export packing firm. This service is usually provided at a moderate cost.

Exported goods are typically packaged in cartons, boxes, crates, drums, bottles or bags of various materials (e.g., wood, cardboard, burlap, plastic, glass, etc.). The packages are loaded into 20-40 foot containers or onto wooden pallets for transport to the foreign destination. Both the packaging and loading need particular care, because exported goods face greater physical risks in transit than domestic shipments. At some exit and entry ports, goods may still be loaded or unloaded in nets or by a sling, conveyor, or chute, putting added strain on the package. While in transit by air or sea, the goods could be damaged by jolting, vibration, pressure, heat/cold, and contamination from moisture, dust, and dirt. When unloaded at less-modern entry ports, the goods might be dragged, pushed, rolled, or even dropped. Moisture from condensation is also a danger, even if the ship's hold is equipped with air conditioning and a dehumidifier. The cargo also might be unloaded in the rain. Some foreign ports do not have covered storage facilities. Goods can also be stolen when poorly packaged.

In addition to keeping packages safe and secure throughout, exporters must also comply with any applicable international-or country-specific packaging requirements. These mostly relate to the materials used (e.g., wood or plastics). For example, the International Plant Protection Convention (IPPC)[2] sets International Standards for Phytosanitary Measures (ISPMs)[3]. ISPM 15, in particular, stipulates how wood packaging materials must be treated to protect against invasive quarantine pests. To comply with ISPM 15, a stamp must be applied to the packaging to show that an inspection agency has certified the facility (i.e. a pallet manufacturer or recycler). Some countries may also impose packaging requirements. So too, buyers may specify their own requirements in purchase orders or contracts. Your freight forwarder can advise and help with these best practices to assure compliance and avoid problems:

For **sea shipments**, containerize your cargo whenever possible. Containers vary in size, material, and construction and are best suited for standard package sizes and shapes. Refrigerated and liquid bulk containers are readily available. If you can't fill an entire container, a freight forwarder can arrange to combine your cargo with others to get the benefit of lower container rates. For **air shipments**, you can use lighter weight packing, but you must still take precautions. Standard domestic packing should suffice, especially if the product is durable. Otherwise, high-test cardboard or tri-wall construction boxes are more than adequate (at least 250 pounds per square inch). In either case, use strong, reinforced boxes or crates, and seal and fill them with lightweight, moisture-resistant material. Distribute the weight evenly to brace the container. To deter theft, use strapping, seals, or shrink wrapping where possible.

Dangerous goods[4]—classified as potentially harmful to any person or animal, or that could damage the environment—must have leak-or break-proof packaging and must be properly marked, labeled, documented, and classified. Dangerous goods fall into nine classifications, each with further subclasses and each requiring its own unique label that identifies the potential dangers the goods present and must appear somewhere on the packaging.

- Class 1 Explosives; Class 2 Gases; Class 3 Flammable Liquids
- Class 4 Flammable solids; substances liable to spontaneous combustion; substances which, in contact with water, emit flammable gases
- Class 5 Oxidizing substances and organic peroxides;
- Class 6 Toxic and Infectious substances; Class 7 Radioactive material
- Class 8 Corrosive substances
- Class 9 Miscellaneous dangerous substances and articles, including environmentally hazardous substances

* * *

8B. Export Marking and Labeling

Many countries and some international organizations have marking and labeling regulations[5] to protect public health and the environment. Your foreign buyers will also likely require certain marks on the cargo to prevent misunderstandings and delays. The required lettering should be stenciled on packages in waterproof ink. Markings should appear on three faces of the package—on the top and on the two ends or the two sides. Old markings must be completely removed. Don't list the contents or show brand names on the outside of the packages.

Standard marks include:

- Shipper's mark
- Country of origin
- Port of entry;

- Gross and net weights (in pounds and in kilograms)
- Number of packages and size of cases (in inches and centimeters)
- Any special handling marks (international pictorial symbols)
- Cautionary markings, such as "This Side Up" or "Use No Hooks" (in English and in the language of the country of destination)
- Labels for hazardous materials (universal symbols adapted by the International Air Transport Association and the International Maritime Organization)
- Ingredients (if applicable, also included in the language of the destination country).

Failure to comply could incur severe penalties and fines for the shipper and seizure or delays for the entire cargo. The importer could also face costly litigation and reputation damage. The risk is particularly high when shipping hazardous materials and dangerous goods.

CHAPTER 9

DELIVER THE EXPORT GOODS

9A. Get Cargo Insurance

Marine insurance[1] (also known as cargo insurance) offers important protection against delays in transit and losses or damage to cargo from bad weather, rough handling, collision, overturn, theft, or non-delivery, jettison (the act of casting goods from a vessel or aircraft to lighten or stabilize it). Liability for export cargo depends on the point at which the buyer takes title to the goods (determined by the Incoterms of sale). For example, if the buyer takes title and picks up the goods at the supplier's factory (ExWorks—EXW)[2], the buyer is liable for any damages from that point on. If the buyer does not take title until the goods arrive at the foreign destination (Cost Insurance & Freight (CIF)[3], the supplier is liable for any loss or damage to the goods to that end point. The responsible party must insure the cargo for its portion of the risk. The needed insurance can be obtained directly from marine insurance companies or through the freight forwarder. Make sure to include a general average[4] clause, which limits liability just to the supplier's own cargo involved. Otherwise, you could be liable for a share of the entire ship's cargo if destroyed for any reason (e.g., if the ship sinks).

If the foreign buyer has responsibility, don't assume (or even take the buyer's word) that the insurance has been purchased. The supplier could still be liable if the buyer fails to obtain coverage or takes too little. The carrier will not insure the cargo. For international shipments, the carrier's liability is frequently limited by international agreements, and the coverage is substantially different from domestic coverage. Check with an international insurance carrier[5] or freight forwarder[6] for options and advice.

* * *

9B. Transport the Goods

You have now come to the last major step in the export development process—getting the goods from here to there. To reach this point, you plowed through the more daunting aspects of exporting—learning how, finding best markets, developing effective market entry strategies, negotiating deals, arranging the payment, and complying with all the requirements. If you're already shipping domestically, except for ocean shipping, the truck, rail, and air modes for export are basically the same. Moreover, the same international freight forwarder that helped you with the regulations and documents can also handle all aspects of the physical delivery. They can compare the costs, lead times, and transit times; pick up the goods from your factory; containerize or palletize them; make the booking; get the goods to the carrier for loading; obtain cargo insurance; and arrange to clear the goods through customs on arrival. Their modest fees can be factored into the export price.

Note that you have **no transportation responsibilities** if the buyer asks for Ex Works (EXW) Incoterms. Under EXW, the buyer will pick up the goods at your premises and handle all transportation from that point on. Under Free Alongside Ship (FAS)[7] or Free on Board (FOB)[8] terms, you would just have to get the goods to the port of exit (purely domestic transportation). You only become responsible for international transportation when the terms specify delivery to the destination country—Cost & Freight (C&F)[9] or Cost, Insurance & Freight (CIF).

If you do have to ship outside the country, you have four main options —rail, truck, air, or sea.

- **Rail and truck** are only viable for destinations reachable by land (e.g., Canada or Mexico). Rail is the least costly method and can handle all types of cargo, including containers. However, rail can only go station to station. Not many foreign buyers have their own rail landing sites, so trucks would also likely be needed beyond the rail station. Trucks can also handle most cargo at relatively low cost, and are a popular option for anywhere by land.
- **Sea and air.** Since neither rail nor trucks are options for any overseas transportation, the choice is most often between sea and air. The buyer will generally decide which mode to use. Air would automatically be ruled out if the cargo is too big or too heavy for the plane. Otherwise, the decision would be based on cost and speed. Air transport costs much more than sea transport, but may be best for low-weight, low volume goods, perishable goods, and any other cargo that needs fast delivery. Air cargo can arrive overnight or the next day. Sea transport could take up to 2 weeks or more. Most cargo goes by sea, because vessels can accommodate cargo of any size or weight, the buyer can often wait for as long as it might take, and the cost is much lower.

Large, frequent exporters often have their own freight departments and book their cargo directly with the carrier at a volume discount. Smaller, less frequent exporters do not have the clout to get carrier discounts, so are much better off piggybacking on the discounts that freight forwarders have with the carriers.

Here are resources to identify sources of help for international transportation:

Freight forwarders are often listed in local Yellow Pages, but it's best to look for freight forwarders that are members of the National Customs Bureau and Freight Forwarders Association (NCBFFA)[10] or any of its regional associations (e.g. Los Angeles Customs Bureau and Freight Forwarders Association (LACBFFA)[11].

Carriers include the airlines, shipping companies, and others that physically transport the goods to their destinations.

- U.S. Airport Information[12]
- FreightWorld[13]
- Container Shipping[14]
- U.S.-Flag Carriers[15]
- World Freight Ship Companies[16]

FITA[17] has a comprehensive directory of associations[18] representing the many different providers of international transportation and logistics services.

* * *

Conclusion

Congratulations on your perseverance to reach this point! I have taken you through a journey that often begins with an epiphany: "maybe exporting really is for me." Since that initial motivation, you have not only shown a willingness to explore what it takes to get started, but then committed to learning what you'll need to know and be able to do to make it happen. The Appendices that follow have many practical tools and resources to backstop your efforts. However, I am not done with you yet. As a longtime export mentor, I also encourage you to explore the free resources that I offer on my website at tradecompliance institute.org and to email me at mkogon@socal.rr.com about anything covered in this book—whether for advice, clarification, or reinforcement. I'll do my best to provide answers and get you headed in the right direction.

APPENDICES

CONTENTS

APPENDIX A: EXPORT READINESS ASSESSMENT SYSTEM (ERAS)

ERAS was developed by Maurice Kogon as an on-line diagnostic tool to assess a company's export potential and "readiness": to export. It is intended mainly for non-exporting manufacturers who see exporting as a possible new or expanded activity, but are uncertain if their product has export potential or how export-ready they are as a company. Trade counselors can also use ERAS as a fast, user-friendly way to "qualify" new clients for export assistance. The Assessment starts with 23 questions about the company's domestic activity, business practices, organization, and products. After answering each question in one of the 3-6 possible ways given, the user gets an immediate export readiness "score" and a detailed diagnostic report that addresses the company's export strengths and weaknesses in each of the 23 areas. The report further suggests specific steps the company can take to build on its strengths and overcome any weaknesses. The user can save, copy, and print the entire report and, if desired, can automatically share the results with a trade counselor of choice.

The 23 ERAS Questions & Possible Responses

1. Company Export Readiness

1. Are you an established presence in your industry domestically?

- Well known
- Somewhat known
- Not well known

2. How extensive is your current domestic sales outreach?

- Sell to large national customer base
- Sell to large regional customer base
- Sell to large local customer base
- Sell to few regional/national customers
- Sell to local customers

3. How do you sell and distribute your products in the domestic market?

- Use combination of own sales force and regional distributors
- Use regional distributors only
- Use own sales force only
- No sales/distribution network

4. Do you customarily conduct market research and planning for your domestic operations?

- Always
- Sometimes
- Rarely

5. To what extent do you advertise and promote your products in the domestic market?

- Very aggressively
- Fairly aggressively
- Modestly
- Not much
- None

6. Do any of your current managers or staff have export marketing or sales experience?

- Considerable experience
- Some experience
- Little or no experience

7. Has your company received any unsolicited inquiries from foreign firms?

- Many
- Some
- None

8. Could you promptly fill any new export orders from present inventory or other sources?

- Easily
- With Some Difficulty
- With Great Difficulty

9. How would you handle any new or additional export business within your organization?

- Establish export department
- Establish export manager
- Hire more staff
- Train existing staff
- Assign to current staff

10. What is the current status of your export activity?

- Export to many markets
- Export to some markets
- Export occasionally
- No export activity

11. Is your top management committed to exporting as a new or expanded area of activity?

- Strongly committed
- Somewhat committed
- Little commitment

12. How much per year could you afford to spend on export development?

- <$5K
- $5-25K
- $26-50K
- $51-100K
- >$100K

13. How long would your management be willing to wait to achieve acceptable export results?

- Up to 3 years
- Up to 2 years
- Up to 1 year
- Up to 6 months
- Need immediate results

2. Product Export Readiness

14. Have domestic sales of your product grown over the past 3 years (average per year)?

- Zero or negative
- <5%
- 6-10%
- 11-20%
- >20%

15. What is your product's current share of the domestic market?

- <5%
- 5-10%
- 11-20%
- 21-40%
- >40%

16. Is your product price-competitive in the domestic market?

- Highly Competitive
- Somewhat Competitive
- Not Competitive

17. What payment terms would you be willing to offer reputable foreign buyers?

- Pay in advance
- Pay on delivery
- Up to 30 days
- 31-60 days
- 61-120 days
- Over 120 days

18. Does your product compare favorably with domestic competitors in features and benefits?

- Very favorably
- Somewhat favorably
- Somewhat unfavorably
- Unfavorably

19. Would you be willing to adapt your product and/or packaging to better suit foreign markets?

- Very willing
- Willing
- Reluctantly
- Unwilling

20. Is your product costly to transport over long distances?

- Not very costly
- Somewhat costly
- Very costly

21. Is any special training required to assemble, install or operate your product?

- No special training
- Some training
- Extensive training

22. Does your product require any special technical support or after-sale service?

- None required
- Some support/service
- Extensive support/service

23. Can your product tolerate harsh or widely varying environmental conditions?

- High tolerance
- Some tolerance
- Low tolerance

APPENDIX B: COMMODITY CLASSIFICATION CODES

The most widely used trade classification codes are the Harmonized System (HS) Code, a universal standard; the Schedule B and Harmonized Tariff Schedule of the United States (HTSUSA); and the Standard International Trade Classification (SITC), used by the United Nations. Other coding systems may be used to categorize products by industry sector rather than for trade purposes, such as the North American Industry Classification System (NAICS), which replaced the Standard Industrial Classification (SIC).

Schedule B Export Codes[1] are used only in the U.S. and only for export shipments. The 10-digit Schedule B codes are required entries on U.S. Electronic Export Information (EEI) filings (formerly Shipper's Export Declarations). At the 6-digit level, Schedule B codes are equivalent to Harmonized System (HS) codes.

Harmonized System (HS) Codes[2] were developed in 1989 by more than 60 countries to provide a uniform classification system for export and import statistics and to determine applicable import duties by product. The first 6 digits of an HS number are the same regardless of country.

Harmonized Tariff Schedule of the United States (HTSUSA) Codes[3] are specific to the U.S. for exports (comparable to 10 digit Schedule B codes) and imports (to determine applicable U.S. import duties.

Standard International Trade Classification (SITC) Codes[4] were developed by the United Nations for use solely by international organizations for reporting international trade. The SITC has been revised several times; the current version is Revision 4

North American Industry Classification System (NAICS) Codes[5] are used to categorize business establishments and industries in the U.S., Canada and Mexico, replacing the **Standard Industrial Classification** (SIC) codes. The NAICS, adopted in 1997-98, was developed to provide a consistent framework for the collection, analysis, and dissemination of industrial statistics.

APPENDIX C: ITCI MARKET RESEARCH PORTAL

The International Trade Compliance Institute (ITCI)[1] Trade Information Database (TID) is an extensive one-stop source of trade information drawn from many different U.S. Government, international, and non-governmental Websites. The TID is organized into 12 broad categories and 74 subcategories for convenient, drill-down searches, Within the 74 subcategories, are over 900 direct links to export/import guides; trade reference tools; product-and country-specific statistics and market research; trade directories, trade opportunities; tariff and non-tariff trade barriers; trade promotion programs; guides to trade finance, documentation, and transportation; and sources of trade assistance.

Trade Readiness Tools: How-to information and tools to prepare and train for international trade

- Export Readiness Assessment
- Internet Export Search Wizard
- Export Guides
- Import Guides
- Trade Tutorials—Webinars, Courses, Videos

Trade Reference Tools: Quick look-ups to commonly needed international commodity codes definitions and conversions.

- Commodity Coding Systems
- Trade Terminology
- International Conversions
- Other Handy References
- Templates for International Contracts & Agreements
- International Standards

Trade & Economic Data/Policy: Worldwide trade and economic data, U.S. trade policy, and U.S. exporter composition and job impacts.

- U.S. Trade Data
- Foreign Trade Data
- World Economic & Demographic Data
- U.S. Industry Profiles
- U.S. Economic Data
- U.S. Trade Policy
- U.S. Exporter Composition & Job Impacts
- California Trade/Economic/Industry Data

Foreign Market Research: Extensive industry country and topical market research to help pinpoint best export markets assess particular markets adapt to local cultures and customs and develop effective market entry strategies.

- Market Identification/Assessment Tools
- Manufactured Products Research
- Food & Agriculture Products Research
- Services Sector Research
- Intercultural Research
- Countries & Regions Research
- Country Risk Assessments
- North America Region Research (U.S./Mexico/Canada)
- South/Central America Region Research

- Western Europe/EU Region Research
- Russia/Eastern Europe Region Research
- Asia/Pacific Region Research
- Africa/Middle East Region Research

Trade Contacts & Leads: Trade directories and specific trade lead to identify prospective suppliers, buyers and distributors.

- U.S. Producers, Exporters and Importers
- Foreign Manufacturers & Importers
- Hot Trade Leads
- Major Project Opportunities

Trade/Investment Regulations: U.S. and worldwide laws and regulations affecting market access and compliance.

- U.S. and Foreign Import Duties
- U.S. National Security Export Controls (EAR, ITAR, FACR)
- Other U.S. Export Laws & Regulations
- Intellectual Property Law & Regulations
- U.S. Import Laws & Regulations
- Invest in USA Incentives & Regulations
- Foreign Trade Laws & Regulations
- International Trade Treaties & Agreements
- International Legal Resources
- California Law & Regulations

Trade Documentation: Requirements procedures and forms needed for documentary compliance

- Documentation Basics
- Sample Export Documents
- Documentation Forms & Software

Trade Promotion: Programs, services and events to promote exports and facilitate international matchmaking.

- U.S. Trade Promotion & Matchmaking Services
- Trade Event Resources & Schedules
- Worldwide Marketing Media
- U.S. & International Trade Promotion Organizations

Trade Finance & Insurance: Guides, programs, and sources of export finance, export credit insurance, and marine insurance.

- Trade Finance Basics
- Trade Finance Programs & Services
- Trade Finance/Insurance Providers
- Export Trade Financing—On-Line Application
- Marine Insurance Basics
- B2B—E-Commerce

Trade Transport & Logistics: Requirements, tools and services to manage international trade logistics and deliver the goods.

- Transportation & Logistics Basics
- Trade Logistics Tools
- Transport Logistics Providers

International Trade News: News feeds, Blogs, periodicals and publications on topics, industries, and regions of interest to international traders

- Daily News Feeds/Blogs
- Periodicals
- Industry Publications

Trade Resources Directory: California U.S. Government international private sector and academic sources of assistance.

- U.S. Government Trade Assistance Organizations
- U.S. Government Trade Regulatory Organizations
- State & Local Economic and Trade Organizations
- California Trade Organizations
- Trade & Industry Associations
- Chambers of Commerce
- Foreign Trade Offices
- Academic Trade Organizations
- International Trade Organizations
- International Trade Career Resources

APPENDIX D: MARKET IDENTIFICATION AIDS

1. Market Potential Matrix Template

The matrix below can provide a first clue to high potential export markets for any U.S. product with a Schedule B or HS Code number. The assessment is based on how well the specified product performed in each country against these 11 "predictor" criteria represented in Matrix Columns 1-11.

1. This country is a large export market for the U.S. product (e.g., top 5 last year)
2. This country is a fast-growing export market for the U.S. product (e.g., +50% over the past 4 years)
3. This country showed continued growth for the U.S. product in the latest year (e.g., +10%)
4. This country is a large world importer of the product (e.g., top 5 last year)
5. This country is a fast-growing importer of the product (e.g., +50% over the past 4 years)
6. This country showed continued import growth for the product in the latest year (e.g., +10%)

7. This country imported a significant share of this product from the U.S. in the latest year (e.g., +15% U.S. market share)
8. This country has no local competitors that already dominate the market for this U.S. product
9. This country is highly receptive to U.S. products, including this U.S. product
10. This country has no significant barriers to entry of this U.S. product in the market
11. This country is "recommended" by the U.S. Embassy as a promising market for this product

Users can fill in the 11 columns in the Matrix by using the Market Potential Statistics Sample Worksheets in **Appendix D2**. As illustrated for 5 hypothetical countries, a **double X** in the Column cell indicates the country met the criterion very well; a **single X** indicates reasonably good performance; a **blank** indicates the country was lacking in that criterion. The countries with the greatest number of XX's and X's across the most number of criteria are presumed to offer greater export potential for the industry.

Export Market Potential Matrix: Selection Criteria

	1	2	3	4	5	6	7	8	9	10	11
Country 1	X	XX	X	XX	X	X	XX	X	XX	XX	XX
Country 2		X			XX			X		X	X
Country 3	XX	X	X	XX	XX	XX	XX	X	XX	XX	XX
Country 4			X	X					X	X	
Country 5		X			X						

	1	2	3	4	5	6	7	8	9	10	11
Argentina											
Australia											
Austria											
Belgium											
Brazil											
Canada											
Chile											
China											
Czech Republic											
Denmark											
France											
Germany											
Hong Kong											
Hungary											
India											
Ireland											
Israel											
Italy											
Japan											
Korea											
Malaysia											
Mexico											
Netherlands											
Poland											
Russia											
Saudi Arabia											
Singapore											
South Africa											
Spain											
Sweden											
Switzerland											
Taiwan											
Thailand											
UAE											

2. Market Potential Statistics Samples

The Sample Worksheets 1-3 below list only 10 countries each for a hypothetical product (widgets). They are based on official U.S. export statistics maintained by the U.S. Census Bureau. Comparable actual data can be accessed at no cost for any specified product for up to nearly 200 countries. Go to USITC Trade Dataweb (https://dataweb.usitc.gov), plug in the desired product's Schedule B # (up to 10 digits) or HS Code # (up to 6 digits), and follow the prompts. The search results can be downloaded into MS Excel for further sorting as desired.

2. Market Potential Statistics Sample – Worksheet 1

Top U.S. Export Markets for Widgets [Past 4 Years]
In Rank Order by Country [Latest Year]

Country	Base Year	2 Years Ago	Last Year	Latest Year	% Change From Base Year	% Change From Last Year	% Share Latest Year
	In 1,000 Dollars						
Canada	5,052,205	4,759,415	5,131,904	5,393,844	6.8%	5.10%	22.5%
Mexico	2,876,758	2,722,342	2,687,602	3,999,975	39.0%	48.80%	16.7%
Japan	2,542,296	1,778,775	1,649,501	1,567,063	-38.4%	-5.00%	6.5%
United Kingdom	1,980,351	1,390,027	1,339,784	1,485,395	-25.0%	10.90%	6.2%
Netherlands	2,118,322	1,463,165	1,379,502	1,318,343	-37.8%	-4.40%	5.5%
Germany	1,123,926	965,580	1,017,171	1,091,621	-2.9%	7.30%	4.6%
China	957,494	738,618	735,760	779,539	-18.6%	6.00%	3.2%
Singapore	923,633	660,386	669,519	649,593	-29.7%	-3.00%	2.7%
Hong Kong	1,250,218	800,819	686,630	633,767	-49.3%	-7.70%	2.6%
France	508,981	415,218	457,123	516,888	1.6%	13.10%	2.2%
Korea	812,728	694,474	518,784	502,270	-38.2%	-3.20%	2.1%

2. Market Potential Statistics Sample – Worksheet 2

Top U.S. Export Markets for Widgets [Past 4 Years]
In Rank Order by Growth Rate [From Base Year to Latest Year]

Country	Base Year	2 Years Ago	Last Year4	Latest Year	% Change From Base Year	% Change From Last Year	% Share Latest Year
	In 1,000 Dollars						
Denmark	62,151	75,932	79,977	105,283	69.40%	31.60%	0.40%
Russia	63,360	59,666	72,001	98,335	55.20%	36.60%	0.40%
Mexico	2,876,758	2,722,342	2,687,602	3,999,975	39.00%	48.80%	16.70%
India	246,348	255,726	274,416	311,686	26.50%	13.60%	1.30%
Spain	107,596	98,865	114,881	135,921	26.30%	18.30%	0.60%
Chile	193,447	187,887	183,373	236,537	22.30%	29.00%	1.00%
Italy	198,878	174,147	191,785	239,779	20.60%	25.00%	1.00%
Canada	5,052,205	4,759,415	5,131,904	5,393,844	6.80%	5.10%	22.50%
Peru	92,703	75,673	92,693	96,024	3.60%	3.60%	0.40%
Paraguay	118,940	170,643	106,546	123,091	3.50%	15.50%	0.50%
France	508,981	415,218	457,123	516,888	1.60%	13.10%	2.20%

2. Market Potential Statistics Sample – Worksheet 3

Top U.S. Export Markets for Widgets, [Past 4 Years]
In Rank Order by Growth Rate [From Last Year to Latest Year]

Country	Base Year	2 Years Ago	Last Year4	Latest Year	% Change From Base Year	% Change From Last Year	% Share Latest Year
	In 1,000 Dollars						
Venezuela	221,331	110,641	65,003	179,424	-18.90%	176.00%	0.70%
Mexico	2,876,758	2,722,342	2,687,602	3,999,975	39.00%	48.80%	16.70%
Russia	63,360	59,666	72,001	98,335	55.20%	36.60%	0.40%
Denmark	62,151	75,932	79,977	105,283	69.40%	31.60%	0.40%
Argentina	246,526	46,589	114,522	150,261	-39.00%	31.20%	0.60%
Chile	193,447	187,887	183,373	236,537	22.30%	29.00%	1.00%
Belgium	221,275	136,483	135,213	174,471	-21.20%	29.00%	0.70%
Italy	198,878	174,147	191,785	239,779	20.60%	25.00%	1.00%
Malaysia	407,250	371,353	288,711	350,984	-13.80%	21.60%	1.50%
Spain	107,596	98,865	114,881	135,921	26.30%	18.30%	0.60%
Paraguay	118,940	170,643	106,546	123,091	3.50%	15.50%	0.50%

The Sample Worksheets 4-6 below list only 10 countries each for a hypothetical product (widgets). They are based on official United Nations trade statistics reported by each member country. Comparable actual data can be accessed at no cost for any specified product for up to nearly 200 countries. Go to UN International Trade Centre (International trade statistics 2001-2020 (intracen.org), plug in the desired product's HS Code # (up to 4 digits), and follow the prompts. The search results can be downloaded into MS Excel for further sorting as desired.

2. Market Potential Statistics Sample – Worksheet 4

Top 30 World Importers of Widgets, [Past 4 Years]
In Rank Order by Country [Latest Year]

Country	Base Year	2 Years Ago	Last Year4	Latest Year	% Change From Base Year	% Change From Last Year	% Share Latest Year
	In 1,000 Dollars						
USA	48,492,144	51,012,784	52,984,512	60,782,880	25.3%	14.7%	23.9%
Netherlands	14,177,290	12,713,590	17,062,944	21,922,432	54.6%	28.5%	8.6%
Germany	16,964,912	16,003,794	17,772,144	20,392,544	20.2%	14.7%	8.0%
United Kingdom	14,597,824	13,785,818	15,233,345	17,904,640	22.7%	17.5%	7.0%
Japan	15,038,005	14,332,633	15,928,690	17,617,440	17.2%	10.6%	6.9%
China	4,980,964	6,733,327	11,411,206	14,456,089	190.2%	26.7%	5.7%
France	8,054,771	7,873,243	9,148,496	11,428,904	41.9%	24.9%	4.5%
Hong Kong	6,448,641	6,846,739	7,028,636	7,441,557	15.4%	5.9%	2.9%
Canada	6,555,357	6,143,934	6,524,289	7,339,777	12.0%	12.5%	2.9%
Italy	4,698,982	4,662,938	5,351,687	6,273,750	33.5%	17.2%	2.5%
Mexico	4,162,375	4,524,254	5,235,837	6,240,103	49.9%	19.2%	2.5%
Belgium	3,840,399	3,627,217	4,824,050	5,394,915	40.5%	11.8%	2.1%

2. Market Potential Statistics Sample – Worksheet 5

Top World Exporters of Widgets, [Past 4 Years]
In Rank Order by Country [Latest Year]

Exporting Country	Base Year	2 Years Ago	Last Year4	Latest Year	% Change From Base Year	% Change From Last Year	% Share Latest Year
	In 1,000 Dollars						
Italy	$2,486,029,568	$2,719,557,901	$3,188,613,603	$3,152,002,685	26.8%	-1.1%	15.1%
Germany	$1,853,634,816	$2,108,984,000	$2,742,899,000	$2,823,024,000	52.3%	2.9%	13.5%
China	$1,313,839,558	$1,612,924,802	$2,028,959,587	$2,756,843,267	109.8%	35.9%	13.2%
USA	$1,250,118,581	$1,378,639,835	$1,659,469,135	$1,972,277,018	57.8%	18.8%	9.4%
Japan	$836,997,952	$1,019,295,658	$1,252,187,175	$1,385,504,259	65.5%	10.6%	6.6%
Belgium	$805,705,088	$999,390,328	$1,157,331,806	$1,220,434,208	51.5%	5.5%	5.8%
United Kingdom	$685,780,288	$818,617,880	$1,011,257,188	$1,130,869,450	64.9%	11.8%	5.4%
France	$805,705,088	$883,498,496	$982,702,252	$1,053,352,707	30.7%	7.2%	5.0%
Canada	$767,516,470	$762,098,853	$864,942,697	$918,421,953	19.7%	6.2%	4.4%
Austria	$399,964,320	$550,824,071	$639,352,516	$672,185,008	68.1%	5.1%	3.2%

2. Market Potential Statistics Sample – Worksheet 6

World Importers of Widgets, [Latest 3 Years]
Total Market, Imports and Imports from the U.S.
In Rank Order by Imports from the U.S. [Latest Year]
In $millions

Country	Total Market			Total Imports			Imports from US			% U.S. Share
	Base Year	Latest Year	% Change	Base Year	Latest Year	% Change	Base Year	Latest Year	% Change	Latest Year
Argentina	175	236	35%	105	156	49%	31	45	45%	29%
Australia	1,787	2,009	12%	1,208	1,310	8%	593	570	-4%	44%
Austria	442	494	12%	827	868	5%	171	178	4%	20%
Brazil	1,602	1,840	15%	851	930	9%	361	360	0%	39%
Bulgaria	111	165	49%	104	160	54%	16	33	106%	21%
Canada	2,981	3,589	20%	1,993	2,594	30%	1,223	1,496	22%	58%
Chile	58	78	34%	43	59	37%	23	25	9%	42%
China	N/A	N/A	N/A	N/A	N/A	N/A	N/A	N/A	N/A	N/A
Colombia	205	231	13%	179	200	12%	76	87	14%	43%
Costa Rica	16	75	369%	17	77	358%	8	34	315%	44%

APPENDIX E: MARKET PLANNING AIDS

1. Export Market Plan Template

The Export Market Plan (EMP) template below can help each company develop a customized export development and market entry plan, with specific recommendations on target markets, prospective buyers and distributors, and effective export pricing, distribution and promotion strategies in each target market. The EMP provides a structure and step-by-step roadmap for the company. It has a three-part focus:

- Available company resources, capabilities and potentials.
- Overall strategic objectives and approach to develop markets, including product and market focus and whether to export directly or through a domestic intermediary.
- Strategy and actions to effectively enter and penetrate specific target markets, including product, pricing, distribution and promotion strategies.

* * *

I. Executive Summary

* * *

II. Company Profile

Provide a concise description of the company to include type of business (manufacturer, other), products supplied, when established, current location, # employees, organization structure and key managers.

* * *

III. SWOT Analysis

A. Strengths
B. Weaknesses
C. Opportunities
D. Threats

* * *

IV. Current Export Status

A. Current export activity (as % of total sales):
B. Current export products and markets:
C. Ability to meet commercially acceptable international product standards:

* * *

V. Product Focus for Export

A. Product 1: _____

1. Classification:
Schedule B/HS# _____
2. Product description & function:
3. Target customers/users:
4. Customary sales/distribution channels:
5. Customer support requirements for export:

- Warranty & replacement policies:
- Installation & maintenance:
- User training:
- Replacements/spare parts stocking:

6. Available supply for export (units per month):

___ currently available for export
___ to be available for export as of _____

B. Product 2: Repeat above for each product

* * *

VI. Current Export Resources, Functions & Requirements

A. Export Budget (last 3 years):

$ _____ 3 Years Ago
$ _____ 2 Years Ago
$ _____ 1 Year Ago

B. Export Organization Structure & Reporting Hierarchy: Which unit has responsibility for the function; where does it fit in the organization?

C. Export Manager(s)/Sales Force: Who supervises the function; how experienced. How large and experienced is the staff?

D. Export Functions Currently Performed (organization unit/persons assigned): How regularly is this function performed; what is done; how and by whom is it used?

1. **Market research, analysis and planning:**
2. **Export marketing and promotion:**
3. **Order taking & processing:**
4. **Export documentation:**
5. **Export finance/insurance:**
6. **Shipping & delivery:**

* * *

VII. Export Market Strategy for [This Year-Next Year]

A. Most Promising Markets:

B. Target Market 1 (Repeat for each target market):

1. Market Profile

- **Market overview:**
- **Demand trends:**
- **End user analysis:**
- **Competitive analysis:**
- **Import requirements and regulations:**
- **Market compatibility:**
- **Marketing & distribution practices:**
- **Advertising and promotion media:**
- **Potential business contacts:**

2. First Year Export Sales Goal: $_____

3. Market Entry Strategy

- **Export Mode:** (Whether to export directly or use domestic export representative)
- **Localization/adaptation:** (Whether/how to adapt product, packaging, literature)
- **Distribution:** (Whether to sell direct to buyer or use local rep, sales office, etc.)
- **Advertising & promotion:** (Whether/how to promote and media to use)
- **Product pricing:** (Base price and whether /how much to discount)
- **Export financing:** (What payment terms/methods to use, for whom)
- **Product delivery:** (What packing, labeling, shipping, storage needs/methods apply)

4. Market Development Action Plan (milestones/dates)

- **Develop marketing collateral:** (Promotional materials, pricing, etc.)
- **Identify prospects in target markets:** (Buyers, agents/distributors, licensees, etc.)
- **Select/appoint partners:** (Conclude agent/distributor/other agreements)
- **Conduct marketing campaign:** (Advertising, trade shows, business visits)
- **Evaluate results:** (apply to ongoing strategic review)

First-Year Export Budget

$ _____ A. Pre-Export Working Capital
$ _____ B. Market Research
$ _____ C. Sales & Distribution
$ _____ D. Market Promotion
$ _____ E. Market Adaptation

$ _____ Total

2. Sample Export Market Plan (Based on Template)

ABC Co.

* * *

I. Executive Summary

* * *

II. Company Profile

ABC Inc., established in 1980 and located in Big City, USA, manufactures digital imaging systems for the medical market. ABC's products are highly regarded for reliability, innovation and quality engineering. The complete ABC line offers diagnostic and review workstations, transcription software, and Web distribution and tele-radiology solutions. This scalable product line allows each facility to transition into the digital environment and grow at its own rate, offering improved productivity with limited financial exposure.

* * *

III. Current Export Status

A. Current Export Activity (as % of total sales): **ABC's e**xports are fairly sporadic and currently account for about 5% of total sales.
B. Current Export Products and Markets—ABC exports digital imaging systems on occasion to Canada, Mexico, Israel, Hong Kong, and Saudi Arabia.
C. Ability to meet commercially acceptable standards: ABC's PACS (Picture Archiving Communication Systems) comply with all FDA and other U.S. standards. CE Mark pending.

* * *

IV. Product Focus for Export

Product 1: Digital imaging systems

1. HS Classification: 902214

2. Product Description

ABC's digital imaging systems bring the best of today's digital imaging technology to hospitals, imaging centers and other institutions in a user-friendly environment that dramatically reduces wasteful administrative time. The systems enable diagnosticians in one location to analyze medical scans taken at the source location and also to easily interface and consult with other medical professionals on a timely basis to improved patient care. See ABC's Web site for further details (www.xxx.xxx).

3. Target Customers/Users

Hospitals, medical centers, imaging centers, doctors' offices.

4. Customary Sales/Distribution Channels

ABC sells to a large customer base domestically, utilizing a combination of their own sales force and regional distributors. The current domestic sales and marketing strategy is to service existing customers and rely on them and word of mouth to attract new customers. Customers are encouraged to visit the plant and talk over their needs with the plant staff.

5. Customer Support Requirements for Export

- **Warranty & replacement policies:** ABC has a strong customer service orientation. We are willing to send or train technicians to replace or repair any system that does not meet customer requirements.
- **Installation & maintenance:** Dealer's responsibility.

- **User Training**: Dealer provides and/or training provided at ABC.
- **Replacements/Spare parts stocking**: Dealer discretion.

6. Available supply for export (units per month):

- **Currently available for export:** ABC could easily fill new export orders from present inventory or other sources.
- **To be available for export as of :** Not applicable.

* * *

V. Current Export Resources, Functions & Requirements

A. Export Budget (last 3 years): ABC's management is strongly committed to exporting and would be willing to commit over $15,000 per year for export development. The company would also be willing to wait up to 3 years to achieve acceptable export results.

3 yrs ago: None
2 yrs ago: None
Last yr: $5,000

B. Export Organization Structure & Reporting Hierarchy (which unit has responsibility for the functions; where does it fit in the organization?**):** For export purposes, existing sales, marketing and distribution managers will report to the president of the company.

C. Export Manager(s)/Sales Force (Who supervises the function; how experienced; how large and experienced is the staff?). The current sales manager, Joe Smith, will initially serve as both the Export Manager/Sales Manager. He has little prior experience in exporting, but will be given opportunities to attend appropriate export training programs. ABC will consider hiring an Export Manager if new export volume warrants.

D. Export Functions Currently Performed (organization unit/persons assigned; How regularly is this function performed; what is done, how and by whom is the work used in the company): Joe Smith handles the majority of the sales and processes the orders through ABC's credit department and then shipping department.

- **Market research, analysis and planning:** At present, ABC invests minimally in market research, analysis and planning.
- **Export marketing and promotion:** ABC has not yet done any export marketing or promotion, although we do have an active website.
- **Order taking & processing:** Will be assigned to the Sales/Export Manager.
- **Export documentation:** Sales/Export Manager to work with freight forwarders.
- **Export finance/insurance:** Sales/Export Manager to work with XYZ Commercial Bank for export transactions by L/C and Documentary Collections and with the U.S. Export-Import Bank export credit insurance.
- **Shipping & delivery:** Sales/Export Manager will handle and work with freight forwarders.

* * *

VI. Export Market Strategy Next 2 Years

Target Markets: ABC will focus on 2 markets considered most promising over the next two years, based on trade statistics and available market research—[Country 1, Country 2]. See Appendices for assessments of these target markets.

U.S. Exports of HS 902214, Latest 4 Years
Apparatus based on the use of X-Rays for medical, surgical, or veterinary uses

U.S. Exports of HS 902214, Latest 4 Years
Apparatus based on the use of X-Rays for medical, surgical, or veterinary uses,
Top 5 Markets in Rank Order, Latest Year

Country	Base Year A	Next Year B	Next Year C	Latest Year D	% Change A-D	% Change C-D	% Total D
	In 1,000 Dollars						
Japan	108,223	72,498	90,234	142,111	31.3%	57.5%	15.54%
China	77,273	100,622	120,372	102,924	33.2%	-14.5%	11.26%
Canada	58,909	67,951	93,589	66,249	12.5%	-29.2%	7.25%
Belgium	69,510	70,477	64,830	63,784	-8.2%	-1.6%	6.98%
Germany	52,224	63,054	54,187	54,837	5.0%	1.2%	6.00%
Subtotal :	366,138	374,602	423,212	429,906	17.4%	1.6%	47.02%
All Other:	426,319	443,271	519,807	484,459	13.6%	-6.8%	52.98%
Total	792,457	817,873	943,018	914,365	15.4%	-3.0%	100.00%

A. First Year Export Sales Goal: $500,000

B. Market Entry Strategy

- **Export Mode: (Whether to export directly or use domestic export intermediary):** ABC will export directly to [Country], not use a U.S. intermediary.
- **Distribution in target markets (Whether to sell direct to foreign buyers or use in-country agent/distributor):** ABC will initially seek a distributor in [Country] that specializes in radiological equipment, can train locally as needed, is not already overloaded with other accounts, and is willing to share costs of market development and promotion. ABC will use the Department of Commerce Gold Key Service in [Country] as a first step.
- **Advertising & promotion (Whether/how to promote to target market and what media to use):** ABC and its distributor will launch an aggressive in-country promotion campaign focused on ads in the major medical imaging trade magazines and exhibiting at the next [Medica show in Germany].

- **Product pricing (Base price and whether /how much to discount)**: Base export prices (Ex Works and FAS Los Angeles) are shown on the attached Price List. CIF pricing can be quoted on a case-by-case basis. The distributor will get a 15% discount on orders below $25,000 and a 25% discount on orders above $25,000.
- **Export financing (What payment terms/methods to use)**:Unless special circumstances apply, or the distributor advises otherwise, ABC will sell on an irrevocable, confirmed Letter of Credit basis or, if warranted, on open account backed by export credit insurance from the U.S. Export-Import Bank.
- **Product delivery (What methods to use for packing, labeling, shipping, and storage)**: ABC will pack and label shipments in compliance with any product marking and labeling requirements. ABC's freight forwarder will arrange delivery from and to whatever point the buyer specifies (from factory only (ex-works), to the U.S. point of exit (FOB, FAS) or to the entry point in the destination country (CIF).
- **Localization/adaptation (Whether/how to adapt product, packaging, literature)**: For the [Country] market, ABC will be able to use current product design and packaging and current English-language product brochures and other marketing collateral.

C. Market Development Action Plan (milestones/dates)

- **Develop marketing collateral** (promotional materials, price lists, legal instruments, etc.): ABC will develop by [Date]
- **Identify prospects in target markets** (Buyers, agents/distributors): ABC will use the Department of Commerce Gold Key Service to identify potential distributor in [Country]. Additional repfind initiatives will be pursued on a case by case basis. by [Date]
- **Select/ appoint partners** (Conclude agent/distributor/other agreements): To be pursued as prospects are identified.

- **Conduct marketing campaign** (Advertising, trade shows, business visits): After selection of distributor(s).
- **Evaluate results:** Quarterly

* * *

VII. First-Year Export Budget

1.	**Pre-Export Working Capital:**	$ None
2.	**Export Training** (8 topics):	$1,800
3.	**Market Research & Planning:**	$1,500
4.	**Sales & Distribution:**	$1,500 for Gold Key
5.	**Market Promotion:**	$10,000 (Medica Trade Show)
6.	**Market Adaptation:**	As needed for regulatory compliance
7.	**Travel:**	$5,000
8.	**Other:**	$200
	Total:	**$20,000**

APPENDIX F: MATCHMAKING AIDS

1. Sample Agent/Distributor Search Letter

Dear _____:

We are seeking representation for our products in your country and would welcome your possible interest. This will briefly describe who we are, what we do, what we are looking for, and how we prefer to operate. Please refer to our Web site (**www.xxxxxxxxx.com**) for additional information.

XYZ, Inc. is a leading U.S. manufacturer of two-way radio communications equipment for professional use. We offer vehicular mounted radios and base station radios. They are used by police, taxis, delivery services, etc. We are currently [exporting to _____ , but not yet in your country] [selling throughout the U.S., but not yet exporting].

Our firm was founded in 19__ with __ employees. We now have ___ employees, and our annual sales this past year totaled over $_____. ABC, Inc. is capitalized at over $____, has modern plant facilities, and excellent profitability. Our financial and operations can be confirmed by national credit agencies. We are also a member of the [any relevant chambers or other organizations].

Our products are sold in the U.S. through a nationwide network of stocking distributors who purchase direct from our factory. The distributors must have the capability to install the equipment and provide local warranty and non-warranty service. The distributor must have adequate test equipment and be willing to not only inventory our radios, but service materials as well.

We prefer to deal with mutually exclusive distributors in each defined territory. We grant a __% discount (__% commission) from our recommended or suggested list prices and fully support our distributors with technical advice, express shipments when needed, and other support services. We would support our overseas representatives in the same way.

It is our policy to select and work with a dealer on a trial basis using either pre-payment or payment by a confirmed, irrevocable letter of credit. After a relationship has been established, and a distributor has demonstrated they can sell and service our products profitably, we are open to other credit and payment terms.

With kind regards,

* * *

2. Agent/Distributor Qualifications Checklist

Consider these factors in evaluating prospective overseas representatives. Their significance varies with the products and countries involved and the needs of the company seeking a rep.

Sales force

- Number and location of sales staff.
- Would the rep need more staff to service your account? Would it be willing add staff?
- How is its sales staff compensated? Are any incentive or motivation programs offered?
- How is its sales staff trained? Would it pay or share costs of Egypt-based training if needed?

Sales performance

- Sales volume for the past five years. If growing, why? If not, why not?
- Sales goals for next year; based on what assumptions?
- What sales volume does it foresee for your products? Based on what? Is this adequate?

Territorial coverage

- Current territory served. Is that the coverage you need?
- How does it serve more distant areas within its territory— resident staff, branch offices?
- Would it be willing to strengthen coverage in areas you consider important?

Companies/products represented

- How many and whose/products does it currently represent? Is this a manageable level?

- Would you be the primary supplier? What priority would you receive?
- Would your products fit well in this mix?
- Do you compete with any of the companies/products represented?

Customer profile

- What end-use sectors does it mainly sell to? Are these the right targets for you?
- Who are its key accounts? What share of sales do they represent? Do they make sense for you as well?

Facilities and equipment

- Communications facilities and preferred methods—phone, fax, cable, E-mail, other?
- Warehouse and stocking capacity. Is there enough for you, if you need it?
- Customer support facilities/capabilities. Can it install and service your products if needed?
- Training facilities/capabilities. Can it train users if needed?

Localization capabilities

- Can it translate your sales literature and ad copy if needed?
- Can it alter the packaging or the product itself if needed to meet local requirement or tastes?

Market development capabilities

- Market research—Does it conduct or use market research in decision-making? Can it help you assess your market potential?
- Promotion—Does it promote itself and the products it

represents? What promotional literature is used for this? What promotional media are used? How are the results measured? How much is spent on each method? If the principals contribute, what formula is used to allocate the costs?

3. Sample Export Sales Representative Agreement

DISCLAIMER

THIS EXPORT SALES REPRESENTATIVE AGREEMENT (this "Agreement") is made and entered into on _____ (date) (the "Effective Date"), by and between _____ ("Manufacturer"), a California corporation with principal offices located at _____ (address), USA, and _____, ("Representative") having its principal offices at _____ (complete address of representative's office).

RECITALS

Manufacturer is in the business of manufacturing and exporting _____;

Representative is in the business of representing manufacturers to sell products; and

Manufacturer desires to retain Representative to act as Manufacturer's sales representative pursuant to the terms and conditions set forth in this Agreement.

AGREEMENT

NOW, THEREFORE, for and in consideration of the mutual covenants contained herein, the Manufacturer and Representative agree as follows:

1. DEFINITION

1.1 "Affiliate" means an entity which, directly or indirectly, controls, is controlled by, or is under common control of a parent company with a party to this Agreement. For purposes of this paragraph, "control" means owning or controlling at least 30% of the voting stock entitled to vote for elections of the members of the board of directors (or, if none, persons performing similar functions) or, in the case of entities not having voting stock, equivalent ownership or control thereof.

1.2 "Commissions" shall mean the commissions to be paid by Manufacturer to Representatives for the Commissionable Orders pursuant to Sections 6.3, 6.4 and 6.5 of this Agreement.

1.3 "Commissionable Orders" shall mean any and all Orders for Products: (a) that have been received by Manufacturer through or from the Representative for orders of Products to be delivered to Manufacturer Customers within the Territory; (b) that have been reported by Representative to Manufacturer promptly after the receipt of the order; (c) that have been confirmed in writing signed by the CEO of, or a person designated by, Manufacturer, confirming that such an Order is a Commissionable Order; (d) that disclose the name of the ultimate Manufacturer Customers and the price or prices quoted for payment by such Manufacturer Customers for Products; (e) that have been delivered to Manufacturer's principal office located at ____; and, (f) that have been accepted by the Manufacturer in writing prior to the termination or expiration of the Term. Any Order submitted by Representative not in compliance with Section 1.3 will not be qualified as a Commissionable Order, and Manufacturer shall not be obligated to pay Commissions on such an Order. Commissionable Orders shall not include any Products sold to Manufacturer Customers outside the Territory for delivery outside the Territory or any Products that are incorporated into, and become a component of, goods or items that are delivered to or sold within the Territory by a third person. Manufacturer agrees that all bona fide inquiries and Orders received by Manufacturer from persons within the Territory will be referred to Representative and may qualify as Commissionable Orders if other requirements set forth in this Section 1.2 of this Agreement are met. With respect to Orders from Manufacturer Customers within the Territory for delivery outside the Territory or from Manufacturer Customers outside the Territory for delivery within the Territory, if there is no exclusive sales representative for any of the territories involved herein other than the Territory, such orders may qualify as Commissionable Orders if all other requirements set forth in this Section 1.2 of this Agreement are met. If, however, there are one or more exclusive sales representatives for the territories involved other than the Territory, then such orders will not qualify as Commissionable Order, and instead, Manufacturer will divide the commission applicable for such orders equally among the sales representatives involved on a case by case basis.

(The above set forth provision is applicable if the Representative is the exclusive representative for Manufacturer in the Territory. If the Representative is a non-exclusive representative, the following should be used instead.)

1.3 "Commissionable Orders" shall mean any and all Orders for Products: (a) that have been received by Manufacturer through or from the Representative for orders of Products to be delivered to Manufacturer Customers within the Territory; (b) that have been reported by Representative to Manufacturer promptly after the receipt of the order; (c) that have been confirmed in writing signed by the CEO of, or a person designated by, Manufacturer, confirming that such an Order is a Commissionable Order; (d) that disclose the name of the ultimate Manufacturer Customers and the price or prices quoted for payment by such Manufacturer Customers for Products; (e) that have been delivered to Manufacturer's principal office located at _____; and, (f) that have been accepted by the Manufacturer in writing prior to the termination or expiration of the Term. Any Order submitted by Representative not in compliance with Section 1.3 will not be qualified as a Commissionable Order, and Manufacturer shall not be obligated to pay Commissions on such an Order. Commissionable Orders shall not include any orders for Products received by Manufacturer not from Representative.

1.4 "Confidential Information" shall mean information provided by Manufacturer or Manufacturer Customers to Representative (i) that is not known by actual or potential competitors of Manufacturer or is generally unavailable to the public, (ii) that has been created, discovered, developed or otherwise become known to Manufacturer or in which property rights have been assigned or otherwise conveyed to Manufacturer, and (iii) that has material economic value or potential material economic value to Manufacturer's present or future business. Confidential Information, subject to exceptions set forth by laws, shall include trade secrets (as defined under California Civil Code section 3426.1) which include all discoveries, developments, designs, improvements, inventions, formulas, software programs, processes, techniques, know-how, negative know-how, data, research, technical data (whether or not patentable or registrable under patent, copyright or similar statutes and including all rights to obtain, register, perfect and enforce those proprietary interests), customer and supplier lists, customer profile and other customer information, customer and price list, business plans, and any modifications or enhancements of any of the forgoing, and all program, marketing, sales, or other financial or business information disclosed to Representative by Manufacturer, either directly or indirectly, in writing or orally or by drawings or observation, which has actual or potential economic value to Manufacturer.

1.5 Effective Date" shall mean _____.

1.6 "Initial Term" shall mean the initial term of this Agreement from __ to __.

1.7 "Manufacturer" shall mean _____ and its Affiliates.

1.8 "Manufacturer Customers" shall mean any individuals or entities, who are current or potential customers or business prospects of Manufacturer, or who are introduced from or by Manufacturer to Representative.

1.9 "Net selling price" shall mean the gross amount actually invoiced to Manufacturer Customers, including components, spare parts, accessories and related services, minus any of the following which may have been included in the gross price or contract value, provided that they are stated separately on the applicable invoice: (a) shipping, freight and insurance charges, inland, air and ocean; (b) packing, crating or handling charges; (c) sales, use, value added or similar taxes, customs duties, import or export taxes or levies applicable to Products but excluding any income, withholding or other tax or assessment imposed on Manufacturer or Manufacturer Customers in the normal course of business; and (d) discounts, allowances or other special deductions granted Manufacturer Customers.

1.10 "Order" shall mean an order placed by a Manufacturer Customer for Products and received by Manufacturer from or through Representative. Only Orders that meet all terms and conditions set forth in Section 1.4 are Commissionable Orders.

1.11 "Party" shall mean Manufacturer or Representative, individually. "Parties shall mean Manufacturer and Representative collectively.

1.12 "Products" shall mean the products set forth in Attachment A, which is hereby incorporated by reference as fully set forth in this Agreement.

1.13 "Renewal Term" shall mean any renewal term of this Agreement pursuant to Section 8.1 of this Agreement.

1.14 "Representative" shall mean _____ and its Affiliates.

1.15 "Term" shall mean the term of this Agreement, including the Initial Term and any Renewal Terms, if any.

"Territory" shall mean the following country / countries: _____ *(or* "_____ *types of customers serviced by Representative in* _____*).*

2. APPOINTMENT

2.1 Manufacturer appoints Representative, and Representative accepts the appointment, to act as Manufacturer's exclusive sales representative in the Territory for the sale of the Products during the Term. *(The word "exclusive" is optional.)*

3. RELATIONSHIP OF THE PARTIES

3.1 Independent Contractor. This Agreement shall not be deemed to create a partnership, joint venture or agent-principal relationship between the parties, and Representative or any of Representative's directors, officers, employees or agents shall not, by virtue of the performance of their obligations under this Agreement, represent themselves as, or be deemed to be, an agent, partner or employee of Manufacturer. The parties agree that Representative is an independent contractor, not an employee, of Manufacturer. Neither party is liable for any acts, omissions to act, contracts, promises, commitments or representations made by the other, except as specified in this Agreement.

3.2 Exclusivity; Most Favored Representative. Representative shall be the exclusive representative for Manufacturer to sell Products in the Territory. If Manufacturer enters into any export sales representative agreement for Product with another sales representative in a different territory in the future, providing that new sales representative more favorable terms, other than commission amount, Manufacturer will immediately amend this Agreement to provide Representative with the benefit of any terms, other than the commission amount, in the new agreement more favorable than those included in this Agreement. *(This Section is optional. Also, the portion after the first sentence is optional, even if this Agreement is an exclusive agreement.)*

4. DUTIES AND RESPONSIBILITIES OF REPRESENTATIVE

4.1 Representative's duties and responsibilities include but are not limited to:

- Obtaining and providing Manufacturer with market forecast information regarding the Products, identifying potential business and contacts, investigating inquiries received by Manufacturer and referred to Representative and making introductions to, and arranging meetings with, potential customers;
- Assisting Manufacturer in preparation and submission of presentations, bids and quotations for Orders and in their negotiation at the time and in the manner reasonably requested by Manufacturer, assisting Manufacturer in arranging and coordinating demonstration of Products, and assisting Manufacturer's installation of Products and the provision of services in connection with the demonstrations;
- Achieving the minimum sales requirements of Products as set forth in Attachment A.
- Providing Manufacturer Customers presales and post-sales customer services, including but not limited to transmitting technical information and providing advice and assistance concerning the implementation of technical and training programs and the provision of Manufacturer's personnel and other assistance;
- Providing logistical and support services in the Territory, including but not limited to providing assistance necessary to Manufacturer in arranging and providing lodging, office space, equipment, translation, transportation, communications, facilities and other related support activities;
- Providing advice to Manufacturer regarding the probable financing requirements and financing sources for acquisition of Products by potential customers;
- Providing advice and assistance to Manufacturer on compliance with laws, regulations, business and financial practices in the Territory, maintenance of contact,

communications and liaison with government officials and obtaining necessary licenses, permits and authorizations in compliance with law, regulations and ordinances;

- Providing information and recommendations concerning local subcontractors that might be necessary for construction, installation, maintenance or service of Products; and
- Providing other assistance and services as Manufacturer may reasonably request.

(This is a suggested list and should be revised to meet the needs of the parties.)

4.2 With fifteen (15) days from the closing of each calendar ____ *(month or quarter)*, or as reasonably requested by Manufacturer, Representative shall submit a written report to Manufacturer setting forth the sales in that quarter, potential sales in the future, information relating to commercial conditions in the Territory, the financial and credit status of Manufacturer Customers and any additional information necessary to enable Manufacturer to manufacture or supply Products to the required specifications, safety codes, regulations and requirements in the Territory. Representative agrees that it is Manufacturer's objective to obtain "sole-source negotiated sales" wherever possible.

4.3 Representative shall not make any representations, warranties or guarantees to any person with respect to Products or related services, other than those representations, warranties or guarantees that Manufacturer has specifically authorized in writing to be given to that person. Representative's authority is limited to the solicitation and forwarding or placing of Orders with Manufacturer and the performance of other functions set forth in this Agreement. Representative shall have no authorities to make or execute any commitment or agreement, accept any Orders or incur any liability on behalf of Manufacturer or bind Manufacturer in any way.

4.4 Except as specified in Section 5, Representative is responsible for all expenses incurred by Representative in connection with the implementation and performance of Representative's duties and obligations under this Agreement, including but not limited to: (a) the expenses incurred in fulfilling its duties and responsibilities as provided in

Section 4; (b) costs, expenses and salaries of its personnel associated with establishing and maintaining its sales organization and offices; (c) advertising and promotion expenses; and (d) any and all taxes, duties, tariffs or charges that may be imposed on Representative in the Territory. Subject to prior written approval by Manufacturer for each specific trip, Manufacturer may reimburse Representative for Representative's actual and reasonable travel, room and board expenses incurred while performing services under this Agreement in a country that is not also the place of Representative's principal business or residence, provided that Representative provides reasonable documentation for those expenses. *(The last sentence is optional.)*

4.5 Representative is solely responsible for the performance of its duties.

5. DUTIES AND RESPONSIBILITIES OF MANUFACTURER

5.1 Manufacturer will use its best efforts to deliver Products pursuant to the dates and other requirements stated in Orders delivered to and accepted by Manufacturer.

5.2 From time to time, Manufacturer will supply Representative with a reasonable amount of descriptive materials and literature, including but not limited to sales brochures, installation, operating and maintenance manuals, technical descriptions and other data and information, to enable Representative to promote the sale of Products and to undertake its duties and responsibilities set forth in this Agreement.

5.3 At reasonable requests by Representative, Manufacturer may, at its discretion, make arrangement for meetings to introduce and demonstrate Products to promotion sale and other services performed by Representative, so as to familiarize Representative with the use and applications of Products and to facilitate Representative's performance of its duties under this Agreement. The locations for such meetings shall be determined by Manufacturer. Except as otherwise agreed by the parties in writing, each party shall bear its own costs and expenses for such meetings, including but not limited to costs for its personnel and travel and lodging expenses.

5.4 Manufacturer will provide, or make available, expert personnel and technical assistance, in the manner and at the time Manufacturer considers reasonable and appropriate, to follow up Representative's promotion and sales activities and to fulfill Manufacturer Customer's Order or requirements received and accepted by Manufacturer. Manufacturer is solely responsible for the design, development, supply and production of Products, the performance of its personnel and the furnishing of technical assistance. In no event is Representative entitled to, nor does Representative have any right to, claim any compensation or loss for clientele or sales or for other reason arising from Manufacturer's performance or failure to perform any of its above-stated functions.

(This is only a suggested list and should be revised to meet the needs of the parties.)

5.5 Manufacturer is solely responsible for the performance of its duties.

6. PRICING, COMMISSIONS AND ACCOUNTING

6.1 Pricing. Manufacturer has the sole right to establish and control all prices, discounts, extension of credit, allowances, refunds, specifications, delivery and other terms governing the sale of Products. Representative shall only quote to Manufacturer Customers the prices and terms of sale for Products provided by Manufacturer and will in no event alter or change the prices or terms of sale unless authorized by Manufacturer in writing. Prices and terms of sale are subject to change by Manufacturer at any time without advance notice. Manufacturer reserves the right to grant or not to grant any discount or allowance, to accept a return or make a refund, or to extend credit, as Manufacturer in its discretion deems advisable. However, after making any change in prices or terms or canceling any approved Order, Manufacturer shall immediately notify Representative of the changes and/or cancellations.

6.2 Acceptance and Cancellation of Orders. No Order is binding on Manufacturer until accepted in writing by Manufacturer. Manufacturer reserves the right to accept, reject, modify or cancel, in whole or in part, any or all Orders received or accepted by Manufacturer. Manufacturer will bill Manufacturer Customers and carry accounts in its own name as creditor, except in cases where a different procedure is agreed upon by the parties in advance in writing. Following Product shipment, Manufacturer will furnish Representative with a copy of Manufacturer's approval of the Order and the invoice or invoices included in the shipping documents. Notwithstanding Manufacturer's acceptance of an Order, Manufacturer has the absolute right to modify or cancel the Order or to consent to Manufacturer Customer's modification or cancellation of the Order at any time for any reason. Manufacturer is not liable to Representative for a cancellation or modification or Manufacturer's failure to deliver any Product.

6.3 Commissions. Manufacturer will pay Representative Commissions at the rates set forth in Attachment B, which is hereby incorporated by reference as fully set forth in this Agreement, of the Net Selling Price of all Products sold pursuant to Commissionable Orders accepted by Manufacturer under, and during the term of, this Agreement. Unless otherwise agreed by the parties in writing, Commissions for a particular Commissionable Order are deemed earned and payable, pro rata, within fifteen (15) days of Manufacturer's receipt of payment from Manufacturer Customer placing the Commissionable Order. In the event of nonpayment by such Customer for any reason, no Commissions may arise or be deemed to be earned with respect to the unpaid amount, and Representative agrees to relinquish and waive any claims against Manufacturer for all of these Orders. *(Commissions can also be paid on a monthly basis.)*

6.4 Payments of Commissions. Any payment of Commissions will be made in U.S. Dollars, unless the parties agree otherwise in writing, and will be made by check or bank transfer to the order of Representative or by any other means as the parties may agree otherwise in writing prior to such payment. No payment of Commissions may be made to any person or entity other than Representative, except pursuant to a written assignment by Representative approved in advance in writing by Manufacturer. No Commission will be paid for any Commissionable Orders placed with Manufacturer for the specific purpose of repairing or replacing defective or damaged Products. If a Product ordered by a Manufacturer Customer is returned by that Customer, Commissions paid by Manufacturer to Representative for such Products will be deducted from future Commissions to be paid by Manufacturer to Representative until the amount is deducted in full. If no future Commissions will be paid to Representative, then Representative shall immediately pay the unpaid balance of such amount to Manufacturer in full.

6.5 Payment of Commissions Following Termination or Expiration. Subject to Sections 6.2 and 6.4, following termination or expiration of this Agreement, within thirty (30) days from the date of termination or expiration, Manufacturer will pay Representative Commissions on Products under Commissionable Orders accepted by Manufacturer and paid by Manufacturer Customers on or before the date of termination or expiration. No Commissions will be paid with respect to any Orders accepted after the termination or expiration date, except that Manufacturer will pay Commissions on the following Order: (a) Any Orders received by Manufacturer prior to the date of termination or expiration but accepted and paid in whole or in part thereafter; and (b) any Order received and accepted by Manufacturer and paid by Manufacturer Customers within __ days of the termination or expiration date if the Term is ___ years or less at the time of termination or expiration; or within___ days of the termination or expiration date, if the Term is __ year or less; or within ___ days of the termination or expiration date if the Term is __ or more. *(The second half of Section 6.6, starting from "except, (a) . . ." to the end of the Section is optional—the parties can use (a), (b) or both.)*

6.6 Audit Rights. During the Term and for a period of one (1) year following the termination expiration of the Agreement, each party shall maintain complete, accurate and detailed books and records with respect to the determination of its revenues and other matters associated with the performance of this Agreement. Each Party (the "requesting party") shall have the right, at its expense and upon prior written notice given to the other party (the "responding party") at least fifteen (15) days prior to the inspection date requested by the requesting party, to inspect and audit all of the responding party's records associated with the performance of this Agreement, and the responding party agrees to reasonably cooperate with and provide access to the requesting party and its financial advisors as may be necessary and appropriate for such inspection and audit.

7. COMPLIANCE WITH LAW

7.1 Representative agrees that in rendering services and in carrying out its duties under this Agreement, Representative will neither undertake nor cause or permit to be undertaken any activity which to Representative's knowledge is illegal under the laws of the Territory or of the U.S. It is a condition of this Agreement that, within __ *(specify number, such as: 30)* days from execution of this Agreement and prior to the initiation of any activities with respect to any Order, Representative will submit to Manufacturer an opinion of Representative's counsel, provided that such counsel and the form and substance of the opinion shall be to Manufacturer's satisfaction, that nothing in this Agreement prevents Representative from carrying out its duties in accordance with laws, decrees, rules and regulations of the Territory, and that Representative may act as representative and sales agent for all Products to any government ministries, agencies and departments, including the armed forces. The submission of this opinion is a condition precedent to the effectiveness of this Agreement. In addition to this opinion, or as an alternative, Manufacturer may require Representative to disclose this relationship to any Manufacturer Customer and, either to provide satisfactory evidence of the disclosure or to secure, prior to, and as a condition of, any Order being accepted pursuant to Section 1.3, Manufacturer Customer's authorization or acknowledgment in writing, in a form acceptable to Manufacturer, of this relationship as to the specific Products involved. If Manufacture, at its own discretion, considers that Representative fails to do so within a reasonable period of time, Manufacturer may conclude such Order for its own account, and Representative shall not be entitled to any Commissions for such an Order.

7.2 Representative understands and agrees that Manufacturer may comply with any legal provision requiring disclosure, or any request from the U.S. Government or the Government of the Territory to disclose, by affidavit or otherwise, the identity of Representative, as well as the identities of Representative's principal and the amount of any payment made or to be made to Representative under this Agreement.

8. TERM AND TERMINATION

8.1 Term. The term of this Agreement will commence on the effective date of this Agreement and will continue for a period of _ (_) years unless earlier terminated by either party accordance with Section 8.2. At the end of each Term, including at the end of the Initial Term and the Renewal Terms, this Agreement will be automatically renewed for an additional _ (_) year period, unless either party give the other party a written notice _ (_) days prior to the expiration of the Initial Term or any Renewal Term. All the terms and conditions contained in this Agreement will remain the same during any renewals beyond the Initial Term, unless this Agreement is amended or modified in written pursuant to Section 15.4 of this Agreement. *(The automatic renewal portion of the provision is optional. Also, restrictions or conditions may be required, such as sales quota, before there will be a renewal term.)*

8.2 Termination. In the event of any of the following, this Agreement, and the rights and licenses granted hereunder, will terminate.

If either party defaults in the performance of or compliance with any provision contained in this Agreement or breach any provisions set forth in this Agreement (except as otherwise provided in this Section 8) and such default or breach is not cured within fifteen (15) days after written notice thereof is received by the defaulting party, the party giving such notice may then give further written notice to the defaulting party terminating this Agreement, in which event this Agreement, and the rights and licenses granted hereunder, will terminate on the date specified in such further notice.

If either party discontinues its primary business for more than fifteen (15) days, either party may terminate this Agreement upon fifteen (15) days' prior written notice to the other party. If the primary business is continued by an Affiliate, the primary business will be deemed continued by the party for purposes of Section 8.2.2.

Either party may terminate this Agreement by written notice to the other party and may regard the other party as in default of this Agreement, if the other party becomes insolvent, makes a general assignment for the benefit of creditors, files a voluntary petition of bankruptcy, suffers or permits the appointment of a receiver for its business or assets, or becomes subject to any proceedings under any bankruptcy or insolvency law, which is not dismissed within ninety (90) days, or has wound up or entered liquidation, voluntarily or otherwise. In the event that any of the above events occur, the defaulting party will immediately notify the other party of its occurrence.

In the event of a breach of Representative's obligations under Sections 7, 11, 12, 13 and 14, Manufacturer may immediately terminate this Agreement in writing without providing any cure period.

If one party is unable to perform its obligations under the Agreement by reason of any law, rule, regulation or order of any municipal, state or federal or foreign authority, including, but not limited to any regulatory authority that has jurisdiction over that party's business, then the either party may terminate this Agreement by given the other party a thirty (30) day written notice.

If the performance of this Agreement becomes impracticable because of the change of situation in the U.S. or Territory, or if the trade between the U.S. and Territory becomes impracticable because of the change in the currency exchange, then either party may terminate this Agreement by given the other party a _ (_) days' prior written notice. (Optional.)

Either party may terminate this Agreement without cause upon __ (_) days' prior written notice to the other party. (Optional.)

8.3 Termination of the Agreement for any reason does not affect (a) obligations that have accrued as of the date of termination; and (b) the obligations under those sections identified in Section 15.12 of this Agreement. Further, in the event of termination, Representative shall return Manufacturer the Confidential Information as provided in Section 12.4 (or 12.1) of this Agreement, and Representative's limited license to use Manufacturer' intellectual property shall cease immediately.

9. REPRESENTATIONS AND WARRANTIES

9.1 Each party represents and warrants that:

9.1.1 It has the authority to enter into this Agreement and the rights and license necessary to enter into, and perform its obligations under, this Agreement.

9.1.2 It is free to enter into this Agreement and is not bound by any agreements, including but not limited to nondisclosure agreement, noncompetition agreement, documents or obligation that may infringe on its ability or in any manner prevent it from performing any of the duties that may be required of it during the Term, or that may result in liability to it in any manner, action, or proceeding.

9.1.3 It has full power and authority to execute and deliver this Agreement, and this Agreement has been duly executed and delivered by or on behalf of itself and constitutes a legal, valid and binding obligation enforceable against it in accordance with its respective terms. Neither the execution, delivery, nor performance of this Agreement violates or conflicts with any applicable laws, decrees, rules, regulations, requires any notice, consent or other action by a third party or creates a default or breach or give rise to any right of termination, cancellation or acceleration of any right or obligation or to lose any benefit to which it is entitled under any agreement or other instrument binding upon it. It will not take any action that would have the effect of causing the other to be in violation of any laws, decrees, rules or regulations.

9.2 Manufacturer represents and warrants that it has all rights, title and interest in and to all copyrights, patents, trademarks and other intellectual property rights associated with Products or otherwise has the right to allow the use thereof which are necessary to use, sell, market and distribute Products, and to manufacture and sell Products without infringing any rights; and that, as of the Effective Date, Manufacturer is not aware of any basis for third party claims of infringement of any patents, trademarks, or trade names with respect to Products. In the event that any action, claim or suit is brought against Representative alleging that the manufacture, use, sale or transfer of any Product or the use of the trademarks or trade names constitutes infringement of any proprietary rights of any third party, Manufacturer shall indemnify Representative pursuant to Section 10.1 of this Agreement, provided that Representative gives written notice of such actions or claims brought against Representative within five (5) days from the receipt of notice of such actions or claims, and that Representative takes reasonable steps as may be requested by Manufacturer to assist in the defense of such action. *(The last sentence, starting with "In the event that . . ." is optional.)*

9.3 Representative represents and warrants that any fees or Commissions paid or to be paid to Representative under this Agreement are for Representative's own account, and that except as appropriate to carry out Representative's duties in this Agreement, Representative has not, has no obligation to and will not, directly or indirectly, give, offer, pay, promise to pay or authorize the payment of money or thing of value to any other person in connection with transactions for which Commissions under this Agreement are to be paid. Representative agrees not to take any actions that would cause Manufacturer to violate section 103 of the Foreign Corrupt Practices Act of 1977 (15 U.S.C.A. § 78dd-1). Representative warrants that none of its officer, director, employee or agent is an "official" of ___ *(name of country)* Government as that term is defined in section 103, nor will Representative employ an "official" of that government.

9.4 Representative represents and warrants that it will make and keep books, records and accounts that, in reasonable detail, accurately and fairly reflect the transactions performed by Representative under this Agreement and the dispositions of the Commissions paid Representative pursuant to this Agreement. Representative specifically agrees that Manufacturer may inspect such books, records and accounts upon reasonable requests made by Manufacturer to Representative.

10. INDEMNIFICATION AND LIMITATION OF LIABILITY

10.1 Indemnification. Each party (the "First Party") hereby indemnifies and agrees to hold the other party (the "Second Party") and its affiliates, and its and their successors and assigns, and its and their directors, officers and employees harmless against any and all claims, causes of actions, loss, demands, penalties, damages, costs, judgments, attorney's fees or any other expenses incurred in connection with, caused by or relating to the First Party's actions or failure to act or any breach by the First Party of the terms, covenants, representations or warranties set forth in this Agreement.

10.2 Limitation of Liability. Regardless of the basis on which any party (the "first party") may be entitled to recover damages from the other party (the "second party"), including but not limited to, breach of warranty, contract or fiduciary duty, fraud, negligence, misrepresentation, other tort or indemnity, the second party's aggregate liability under this agreement or related to products or the use thereof is limited to actual, direct damages that can be proven up to an amount not to exceed the aggregate of commissions paid by manufacturer to representative for the six-month period prior to the date when such problem occurred. The party suffering such damages or losses must first exhaust any available legal and equitable remedies against parties other than the second party. The second party shall in no event be liable to the first party or any third party for any special, incidental, indirect or consequential damages (including lost profits, savings, revenues, business opportunities or business advantages) under this agreement or in any way in connection with products or the use thereof whatsoever, even if second party has been advised of the possibility of such damages. Notwithstanding the foregoing, the limitations of liability set forth above in this section 10.2 shall not apply to losses against which the parties have agreed to indemnify each other pursuant to the terms and provisions of this agreement or the damages incurred by manufacturer because of representative's breach of sections 11, 12, 13 and 14 of this agreement by representative. *(Optional.)*

10.3 Disclaimer. Except or as otherwise expressly set forth in this agreement, each party disclaims all other warranties or conditions, express or implied, including, but not limited to the implied warranties or conditions of merchantability, fitness for a particular purpose of the services or products, quiet enjoyment, as well as implied warranties arising from course of dealing or course of performance.

10.4 Some jurisdictions do not allow the exclusion or limitation of incidental or consequential damages, so the above limitation or exclusion may not apply.

(The sections on limitation of liability will limit the liability for both parties. If the parties or either party does not want to set a limitation on liability, then please delete Sections 10.2 to 10.4 and delete the reference of limitation of liability in the header. If the limitation is applicable as to one party only, then revise these sections accordingly.)

11. OWNERSHIP OF INTELLECTUAL PROPERTY

11.1 Manufacturer shall at all times own and retain all respective right, title and interest in and to, and is the sole and exclusive owner of, any intellectual property rights in Products. Such right, title and interest include, but are not limited to, all patents, copyrights, trademarks, trade names, trade dress and trade secrets, names and marks now and subsequently used to identify Products, any proprietary information used in or applying to Products, rights of privacy or publicity, rights to the graphical user interface, source code, object code and other intellectual property rights. Representative agrees that (a) the intellectual property rights in Products are Manufacturer' property and contain valuable proprietary materials of Manufacturer; (b) Manufacturer hereby grants a limited license to Representative to use the names and trademarks of Manufacturer and Product and manuals in order to market and sell Product in strict conformity with this Agreement; and (c) Representative shall not have any rights in and to the intellectual property rights in Products, except as otherwise explicitly stated in this Agreement. If requested by Manufacturer, Representative shall assist Manufacturer or Manufacturer's designees at Manufacturer's expense to file any application for registration of a patent, trademark, trade name, service mark or other trade-identifying symbol used in connection with the Products and to establish any right of prior use by Manufacturer that may be required for the registration or protection of the patent, trademark, tradename, service mark or other symbol under the laws of the Territory. Upon expiration or sooner termination of this Agreement, Representative's limited license to use Manufacturer' intellectual property shall cease immediately.

12. CONFIDENTIALITY

12.1 Confidential Information. In the course of performing its obligations hereunder, it may be necessary for Manufacturer or Manufacturer Customers to disclose Confidential Information. Manufacturer shall be the sole owner of the Confidential Information. Such Confidential Information is considered by Manufacturer to be commercially valuable, confidential and proprietary including information furnished by a third party. Manufacturer makes no representations or warranties, express or implied, with respect to any Confidential Information. Manufacturer will not be liable for any damages arising out of use of Confidential Information by Representative. Any use of Confidential Information is at Representative's own risk. Also, nothing in this Agreement will be construed as granting or conferring any rights by license or otherwise in Confidential Information, except for the use as expressly provided in this Agreement.

12.2 Notice to Manufacturer re Disclosure. If, at any time, Representative become aware of any unauthorized access, use, possession or knowledge of any Confidential Information, or if Representative receives any request of a governmental agency or third party pursuant to operation of law, regulation or court order, Representative shall (1) give Manufacturer sufficient prior written notice of such proposed disclosure to enable Manufacturer to obtain an appropriate protective order, if it so desires; and (2) take such reasonable steps as are available to Representative to prevent disclosure of such Confidential Information until the Manufacturer has been informed of such requested disclosure and Manufacturer has an opportunity to take any necessary action to respond to such requested disclosure. In addition, Representative shall provide all reasonable assistance to Manufacturer to protect the confidentiality of any such Confidential Information that Representative may have directly or indirectly disclosed, published, or made available to third parties in breach of this Agreement, including reimbursement for any and all attorney fees and costs that Manufacturer may incur to protect the rights in such Confidential Information.

12.3 Nondisclosure. Representative: (1) shall hold and maintain the Confidential Information in strictest confidence and in trust for the sole and exclusive benefit of Manufacturer; (2) shall not, without the prior written approval of Manufacturer, use for its own benefit, publish or otherwise disclose to others, or permit the use by others for their benefit or to the detriment of Manufacturer, any of the Confidential Information; and (3) shall only disclose the Confidential Information to its employees and/or consultants with a need to know, and only if such employees and/or consultants have executed agreements that impose on them substantially the same duty with respect to confidentiality as is imposed hereunder.

12.4 Effect of Termination. Upon the expiration or termination of this Agreement, Representative shall immediately cease the use of the Confidential Information and shall have thirty (30) days from the expiration or termination date of this Agreement to return any Confidential Information received from Manufacturer. Representative shall not reproduce or permit the reproduction of any such Confidential Information, nor circulate such to any individual or entity. If it is physically impossible to return any Confidential Information received by Representative, Representative shall delete such undeliverable files and data items transferred from Manufacturer.

12.5 Injunctive Relief. Representative understands and acknowledges that any disclosure or misappropriation of any Confidential Information in violation of this Agreement may cause Manufacturer irreparable harm, the amount of which may be difficult to ascertain, and agrees that Manufacturer shall have the right to apply to a court of competent jurisdiction for an order restraining any such further disclosure or misappropriation and for such other relief as Manufacturer shall deem appropriate, and Representative expressly agrees that Manufacturer shall be entitled, in addition to any other remedy provided by law, to obtain an injunction or other equitable remedy respecting such violation or continued violation. Such right is to be in addition to the remedies otherwise available to Manufacturer at law or in equity.

(This section is a long version with complete protection of intellectual property rights. Below is a shorter version of "Confidentiality.")

12.1 In the course of performing its obligations hereunder, it may be necessary for Manufacturer or Manufacturer Customers to disclose Confidential Information to Representative. Manufacturer is the sole owner of the Confidential Information. Representative shall hold and maintain Confidential Information in strictest confidence and in trust for the sole and exclusive benefit of Manufacturer and shall not, without the prior written approval of Manufacturer, use for its own benefit, publish or otherwise disclose to others or permit the use by others for their benefit or to the detriment of Manufacturer, any of Confidential Information. Any disclosure of Confidential Information to Representative's employees and/or consultants shall be on a need to know basis. If, at any time, Representative become aware of any unauthorized access, use, possession or knowledge of any Confidential Information, or if Representative receives any request of disclosure by a governmental agency or third party pursuant to operation of law, regulation or court order, Representative shall (1) give Manufacturer sufficient prior written notice of such proposed disclosure to enable Manufacturer to obtain an appropriate protective order, if it so desires; and (2) prevent disclosure of such Confidential Information until Manufacturer has an opportunity to take any necessary action to respond to such requested disclosure. Representative shall also provide all reasonable assistance to Manufacturer to protect the confidentiality of such Confidential Information. Upon the expiration or sooner termination of this Agreement, Representative shall have thirty (30) days from the expiration or termination date of this Agreement to return Confidential Information received from Manufacturer or delete Confidential Information, which cannot be returned physically. Representative shall not reproduce or permit the reproduction of any such Confidential Information, nor circulate such to any individual or entity. Representative understands and acknowledges that any disclosure or misappropriation of any Confidential Information in violation of this

Agreement may cause Manufacturer irreparable harm, the amount of which may be difficult to ascertain, and agrees that Manufacturer shall have the right to apply to a court of competent jurisdiction for an order restraining any such further disclosure or misappropriation and for such other relief as Manufacturer shall deem appropriate, and Representative expressly agrees that Manufacturer shall be entitled, in addition to any other remedy provided by law, to obtain an injunction or other equitable remedy respecting such violation or continued violation. Such right is to be in addition to the remedies otherwise available to Manufacturer at law or in equity.

13. NO CONFLICT DURING TERM

13.1 No Representation of Competitor. During the Term, Representative shall not act as a representative for products competitive in substantial respects, or bearing substantial similarities with Products or other products produced by Manufacturer, except as otherwise agreed upon by the parties in writing. Representative agrees that at the end of each calendar year, or from time to time at Manufacturer's reasonable requests, it will provide Manufacturer, in writing, with the identity of Representative's other principals.

14. NO UNFAIR COMPETITION AND NON-INTERFERENCE WITH BUSINESS

(These subsections are optional and should be revised to fit the specific situation for each matter.)

14.1 General. Representative understands that during the Term, Representative will receive from the Manufacturer or Manufacturer Customers Confidential Information belongs to Manufacturer and/or Manufacturer Customers. This Section 14 in no way unnecessarily restricts Representative from continuing to undertake and perform all activities and functions, which Representative is undertaking and performing as of the execution of this Agreement. Representative specifically agrees that this Section 14 is an essential incentive to induce Manufacturer to enter into this Agreement, and that this Section 14 shall be specifically enforceable by Manufacturer, its related entities and its and their successors and assigns. Representative acknowledges that the limitations as to time, geographical area and scope of activity restrained as set forth herein are reasonable and do not impose a greater restraint on Representative than is necessary to protect the integrity of the Confidential Information, the goodwill and other business interests of Manufacturer, as well as the competitive benefit of Manufacturer. As one of the considerations for Manufacturer to enter into this Agreement and without in any way limiting any other provisions herein, Representative agrees to be bound by Section 14.

14.2 No Unfair Competition. Representative shall not (1) during the Term and for one (1) year after the expiration or termination of this Agreement, including but not limited to using Confidential Information, directly or indirectly engage or participate in services for, work for, involved in, engaged in, own, manage or operate any business competitive with, or similar to, that of the Manufacturer in the Territory, so long as the Manufacturer carriers on a like business in the Territory; (2) engage in unfair competition with Manufacturer, including but not limited to doing so by using Confidential Information; (3) aid others in any unfair competition with Manufacturer, including but not limited to doing so by using Confidential Information; (4) in any way breach the confidence that Manufacturer placed in Representative during the Term; (5) misappropriate any Confidential Information; or (6) breach any of the provisions of this Section 14 of the Agreement.

14.3 Non-Interference with Business. During the Term of this Agreement and for one (1) year after the expiration of the Agreement, Representative shall not, including but not limited to by using Confidential Information, (1) influence or attempt to influence any Manufacturer Customers to divert their business to any individual or entity then in competition with Manufacturer; (2) disrupt, damage, impair or interfere with the business of Manufacturer by disrupting its relationships with Manufacturer Customers or prospects or Manufacturer's Customers' agents, representatives or vendors; or (3) solicit, contract with or join in with any Manufacturer Customers or prospects without the involvement of Manufacturer for any purpose without first applying for and receiving the express written consent of Manufacturer.

14.4 Non-Solicitation of Employees. Representative acknowledges and agrees that Manufacturer has made a substantial investment in bringing qualified and professional employees, contractors, agents and/or representatives and would suffer a loss if they are hired by others due to the conduct by Representative. Representative agrees that, during the Term of this Agreement and for one (1) year after the expiration or sooner termination of the Agreement, Manufacturer shall not disrupt, damage, impair or interfere with the business of Manufacturer by interfering with Manufacturer's relationship with its employees by directly or indirectly soliciting Manufacturer's employees who earned _____ ($_____) or more on an annual basis to work for any individual or entity then in competition with Manufacturer.

14.5 Non-Circumvention. Representative and Manufacturer mutually agree not to directly or indirectly circumvent, avoid, bypass or obviate each other in any way, including but not limited to entering into any separate business transactions in any manner with Manufacturer's or Representative's Customers without first applying for and receiving each other's express written consent. Such "business transactions" shall include, but not be limited to any transactions, purchases, sales, manufacturing, joint ventures, investment, mergers, acquisitions, projects, any loans or collateral, or other transaction involving any products, transfers or services or addition, renewal extension, rollover, amendment, renegotiations, new contracts, parallel contracts/agreements or third party assignments thereof.

14.6 Application of this Section. Representative agrees that Section 15.6 shall apply to any transaction between the parties and/or between Representatives and any and all Manufacturer Customers, which makes use of, or involves, Confidential Information, or relates to any sources, introduced by, or disclosed by or from, Manufacturer.

14.7 Injunctive Relief. Representative agrees that a breach of Representative's obligations under this Agreement shall result from any efforts of the Representative or its associates, including but not limited to any of Representative's agents, representatives, employees, affiliates, solicitors, bankers, buyers or sellers, who directly or indirectly, attempt to conduct business of or in any manner, to the exclusion of Manufacturer based upon, or pertaining to, Confidential Information or relating to Manufacturer Customers.

15. MISCELLANEOUS

15.1 Binding Effect. This Agreement shall be binding upon both parties and their permitted successors and assigns from the Effective Date.

15.2 Governing Law. This Agreement shall be construed, interpreted and governed as to procedural and substantive matters according to the laws of _____ (*such as the State of California, United States of America,*) without regard to its choice of law, conflict of law's provisions.

15.3 Arbitration; Choice of Forum.

15.3.1 All claims, disputes, controversies, or disagreements of any kind whatsoever ("claims"), including any claims arising out of, relating to or in connection with this Agreement, shall be submitted to final and binding arbitration before _____ (*name of an arbitration agency*) in _____ (*name of location*) in accordance with the rules and procedures of

_____ *(specify governing rules and provider such as* American Arbitration Association*)* then existing. The arbitration shall be held before one arbitrator mutually agreed by the parties. Either party may request to submit any claims to arbitration and make a written request to the other party to select an arbitrator within __ (_) days. If the parties cannot agree on one arbitrator within __ (_) days from the first written request to select an arbitrator by either party, then each party shall select one arbitrator, those two arbitrator shall select a third mutual arbitrator, and the arbitration shall be held before these three arbitrators. If parties fail to select any arbitrator within ___ (_) days from the first written request to select an arbitrator by either party, then an arbitrator shall be appointed by _____ *(specify governing rules and provider such as* American Arbitration Association*)*, and the arbitration shall proceed in _____ *(name of location)* before the arbitrator so appointed. The arbitration must be conducted in the English language. The parties agree that the arbitration award is final and binding, and that the judgment on any arbitration award may be entered in any court of competent jurisdiction, and either party may file an action to compel arbitration with any court of competent jurisdiction. This Agreement is a waiver of all rights the parties may have to a civil court action on any dispute outlined by this Agreement. The fees and costs of the arbitration shall be borne equally by the parties, except that each party shall each pay for their own attorney fees or costs of representation for purposes of the arbitration unless otherwise provided by law.

15.3.2 The parties agree that the following claims may be excluded from this arbitration provision: (1) claims relating to Representative's violations or breach of Sections ____ of this Agreement; and (2) claims that are expressly excluded by applicable laws. Either party may choose to file any actions concerning disputes or controversies arising out of such claims or the interpretation of any provisions contained therein with ____ *(specify name of court, such as the Los Angeles County Superior Court in Los Angeles, California). (This Section is optional.)*

(The parties may choose to use the following arbitration clause instead.)

15.3 Arbitration; Choice of Forum.

Arbitration. All claims, disputes, controversies, or disagreements of any kind whatsoever ("claims"), including any claims arising out of or in connection with this Agreement, shall be submitted to final and binding arbitration before _____ *(name of an arbitration agency)* in _____ *(name of location)* in accordance with the rules and procedures of *(if applicable, add:* the supervision of _____ *(specify appointing authority) and)* the Rules of the United Nations Commission on International Trade Law ("UNCITRAL") in effect on the date of this contract (the "Rules"). In the event of any conflict between the Rules and this Section, the provisions of this Section govern. Arbitration under this Agreement is the parties' exclusive remedy, and no party to any arbitration is required to exhaust any local administrative or judicial remedy first.

Arbitrator. Each party must appoint one arbitrator within ___ *(specify time period, such as: 30 days)* after receipt by the respondent of the notice of arbitration. The two arbitrators appointed by the parties must, within ___ *(specify time period, such as: 30 days)* after their appointment, appoint a third, presiding arbitrator, who may not be a citizen or resident of ___*(specify country)* or _____ *(specify country)*. If either party fails to nominate an arbitrator, or the two arbitrators appointed by the parties are unable to appoint a presiding arbitrator within the stated periods, the arbitrator or arbitrators will be appointed by the _____ *(appointing authority)* according to the Rules. All arbitrators must be fluent in ___ *(specify language, such as: English)* and must _____ *(specify desired expertise, if any)*.

Procedure. The arbitrators will hold hearings where written, documentary and oral evidence may be presented. Evidence may not be accepted except in the presence of both parties. All witnesses may be questioned by both parties. Unless the parties otherwise agree, or a witness is dead, ill, or unavailable for other good reasons, the arbitrators may not accept a witness' written statement unless the other party has an opportunity to question the witness in the arbitrators' presence. All proceedings must be conducted in the _____ *(specify language, such as: English)* language.

Award. The arbitrators must, by majority vote, render a written decision, stating reasons for their decision, within ___ *(specify number)* months after the respondent receives the request for arbitration. Any cash award must be payable in U.S. Dollars through a bank in the U.S. and determined, to the extent necessary, on the basis of the rate of exchange in effect at the time the claim arose, as published in the Wall Street Journal. Each party must bear its own costs and attorney's fees *(or the prevailing party is entitled to recover its costs of arbitration and reasonable attorney's fees, as determined by the arbitrators)*. The award is deemed an award issued in ____ *(specify nation)*.

Enforcement. The award is final and enforceable and may be confirmed by the judgment of, or enforced by, a court of competent jurisdiction. To the extent that an award or confirming judgment is unsatisfied, it may be enforced in the manner provided by law in all countries. The prevailing party is entitled to recover its costs and attorney's fees in any proceedings to enforce the award or confirming judgment.

Reservation of Rights. The right to refer a claim or dispute to arbitration under this Agreement is not affected by the fact that a claimant or respondent has received full or partial compensation from a third party for the loss or injury that is the object of the claim or dispute, and any third party may participate in these proceedings by right of subrogation.

The parties agree that the following claims may be excluded from this arbitration provision: (1) claims relating to Representative's violations or breach of Sections 11, 12, 13 and 14 of this Agreement; and (2) claims that are expressly excluded by applicable laws. Either party may choose to file an action concerning disputes or controversies arising out of such claims or the interpretation of any provisions contained therein with _____ *(specify name of court, such as the Los Angeles County Superior Court in Los Angeles, California)*.

(The parties may choose to use the following "Choice of Forum" clause instead.)

15.3 Choice of Forum. The parties further agree that any actions concerning disputes or controversies arising out of this Agreement or the interpretation of any provisions contained therein shall be filed with the_____ Court in ___ *(specify location).*

15.4 Entire Agreement; Language; Amendments. This Agreement constitutes the entire Agreement between the parties hereto with respect to the subject matter of this Agreement and supersedes and cancels any other prior agreements or understandings whether written, oral or implied relating to the subject of this Agreement. There are no restrictions, promises, representations, warranties covenants or undertakings other than those expressly set forth or referred to in this Agreement. The parties further agree that neither they nor anyone acting on their behalf made any inducements, agreements, promises, or representations other than those set forth in this Agreement. This Agreement is written in English only, which is the controlling language in all respects. Any version in any other language is for accommodation only and is not binding upon the parties. All formal notices given pursuant to this Agreement must be in English. This Agreement may be amended, modified, and supplemented only by written agreement signed by the parties' authorized personnel hereto.

15.5 Waiver of Breach. The waiver by either party of a breach or violation of any provision of the Agreement shall not operate as, or be construed to be, a waiver of any prior, concurrent or subsequent breach hereof. No waiver or purported waiver will be valid or enforceable unless it is in writing and signed by the party against whom it is sought to be enforced.

15.6 Assignment. No portion of this Agreement or any right or obligation under this Agreement can be transferred or assigned, in whole or in part, whether by operation of law or otherwise, by either party without the prior written consent of the other party, except that Manufacturer may freely transfer and assign its rights and obligations under this Agreement to any of Manufacturer's wholly owned subsidiaries, provided that Manufacturer provides guarantees of the obligations of the wholly owned subsidiaries in form and substance satisfactory to Representative.

15.7 Force Majeure. If either party fails to perform its obligations hereunder (except for the obligation to pay money) because of fires, floods, earthquakes, riots, civil unrest, war, epidemics, shortages, labor unrest, strikes, accidents, acts of God, weather conditions, or action or inaction of any government body or other proper authority, delays caused beyond its reasonable control, then such failure to perform will not be deemed a default hereunder and will be excused without penalty until such time as such party is capable of performing and will not be liable to the other party for any loss, cost or damages arising out of, or resulting from, such failure to perform.

15.8 Notice. All notices which are required or permitted to be given pursuant to this Agreement shall be in writing and shall be sufficient in all respects if delivered personally, by facsimile, by email, by overnight courier using a nationally recognized courier company, or by registered or certified mail, postage prepaid, addressed to a party as indicated below: Manufacturer: _____; and, Representative: _____. Notice shall be deemed to have been received upon delivery thereof as to communications which are personally delivered, are sent by facsimile or by email; on the third (3rd) day after mailing as to communications which are sent by overnight courier; and on the seventh (7th) day after mailing as to communications made by mail. The above addresses may be changed by giving written notice of such change in the manner provided above for giving notice.

15.9 Severability. Any provision of this Agreement which is prohibited or unenforceable in any jurisdiction will, as to such jurisdiction, be ineffective to the extent of such prohibition or unenforceability without invalidating the remaining provisions hereof, and any such prohibition or unenforceability in any jurisdiction will not invalidate or render unenforceable such provision or other provision hereof in any other jurisdiction.

15.10 Attorney's Fees. The prevailing party in any arbitration or litigation brought by either party to this Agreement in connection with this Agreement will be entitled to recover from the other party all reasonable costs, attorney's fees, and other expenses incurred by the prevailing party in such arbitration or litigation.

15.11 Third Parties. Nothing herein expressed or implied is intended or will be construed to confer upon or give to any person or entity other than the parties hereto and their successors or permitted assigns, any rights or remedies under or by reason of this Agreement.

15.12 Survival. The provisions of Sections 1, 6.5, 7, 8.2, 9, 10, 11, 12, 13, 14 and 15 of this Agreement will survive any expiration or termination of this Agreement.

15.13 Headings. The headings of the Sections of this Agreement are inserted for convenience of reference only and do not constitute a part hereof or affect in any way the meaning or interpretation of this Agreement.

15.14 Dollar Amount. Any dollar amount in the Agreement is in U.S. dollars.

15.15 Counterparts. This Agreement may be executed in one or more counterparts, each of which shall be deemed an original, but all of which taken together shall constitute one and the same instrument. Each party hereto acknowledges and agrees that the other party may rely on electronic facsimile signatures as conclusive evidence of the valid and binding execution of this Agreement.

MAURICE KOGON

IN WITNESS WHEREOF, the parties hereto have executed this Agreement as of the date set forth in the first paragraph hereof.

Dated:

_____

MANUFACTURER:

_____

By:

_____

Name:

_____

Title:

_____

Dated:

_____

MANUFACTURER:

_____

By:

_____

Name:

_____

Title:

_____

ATTACHMENT A

LIST OF PRODUCTS

(Manufacturer may retain the right to change Products during the Term. Manufacturer may grant the right of approval or first right of refusal to Distributor for such change of Products during the Term.)

ATTACHMENT B

COMMISSION RATES

* * *

4. Sample Foreign Representation Agreement

DISCLAIMER

THIS DISTRIBUTION AGREEMENT (this "Agreement") is made and entered into on _____ (*date*) (the "Effective Date"), by and between _____ ("Manufacturer"), a California corporation with principal offices located at _____ (*address*), USA, and _____, ("Distributor") having its principal offices at _____ (*complete address of Distributor's office*).

RECITALS

A. Manufacturer is in the business of manufacturing and export
_____;

B. Distributor is in the business of importing _____ *(types of products)*
into _____ *(name(s) of country/countries)*; and

C. Manufacturer desires to retain Distributor to sell Manufacturer's
_____ *(types of products)* in _____*(name(s) of country/countries)*
pursuant to the terms and conditions set forth in this Agreement.

AGREEMENT

NOW, THEREFORE, for and in consideration of the mutual covenants
contained herein, the Manufacturer and Distributor agree as follows:

1. DEFINITION

1.1 "Affiliate" means an entity which, directly or indirectly, controls, is
controlled by, or is under common control of a parent company with a
party to this Agreement. For purposes of this paragraph, "control"
means owning or controlling at least 30% of the voting stock entitled to
vote for elections of the members of the board of directors (or, if none,
persons performing similar functions) or, in the case of entities not
having voting stock, equivalent ownership or control thereof.

1.2 "Confidential Information" shall mean information provided by
Manufacturer or Manufacturer Customers to Distributor (i) that is not
known by actual or potential competitors of Manufacturer or is generally unavailable to the public, (ii) that has been created, discovered,
developed or otherwise become known to Manufacturer or in which
property rights have been assigned or otherwise conveyed to Manufacturer, and (iii) that has material economic value or potential material
economic value to Manufacturer's present or future business. Confidential Information, subject to exceptions set forth by laws, shall
include trade secrets (as defined under California Civil Code section
3426.1) which include all discoveries, developments, designs, improvements, inventions, formulas, software programs, processes, techniques,
know-how, negative know-how, data, research, technical data (whether

or not patentable or registrable under patent, copyright or similar statues and including all rights to obtain, register, perfect and enforce those proprietary interests), customer and supplier lists, customer profile and other customer information, customer and price list, business plans, and any modifications or enhancements of any of the forgoing, and all program, marketing, sales, or other financial or business information disclosed to Distributor by Manufacturer, either directly or indirectly, in writing or orally or by drawings or observation, which has actual or potential economic value to Manufacturer.

1.3 "Distributor" shall mean _____ and its Affiliates.

1.4 "Effective Date" shall mean _____.

1.5 "Initial Term" shall mean the initial term of this Agreement from __ to __.

1.6 "Manufacturer" shall mean _____ and its Affiliates.

1.7 "Manufacturer Customers" shall mean any individuals or entities, who are current or potential customers or business prospects of Manufacturer, or who are introduced from or by Manufacturer to Representative.

1.8 "Order" shall mean orders placed by Distributor for Products, which are received by Manufacturer and accepted by Manufacturer in writing.

1.9 "Party" shall mean Manufacturer or Distributor, individually. "Parties shall mean Manufacturer and Distributor collectively.

1.10 "Products" shall mean the products set forth in Attachment A, which is hereby incorporated by reference as fully set forth in this Agreement.

1.11 "Renewal Term" shall mean any renewal term of this Agreement pursuant to Section 8.1 of this Agreement.

1.12 "Term" shall mean the term of this Agreement, including the Initial Term and any Renewal Terms, if any.

1.13 "Territory" shall mean the following country / countries: _____ *(or "_____ types of customers serviced by Distributor in _____).*

2. GRANT OF DISTRIBUTORSHIP

2.1 Manufacturer hereby grants Distributor, subject to the terms and conditions of this Agreement, the exclusive right to sell, distribute and service Products in Territory during the Term. *(The word "exclusive" is optional. Also, the right to sell can also be limited to selling Products to specified types of customers.)*

3. RELATIONSHIP OF THE PARTIES

3.1 Independent Contractor. This Agreement shall not be deemed to create a partnership, joint venture or an agent and principal relationship between the parties, and Distributor or any of Distributor's directors, officers, employees or agents shall not, by virtue of the performance of their obligations under this Agreement, represent themselves as, or be deemed to be, an agent, partner or employee of Manufacturer. The parties mutually agree that Distributor is an independent contractor, not an employee, of Manufacturer. Neither party is liable for any acts, omissions to act, contracts, promises, commitments or representations made by the other, except as specified in this Agreement.

3.2 Exclusivity. Distributor shall be the exclusive distributor for Manufacturer to sell Products in Territory and shall not act as a distributor or a sales representative for, or design, manufacture, sell, distribute, service or market, any products in competition with any products manufactured by Manufacturer. Distributor shall disclose to Manufacturer the identities of all products and manufacturers, which it distributes or represents, and notify, and obtain prior written consent from, Manufacturer of any future products or manufacturers that it will distribute or represent prior to making such commitment to do so. *(Optional.)*

3.3 Most Favorable Terms. If Manufacturer enters into any other export distribution agreement for Product with another distributor in a different territory in the future, which provides that new distributor more favorable terms, other than pricing for Products, Manufacturer will immediately amend this Agreement to provide Distributor with the benefit of any terms, other than the pricing for Products, in the new agreement more favorable than those included in this Agreement. *(Optional.)*

4. DUTIES AND RESPONSIBILITIES OF DISTRIBUTOR

4.1 Distributor's duties and responsibilities include but not be limited to:

a. Using its best effort to market, offer, sell, promote and develop a market for Products within Territory, referring all inquiries regarding Products or other products manufactured by Manufacturer to Manufacturer and maintaining qualified sales distribution organization and channels within Territory;

b. Engaging in sales promotion activities, in which designate Products with its correct name and identify Products as being manufactured by Manufacturer and marketed and sold by Distributor as an independent contractor;

c. attached to this Establishing and maintaining place of business in Territory with display of Products for demonstration, a staff of trained technicians and a stock of spare parts and technical literature in order to provide technical support and services to customers; and providing technical support and services to customers;

d. Purchasing the minimum dollar amounts of Products as set forth in Attachment A, a copy of which is Agreement and is hereby incorporate by reference as fully set forth herein; and maintaining an inventory of products sufficient to satisfy customer Orders as they are received.

e. Providing reports concerning inventory, sales and potential sales with fifteen (15) days from the closing of each calendar __ *(month or quarter)*, or as reasonably requested by Manufacturer, and forecasts of anticipated sales over __ month period on a __ *(quarter or yearly)* basis to assist Manufacturer in planning production activities; and assisting

Manufacturer in assessing customer requirements for Products and developing modifications and improvements of Products;

f. Providing logistical and support services in Territory concerning the sale or service of Products, including but not limited to providing assistance necessary to Manufacturer in arranging and providing lodging, office space, equipment, translation, transportation, communications, facilities and other related support activities;

g. Conducting its business at all times in a manner, which shall reflect favorably on Manufacturer and Products, and which is not deceptive, misleading, illegal or unethical, and providing advice and assistance concerning compliance of laws, regulations, business and financial practices in Territory, maintenance of contact, communications and liaison with government officials and obtaining necessary licenses, permits and authorizations in compliance with law, regulations and ordinances;

h. Obtaining all necessary export and import licenses and permits, paying all customs duty and other charges and fees and taking all other actions required to accomplish the export and import of Products;

i. Providing advice and assistance to Manufacturer on compliance of laws, regulations, business and financial practices in Territory, maintenance of contact, communications and liaison with government officials and obtaining necessary licenses, permits and authorizations in compliance with law, regulations and ordinances;

j. Providing Manufacturer, upon reasonable notice by Manufacturer and during regular business hours, access to Distributor's place of business and inventory stock to ascertain Distributor's compliance with this Agreement;

k. Providing Manufacturer with a copy of all Distributor's sales, advertising and promotion materials mentioned Products, and a copy of any translation of materials relating to Products prior to the use of such materials and translations; and

l. Providing other assistance and services as Manufacturer may reasonably request.

(This is a suggested list and should be revised to meet the needs of the parties.)

4.2 Distributor shall not advertise, market, sell or distribute Products outside Territory or to establish or maintain a warehouse located outside Territory for the distribution of Products outside Territory.

4.3 Distributor shall have no authorities to make any representations, warranties or guarantees or make or execute any commitment or agreement, accept any Orders or incur any liability on behalf of Manufacturer or bind Manufacturer in any way.

4.4 Distributor is responsible for all expenses incurred by Distributor in connection with the implementation and performance of Distributor's duties and obligations under this Agreement, including but not limited to: (a) the expenses incurred in fulfilling its duties and responsibilities as provided in Section 4; (b) costs, expenses and salaries of its personnel associated with establishing and maintaining its sales organization and offices; (c) advertising and promotion expenses; and (e) any and all taxes, duties, tariffs or charges that may be imposed on Distributor in Territory.

4.5 Distributor is solely responsible for the performance of its duties.

5. DUTIES AND RESPONSIBILITIES OF MANUFACTURER

5.1 Manufacturer will use its best efforts to deliver Products pursuant to the dates and other requirements stated in Orders delivered to and accepted by Manufacturer, however, Manufacturer is under no obligation to sell or continue to product any model or type of any Products, whether or not listed on Attachment A beyond ___ (__) days of notice of discontinuation sent by Manufacturer to Distributor, and Manufacturer reserves the right to make substitutions and/or modifications to Products if such substitutions or modifications will not materially adversely affect overall performance of Products. In addition, Manufacturer will keep Distributor informed of changes in Products, specifications and deliveries.

5.2 Manufacturer will provide Distributor, from time to time, advertising matter, price lists and technical assistance when Manufacturer deems necessary

5.3 Manufacturer, from time to time, may, at Manufacturer's sole discretion, make special purchase offers and/or quantity discounts available to Distributor.

5.4 Manufacturer may, from time to time, send representatives to consult with Distributor concerning the promotion and increase of market of Products and technical support and service of Products and provide training to Distributor's personnel as reasonably requested by Distributor.

5.5 Manufacturer shall make repair or replacement parts available to Distributor. Further, during the Term and during a period of ___ *(months, years)* after the expiration or termination of the Agreement, Manufacturer will sell Distributor repair and replacement parts necessary to maintain Products in good and serviceable condition at all times, unless the parts have been discontinued by Manufacturer. Manufacturer shall provide Distributor __ (_) day prior notice of any discontinuance.

5.6 Manufacturer shall not make any direct sales within Territory, except for accommodation sales or as otherwise agreed upon by the parties. In those cases, commissions shall be credited to Distributor on a case by case basis.

5.7 Manufacturer is solely responsible for the performance of its duties.

(This is a suggested list and should be revised to meet the needs of the parties.)

6. PRICING, ORDER, PAYMENT, SHIPMENT AND ACCOUNTING

6.1 Pricing. The initial pricing for Products is provided in Attachment A. However, the pricing is subject to change by Manufacturer at its sole discretion at any time. Such changes shall be effective upon sending notice by Manufacturer to Distributor pursuant to Section 15.8 of this Agreement *(or by email, facsimile or other means)*. All pricing is quoted

FOB _____ *(name of city and country.)* and shall include the cost of packaging and crating for export.

6.2 Orders. Any Order placed by Distributor shall be submitted to Manufacturer. An Order shall designate the delivery date for at least __ days from the day such Order is submitted to Manufacturer. The Order shall not contain a shipment date fewer than __ (_) days from the date that such Order is submitted to Manufacturer. After receiving the Order, Manufacturer shall either reject or accept the Order in writing within ___ hours and notify Distributor of its decision pursuant to Section 15.8 of this Agreement. Manufacture has sole discretion to determine if it will accept such an Order. Prior to receiving an acceptance of the Order, Distributor may cancel the Order without further obligations. Upon acceptance of any Order, it shall become a binding agreement between Distributor and Manufacturer, wherein Distributor agrees to purchase Products set forth on the Order pursuant to the terms and conditions in this Agreement. Should Distributor intend to either cancel or change an Order after such Order has been accepted by Manufacturer, Manufacture has the sole discretion to determine if Manufacturer will (1) allow such a cancellation or change, (2) impose a cancellation or change order charge, or (3) declare that Distributor has breached the Agreement and terminate the Agreement pursuant to Section 8.2.1 of this Agreement. Furthermore, Distributor shall meet the minimum dollar amount set forth in Attachment A. Otherwise, Manufacturer may declare that Distributor has breached this Agreement and terminate the Agreement pursuant to Section 8.2.1 of this Agreement.

6.3 Payments. For each Order, Distributor shall establish an applicable irrevocable letter of credit in favor of Manufacturer's bank within __ days after receipt of the acceptance of the Order from Manufacturer. The letter of credit must be confirmed by a United States bank and for the entire amount of each shipment of the Order when made. The letter of credit shall allow negotiation time of ___ days from the day of the Order's confirmed shipment date. The Order shall be paid, upon presentation of shipping documents to Distributor's bank in ___*(name of city, country)*, net cash in U.S. currency.

6.4 Shipment. Distributor is liable to pay for all costs and expenses associated with the shipment of Products. At Distributor's request, Manufacturer may arrange for shipment of Products, with all costs and expenses associated with the shipment paid by Distributor in accordance with Section 6.3 of this Agreement. Title and risk of loss or damage of Products shall pass from Manufacturer to Distributor upon delivery of Product to the shipping company or Distributor's representative for shipment, regardless of which party makes the shipping arrangements. After the acceptance of an Order by Manufacturer, if Distributor requests delay in shipment, any storage, insurance or other costs incurred because of the delay shall be paid by Distributor pursuant to Section 6.3 of this Agreement. If any Product is not correctly shipped due an error by Manufacturer, Manufacturer will replace such Product as promptly as possible free of charge and freight prepaid to Distributor's destination. *(Last sentence is optional.)*

6.5 Inspection of Products. Manufacturer shall inspect all Products prior to shipment to confirm that such Products are in first-class condition. Distributor shall have the right to inspect the Products dockside in __ *(name of city, country)*. Manufacturer has the right to appoint a third party for inspection purpose. If Distributor discovers any damaged or defective Products, Distributor shall notify Manufacturer within __ (_) days of such discovery. Upon a written confirmation of an independent merchandise surveyor and a written confirmation from Manufacturer, Distributor shall have damaged and defective merchandise repaired in __ *(name of city, country)* at Manufacturer's expense.

6.6 Payments Following Termination or Expiration. Following termination or expiration of this Agreement, Distributor shall pay Manufacturer for Products ordered by Distributor and accepted by Manufacturer prior to the termination or expiration within __ (__) from the date of termination or expiration, even though such Products have not been shipped by Manufacturer.

6.7 Audit Rights. During the Term and for a period of one (1) year following the termination or expiration of the Agreement, each party shall maintain complete, accurate and detailed books and records with respect to the determination of its revenues and other matters associated with the performance of this Agreement. Each Party (the "requesting party") shall have the right, at its expense and upon prior written notice given to the other party (the "responding party") at least fifteen (15) days prior to the inspection date requested by the requesting party, to inspect and audit all of the responding party's records associated with the performance of this Agreement, and the responding party agrees to reasonably cooperate with and provide access to the requesting party and its financial advisors as may be necessary and appropriate for such inspection and audit.

7. COMPLIANCE WITH LAW

7.1 Distributor agrees that in carrying out its duties under this Agreement, Distributor will neither undertake nor cause or permit to be undertaken any activity which to Distributor's knowledge is illegal under the laws of the Territory or of the United States. It is a condition of this Agreement that, within __ *(specify number, such as: 30)* days from execution of this Agreement and prior to the initiation of any activities with respect to any Order, Distributor will submit to Manufacturer an opinion of Distributor's counsel, provided that such counsel and the form and substance of the opinion shall be to Manufacturer's satisfaction, that nothing in this Agreement prevents Distributor from carrying out its duties in accordance with laws, decrees, rules and regulations of the Territory, and that Distributor may act as Distributor for all Products to any government ministries, agencies and departments, including the armed forces. The submission of this opinion is a condition precedent to the effectiveness of this Agreement.

7.2 Distributor understands and agrees that Manufacturer may comply with any legal provision requiring disclosure, or any request from the U.S. Government or the Government of the Territory to disclose, by affidavit or otherwise, the identity of Distributor, as well as the identities of Distributor's principal and the amount of any payment made or to be made to Distributor under this Agreement.

8. TERM AND TERMINATION

8.1 Term. The term of this Agreement will commence on the effective date of this Agreement and will continue for a period of __ (__) years unless earlier terminated by either party accordance with Section __. At the end of each Term, including at the end of the Initial Term and the Renewal Terms, this Agreement will be automatically renewed for an additional __ (__) year period, unless either party give the other party a written notice __ (__) days prior to the expiration of the Initial Term or any Renewal Term. All the terms and conditions contained in this Agreement will remain the same during any renewals beyond the Initial Term, unless this Agreement is amended or modified in written pursuant to Section __ of this Agreement. *(The automatic renewal portion of the provision is optional. Also, restrictions or conditions may be required, such as sales quota, before there will be a renewal.)*

8.2 Termination. In the event of any of the following, this Agreement, and the rights and licenses granted hereunder, will terminate.

If either party defaults in the performance of or compliance with any provision contained in this Agreement or breach any provisions set forth in this Agreement (except as otherwise provided in this Section 8) and such default or breach is not cured within fifteen (15) days after written notice thereof is received by the defaulting party, the party giving such notice may then give further written notice to the defaulting party terminating this Agreement, in which event this Agreement, and the rights and licenses granted hereunder, will terminate on the date specified in such further notice.

If either party discontinues its primary business for more than fifteen (15) days, either party may terminate this Agreement upon fifteen (15) days' prior written notice to the other party. If the primary business is continued by an Affiliate, the primary business will be deemed continued by the party for purposes of Section 8.2.2.

Either party may terminate this Agreement by written notice to the other party and may regard the other party as in default of this Agreement, if the other party becomes insolvent, makes a general assignment for the benefit of creditors, files a voluntary petition of bankruptcy, suffers or permits the appointment of a receiver for its business or assets, or becomes subject to any proceedings under any bankruptcy or insolvency law, which is not dismissed within ninety

(90) days, or has wound up or entered liquidation, voluntarily or otherwise. In the event that any of the above events occur, the defaulting party will immediately notify the other party of its occurrence.

In the event of a breach of Distributor's obligations under Sections 7, 11, 12, 13 and/or 14, Manufacturer may immediately terminate this Agreement in writing without providing any cure period.

If one party is unable to perform its obligations under the Agreement by reason of any law, rule, regulation or order of any municipal, state or federal or foreign authority, including, but not limited to any regulatory authority that has jurisdiction over that party's business, then the either party may terminate this Agreement by given the other party a thirty (30) day written notice.

If the performance of this Agreement becomes impracticable because of the change of the situation of the U.S., or if the trade between the U.S. and the Territory becomes impracticable because of the change in the currency controls renders, then either party may terminate this Agreement by given the other party a _ (_) days' prior written notice. (Optional.)

Either party may terminate this Agreement without cause upon _ (_) days' prior written notice to the other party. (Optional.)

8.3 Termination of the Agreement for any reason does not affect (a) obligations that have accrued as of the date of termination; and (b) the obligations under those sections identified in Section 15.12 of this Agreement. Further, in the event of termination, Distributor shall return Manufacturer the Confidential Information as provided in Section 12.4 (or 12.1) of this Agreement, and Distributor's limited license to use Manufacturer' intellectual property shall cease immediately.

9. REPRESENTATIONS AND WARRANTIES

9.1 Each party represents and warrants that:

It has the authority to enter into this Agreement and the rights and license necessary to enter into, and perform its obligations under, this Agreement.

It is free to enter into this Agreement and is not bound by any agreements, including but not limited to nondisclosure agreement, noncompetition agreement, documents or obligation that may infringe on its ability or in any manner prevent it from performing any of the duties that may be required of it during the Term, or that may result in liability to it in any manner, action, or proceeding.

It has full power and authority to execute and deliver this Agreement, and this Agreement has been duly executed and delivered by or on behalf of itself and constitutes a legal, valid and binding obligation enforceable against it in accordance with its respective terms. Neither the execution, delivery, nor performance of this Agreement violates or conflicts with any applicable laws, decrees, rules, regulations, requires any notice, consent or other action by a third party or creates a default or breach or give rise to any right of termination, cancellation or acceleration of any right or obligation or to lose any benefit to which it is entitled under any agreement or other instrument binding upon it. It will not take any action that would have the effect of causing the other to be in violation of any laws, decrees, rules or regulations.

9.2 Manufacturer represents and warrants that it has all rights, title and interest in and to all copyrights, patents, trademarks and other intellectual property rights associated with Products or otherwise has the right to allow the use thereof which are necessary to use, sell, market and distribute Products, and to manufacture and sell Products without infringing any rights; and that, as of the Effective Date, Manufacturer is not aware of any basis for third party claims of infringement of any patents, trademarks, or tradenames with respect to Products. In the event that any action, claim or suit is brought against Distributor alleging that the manufacture, use, sale or transfer of any Product or the use of the trademarks or tradenames constitutes infringement of

any proprietary rights of any third party, Manufacturer shall indemnify Distributor pursuant to Section 10.1 of this Agreement, provided
that Distributor gives written notice of such actions or claims brought
against Distributor within five (5) days from the receipt of notice of
such actions or claims, and that Distributor takes reasonable steps as
may be requested by Manufacturer to assist in the defense of such
action. *(The last sentence, starting with "In the event that . . ." is optional.)*

9.3 Manufacturer further represents and warrants that Products shall
conform in all material aspects with Manufacturer's written specifications for Products and are free of defects in material or workmanship.
This representation and warranty will extend for __ *(months or years)*
from the shipment date of Products. Manufacturer's obligations for
breaching this representation and warranty shall be limited to
replacing or repairing defective Products at Manufacturer's choice.
However, Manufacturer is not liable for any defects in Products, if
Products were used to operate in manner inconsistent with use
intended by Manufacturer, or if there were modifications or repairs
made to Products by party other than Manufacturer's personnel in
manner that adversely affects Products' operation or reliability, or if
Products were damaged because of accident, neglect or misuse by
party other than Manufacturer's personnel.

9.4 Distributor represents and warrants that except as appropriate to
carry out Distributor's duties in this Agreement, Distributor has not,
has no obligation to and will not, directly or indirectly, give, offer, pay,
promise to pay or authorize the payment of money or thing of value to
any other person in connection with transactions under this Agreement are to be paid. Distributor agrees not to take any actions that
would cause Manufacturer to violate section 103 of the Foreign
Corrupt Practices Act of 1977 (15 U.S.C.A. § 78dd-l). Distributor
warrants that none of its officer, director, employee or agent is an "official" of __ *(name of country)* Government as that term is defined in
section 103, nor will Distributor employ an "official" of that
government.

9.5 Distributor represents and warrants that it will make and keep
books, records and accounts that, in reasonable detail, accurately and

fairly reflect the transactions performed by Distributor under this Agreement and the dispositions of Products. Distributor specifically agrees that Manufacturer may inspect such books, records and accounts upon reasonable requests made by Manufacturer to Distributor.

10. INDEMNIFICATION AND LIMITATION OF LIABILITY

10.1 Indemnification. Each party (the "First Party") hereby indemnifies and agrees to hold the other party (the "Second Party") and its affiliates, and its and their successors and assigns, and its and their directors, officers and employees harmless against any and all claims, causes of actions, loss, demands, penalties, damages, costs, judgments, attorney's fees or any other expenses incurred in connection with, caused by or relating to the First Party's actions or failure to act or any breach by the First Party of the terms, covenants, representations or warranties set forth in this Agreement.

10.2 Limitation of Liability. Regardless of the basis on which any party (the "first party") may be entitled to recover damages from the other party (the "second party"), including but not limited to, breach of warranty, contract or fiduciary duty, fraud, negligence, misrepresentation, other tort or indemnity, the second party's aggregate liability under this agreement or related to products or the use thereof is limited to actual, direct damages that can be proven up to an amount not to exceed the aggregate of amount paid by manufacturer to distributor for the six-month period prior to the date when such problem occurred. The party suffering such damages or losses must first exhaust any available legal and equitable remedies against parties other than the second party. The second party shall in no event be liable to the first party or any third party for any special, incidental, indirect or consequential damages (including lost profits, savings, revenues, business opportunities or business advantages) under this agreement or in any way in connection with products or the use thereof whatsoever, even if second party has been advised of the possibility of such damages. Notwithstanding the foregoing, the limitations of liability set forth above in this section 10.2 shall not apply to losses against which the parties have agreed to indemnify each other pursuant to the terms and provisions of this agreement or the damages incurred by manufacturer because of the breach of sections 11, 12, 13 and 14 of this agreement by distributor.

10.3 Disclaimer. Except or as otherwise expressly set forth in this agreement, each party disclaims all other warranties or conditions, express or implied, including, but not limited to the implied warranties or conditions of merchantability, fitness for a particular purpose of the services or products, quiet enjoyment, as well as implied warranties arising from course of dealing or course of performance.

10.4 Some jurisdictions do not allow the exclusion or limitation of incidental or consequential damages, so the above limitation or exclusion may not apply.

(The sections on limitation of liability will limit the liability for both parties. If the parties or either party does not want to set a limitation on liability, then please delete Sections 10.2 to 10.4 and delete the reference of limitation of liability in the header. If the limitation is applicable as to one party only, then revise these sections accordingly.)

11. OWNERSHIP OF INTELLECTUAL PROPERTY

11.1 Manufacturer shall at all times own and retain all respective right, title and interest in and to, and is the sole and exclusive owner of, any intellectual property rights in Products. Such right, title and interest include, but are not limited to, all patents, copyrights, trademarks, trade names, trade dress and trade secrets, names and marks now and subsequently used to identify Products, any proprietary information used in or applying to Products, rights of privacy or publicity, rights to the graphical user interface, source code, object code and other intellectual property rights. Distributor agrees that (a) the intellectual property rights in Products are Manufacturer' property and contain valuable proprietary materials of Manufacturer; (b) Manufacturer hereby grants a limited license to Distributor to use the name of Product to market and sell Product in strict conformity with this Agreement; and (c) Distributor shall not have any rights in and to the intellectual property rights in Products, except as otherwise explicitly stated in this Agreement. If requested by Manufacturer, Distributor shall assist Manufacturer or Manufacturer's designees at Manufacturer's expense to file any application for registration of a patent, trademark, tradename, service mark or other trade-identifying symbol used in connection with the Products and to establish any right of prior use by Manufacturer that may be required for the registration or protection of the patent, trademark, tradename, service mark or other symbol under the laws of the Territory. Upon expiration or sooner termination of this Agreement, Distributor's limited license to use Manufacturer' intellectual property shall cease immediately.

12. CONFIDENTIALITY

12.1 Confidential Information. In the course of performing its obligations hereunder, it may be necessary for Manufacturer or Manufacturer Customers to disclose Confidential Information. Manufacturer shall be the sole owner of the Confidential Information. Such Confidential Information is considered by Manufacturer to be commercially valuable, confidential and proprietary including information furnished by a third party. Manufacturer makes no representations or warranties, express or implied, with respect to any Confidential Information.

Manufacturer will not be liable for any damages arising out of use of Confidential Information by Distributor. Any use of Confidential Information is at Distributor's own risk. Also, nothing in this Agreement will be construed as granting or conferring any rights by license or otherwise in Confidential Information, except for the use as expressly provided in this Agreement.

12.2 Notice to Manufacturer re Disclosure. If, at any time, Distributor become aware of any unauthorized access, use, possession or knowledge of any Confidential Information, or if Distributor receives any request of a governmental agency or third party pursuant to operation of law, regulation or court order, Distributor shall (1) give Manufacturer sufficient prior written notice of such proposed disclosure to enable Manufacturer to obtain an appropriate protective order, if it so desires; and (2) take such reasonable steps as are available to Distributor to prevent disclosure of such Confidential Information until the Manufacturer has been informed of such requested disclosure and Manufacturer has an opportunity to take any necessary action to respond to such requested disclosure. In addition, Distributor shall provide all reasonable assistance to Manufacturer to protect the confidentiality of any such Confidential Information that Distributor may have directly or indirectly disclosed, published, or made available to third parties in breach of this Agreement, including reimbursement for any and all attorney fees and costs that Manufacturer may incur to protect the rights in such Confidential Information.

12.3 Nondisclosure. Distributor: (1) shall hold and maintain Confidential Information in strictest confidence and in trust for the sole and exclusive benefit of Manufacturer; (2) shall not, without the prior written approval of Manufacturer, use for its own benefit, publish or otherwise disclose to others, or permit the use by others for their benefit or to the detriment of Manufacturer, any of Confidential Information; and (3) shall only disclose Confidential Information to its employees and/or consultants with a need to know, and only if such employees and/or consultants have executed agreements that impose on them substantially the same duty with respect to confidentiality as is imposed hereunder.

12.4 Effect of Termination. Upon the expiration or termination of this Agreement, Distributor shall immediately cease the use of the Confidential Information and shall have thirty (30) days from the expiration or termination date of this Agreement to return any Confidential Information received from Manufacturer. Distributor shall not reproduce or permit the reproduction of any such Confidential Information, nor circulate such to any individual or entity. If it is physically impossible to return any Confidential Information received by Distributor, Distributor shall delete such undeliverable files and data items transferred from Manufacturer.

12.5 Injunctive Relief. Distributor understands and acknowledges that any disclosure or misappropriation of any Confidential Information in violation of this Agreement may cause Manufacturer irreparable harm, the amount of which may be difficult to ascertain, and agrees that Manufacturer shall have the right to apply to a court of competent jurisdiction for an order restraining any such further disclosure or misappropriation and for such other relief as Manufacturer shall deem appropriate, and Distributor expressly agrees that Manufacturer shall be entitled, in addition to any other remedy provided by law, to obtain an injunction or other equitable remedy respecting such violation or continued violation. Such right is to be in addition to the remedies otherwise available to Manufacturer at law or in equity.

(This section is a long version with complete protection of intellectual property rights. Below is a shorter version of "Confidentiality.")

12.1 In the course of performing its obligations hereunder, it may be necessary for Manufacturer or Manufacturer Customers to disclose Confidential Information to Distributor. Manufacturer is the sole owner of the Confidential Information. Distributor shall hold and maintain Confidential Information in strictest confidence and in trust for the sole and exclusive benefit of Manufacturer and shall not, without the prior written approval of Manufacturer, use for its own benefit, publish or otherwise disclose to others or permit the use by others for their benefit or to the detriment of Manufacturer, any of Confidential Information. Any disclosure of Confidential Information to Distributor's employees and/or consultants shall be on a need to know basis. If, at any time, Distributor become aware of any unauthorized access, use, possession or knowledge of any Confidential Information, or if Distributor receives any request of disclosure by a governmental agency or third party pursuant to operation of law, regulation or court order, Distributor shall (1) give Manufacturer sufficient prior written notice of such proposed disclosure to enable Manufacturer to obtain an appropriate protective order, if it so desires; and (2) prevent disclosure of such Confidential Information until Manufacturer has an opportunity to take any necessary action to respond to such requested disclosure. Distributor shall also provide all reasonable assistance to Manufacturer to protect the confidentiality of such Confidential Information. Upon the expiration or sooner termination of this Agreement, Distributor shall have thirty (30) days from the expiration or termination date of this Agreement to return Confidential Information received from Manufacturer or delete Confidential Information, which cannot be returned physically. Distributor shall not reproduce or permit the reproduction of any such Confidential Information, nor circulate such to any individual or entity. Distributor understands and acknowledges that any disclosure or misappropriation of any Confidential Information in violation of this Agreement may cause Manufacturer irreparable harm, the amount of which may be difficult to ascertain, and agrees that Manufacturer shall have the right to apply to a court of competent jurisdiction for an order restraining any such further disclosure or misappropriation and for such other relief as Manufacturer shall deem appropriate, and Distributor agrees that Manufacturer shall be entitled, in addition to any other remedy provided by law, to obtain an injunction or other equitable remedy respecting such violation or continued violation. Such right is to be in addition to the remedies otherwise available to Manufacturer at law or in equity.

13. NO CONFLICT DURING TERM

13.1 No Representation of Competitor. During the Term, Distributor shall not act as a distributor for products competitive in substantial respects, or bearing substantial similarities with Products or other products produced by Manufacturer, except as otherwise agreed upon by the parties in writing. Distributor agrees that at the end of each calendar year, or from time to time at Manufacturer's reasonable requests, it will provide Manufacturer, in writing, with the identity of other manufacturers for whom Distributor has been granted distributorship. *(This Section is optional. If the parties agree that Distributor may represent other manufacturer, then use the following Section instead.)*

14. NON-EXCLUSIVITY

14.1 Non-Exclusivity. The parties agree that Distributor is not the exclusive distributor for Manufacturer in the Territory, that Distributor is free to act as a distributor for other manufacturers, and that Manufacture may retainer other distributor to distribute Products in the Territory.

15. NO UNFAIR COMPETITION AND NON-INTERFERENCE WITH BUSINESS

(NOTE: These subsections are optional.)

15.1 General. Distributor understands that during the Term, Distributor will receive from the Manufacturer or Manufacturer Customers Confidential Information belongs to Manufacturer and/or Manufacturer Customers. This Section 14 in no way unnecessarily restricts Distributor from continuing to undertake and perform all activities and functions, which Distributor is undertaking and performing as of the execution of this Agreement. Distributor specifically agrees that this Section 14 is an essential incentive to induce Manufacturer to enter into this Agreement, and that this Section 14 shall be specifically enforceable by Manufacturer, its related entities and its and their successors and assigns. Distributor acknowledges that the limitations as to time, geographical area and scope of activity restrained as set forth herein are reasonable and do not impose a greater restraint on Distributor than is necessary to protect the integrity of the Confidential Information, the goodwill and other business interests of Manufacturer, as well as the competitive benefit of Manufacturer. As one of the considerations for Manufacturer to enter into this Agreement and without in any way limiting any other provisions herein, Distributor agrees to be bound by this Section 14.

15.2 No Unfair Competition. Distributor shall not (1) during the Term and for one (1) year after the expiration or termination of this Agreement, including but not limited to using Confidential Information, directly or indirectly engage or participate in services for, work for, involved in, engaged in, own, manage or operate any business competitive with, or similar to, that of the Manufacturer in the Territory, so long as the Manufacturer carriers on a like business in the Territory; (2) engage in unfair competition with Manufacturer, including but not limited to doing so by using Confidential Information; (3) aid others in any unfair competition with Manufacturer, including but not limited to doing so by using Confidential Information; (4) in any way breach the confidence that Manufacturer placed in Distributor during the Term; (5) misappropriate any Confidential Information; or (6) breach any of the provisions of this Section 14 of the Agreement.

15.3 Non-Interference with Business. During the Term of this Agreement and for one (1) year after the expiration of the Agreement, Distributor shall not, including but not limited to by using Confidential Information, (1) influence or attempt to influence any Manufacturer Customers to divert their business to any individual or entity then in competition with Manufacturer; (2) disrupt, damage, impair or interfere with the business of Manufacturer by disrupting its relationships with Manufacturer Customers or prospects or Manufacturer's Customers' agents, Distributors or vendors; or (3) solicit, contract with or join in with any Manufacturer Customers or prospects without the involvement of Manufacturer for any purpose without first applying for and receiving the express written consent of Manufacturer.

15.4 Non-Solicitation of Employees. Distributor acknowledges and agrees that Manufacturer has made a substantial investment in bringing qualified and professional employees, contractors, agents and/or Distributors and would suffer a loss if they are hired by others due to the conduct by Distributor. Distributor agrees that, during the Term of this Agreement and for one (1) year after the expiration or sooner termination of the Agreement, Manufacturer shall not disrupt, damage, impair or interfere with the business of Manufacturer by interfering with Manufacturer's relationship with its employees by directly or indirectly soliciting Manufacturer's employees who earned ____ ($__) or more on an annual basis to work for any individual or entity then in competition with Manufacturer.

15.5 Non-Circumvention. Distributor agrees that it shall not, directly or indirectly, circumvent, avoid, bypass or obviate Manufacturer in any way, including but not limited to entering into any separate business transactions in any manner with Manufacturer Customers without first applying for and receiving the express written consent of Manufacturer. Such "business transactions" shall include, but not be limited to any transactions, purchases, sales, manufacturing, joint ventures, investment, mergers, acquisitions, projects, any loans or collateral, or other transaction involving any products, transfers or services or addition, renewal extension, rollover, amendment, renegotiations, new contracts, parallel contracts/agreements or third party assignments thereof.

15.6 Application of this Section. Distributor agrees that Section 15.6 shall apply to any transaction between the parties and/or between Distributors and any and all Manufacturer Customers, which makes use of, or involves, Confidential Information, or relates to any sources, introduced by, or disclosed by or from, Manufacturer.

15.7 Injunctive Relief. Distributor agrees that a breach of Distributor's obligations under this Agreement shall result from any efforts of the Distributor or its associates, including but not limited to any of Distributor's agents, Distributors, employees, affiliates, solicitors, bankers, buyers or sellers, who directly or indirectly, attempt to conduct business of or in any manner, to the exclusion of Manufacturer based upon, or pertaining to, Confidential Information or relating to Manufacturer Customers.

16. MISCELLANEOUS

16.1 Binding Effect. This Agreement shall be binding upon both parties and their permitted successors and assigns from the Effective Date.

16.2 Governing Law. This Agreement shall be construed, interpreted and governed as to procedural and substantive matters according to the laws of _____ (*such as the State of California, United States of America,*) without regard to its choice of law, conflict of law's provisions.

16.3 Arbitration; Choice of Forum.

16.3.1 Arbitration. All claims, disputes, controversies, or disagreements of any kind whatsoever ("claims"), including any claims arising out of, relating to or in connection with this Agreement, shall be submitted to final and binding arbitration before _____ (*name of an arbitration agency*) in _____ (*name of location*) in accordance with the rules and procedures of _____ (*specify governing rules and provider such as* American Arbitration Association) then existing. The arbitration shall be held before one arbitrator mutually agreed by the parties. Either party may request to submit any claims to arbitration and make a written request to the other party to select an arbitrator within __ (_) days. If the parties cannot agree on one arbitrator within __ (_) days from the first written request to select an arbitrator by either party, then each party shall select one arbitrator, those two arbitrator shall select a third mutual arbitrator, and the arbitration shall be held before these three arbitrators. If parties fail to select any arbitrator within __ (_) days from the first written request to select an arbitrator by either party, then an arbitrator shall be appointed by _____ (*specify governing rules and provider such as* American Arbitration Association), and the arbitration shall proceed in _____ (*name of location*) before the arbitrator so appointed. The arbitration must be conducted in the English language. The parties agree that the arbitration award is final and binding, and that the judgment on any arbitration award may be entered in any court of competent jurisdiction, and either party may file an action to compel arbitration with any court of competent jurisdiction. This Agreement is a waiver of all rights the parties may have to a civil court action on any dispute outlined by this Agreement. The fees and costs of the arbitration shall be borne equally by the parties, except that each party shall each pay for their own attorney fees or costs of representation for purposes of the arbitration unless otherwise provided by law.

16.3.2 The parties agree that the following claims may be excluded from this arbitration provision: (1) claims relating to Distributor's violations or breach of Sections _____ of this Agreement; and (2) claims that are expressly excluded by applicable laws. Either party may choose to file any actions concerning disputes or controversies arising out of such claims or the interpretation of any provisions contained therein with _____ *(specify name of court, such as the Los Angeles County Superior Court in Los Angeles, California).*

(The parties may choose to use the following arbitration clause instead.)

16.3 Arbitration; Choice of Forum.

Arbitration. All claims, disputes, controversies, or disagreements of any kind whatsoever ("claims"), including any claims arising out of or in connection with this Agreement, shall be submitted to final and binding arbitration before _____ *(name of an arbitration agency)* in _____ *(name of location)* in accordance with the rules and procedures of *(if applicable, add:* the supervision of _____ *(specify appointing authority) and)* the Rules of the United Nations Commission on International Trade Law ("UNCITRAL") in effect on the date of this contract (the "Rules"). In the event of any conflict between the Rules and this Section, the provisions of this Section govern. Arbitration under this Agreement is the parties' exclusive remedy, and no party to any arbitration is required to exhaust any local administrative or judicial remedy first

Arbitrator. Each party must appoint one arbitrator within ___ *(specify time period, such as: 30 days)* after receipt by the respondent of the notice of arbitration. The two arbitrators appointed by the parties must, within ___ *(specify time period, such as: 30 days)* after their appointment, appoint a third, presiding arbitrator, who may not be a citizen or resident of ____*(specify country)* or _____ *(specify country).* If either party fails to nominate an arbitrator, or the two arbitrators appointed by the parties are unable to appoint a presiding arbitrator within the stated periods, the arbitrator or arbitrators will be appointed by the _____ *(appointing authority)* according to the Rules. All arbitrators must be fluent in ___ *(specify language, such as: English)* and must ____ *(specify desired expertise, if any).*

Procedure. The arbitrators will hold hearings where written, documentary and oral evidence may be presented. Evidence may not be taken except in the presence of both parties, and all witnesses may be questioned by both parties. Unless the parties otherwise agree, or a witness is dead, ill, or unavailable for other good reasons, the arbitrators may not accept a witness' written statement unless the other party has an opportunity to question the witness in the arbitrators' presence. All proceedings must be conducted in the _____ (specify language, such as: English) language.

Award. The arbitrators must, by majority vote, render a written decision, stating reasons for their decision, within ___ (specify number) months after the respondent receives the request for arbitration. Any cash award must be payable in U.S. Dollars through a bank in the U.S. and determined, to the extent necessary, on the basis of the rate of exchange in effect at the time the claim arose, as published in the Wall Street Journal. Each party must bear its own costs and attorney's fees or the prevailing party is entitled to recover its costs of arbitration and reasonable attorney's fees, as determined by the arbitrators. The award is deemed a _____ (specify nationality) award.

Enforcement. The award is final and enforceable and may be confirmed by the judgment of a court of competent jurisdiction. To the extent that an award or confirming judgment is unsatisfied, it may be enforced in the manner provided by law in all countries. The prevailing party is entitled to recover its costs and attorney's fees in any proceedings to enforce the award or confirming judgment.

Reservation of Rights. The right to refer a claim or dispute to arbitration under this Agreement is not affected by the fact that a claimant or respondent has received full or partial compensation from a third party for the loss or injury that is the object of the claim or dispute, and any third party may participate in these proceedings by right of subrogation.

The parties agree that the following claims may be excluded from this arbitration provision: (1) claims relating to Distributor's violations or breach of Sections 11, 12, 13 and 14 of this Agreement; and (2) claims that are expressly excluded by applicable laws. Either party may choose to file an action concerning disputes or controversies arising out of such claims or the interpretation of any provisions contained therein with _____ *(specify name of court, such as the Los Angeles County Superior Court in Los Angeles, California).*

(The parties may choose to use the following "Choice of Forum" clause instead.)

16.3 Choice of Forum. The parties further agree that any actions concerning disputes or controversies arising out of this Agreement or the interpretation of any provisions contained therein shall be filed with the_____ Court in ___ *(specify location).*

16.4 Entire Agreement; Language; Amendments. This Agreement constitutes the entire Agreement between the parties hereto with respect to the subject matter of this Agreement and supersedes and cancels any other prior agreements or understandings whether written, oral or implied relating to the subject of this Agreement. There are no restrictions, promises, representations, warranties covenants or undertakings other than those expressly set forth or referred to in this Agreement. The parties further agree that neither they nor anyone acting on their behalf made any inducements, agreements, promises, or representations other than those set forth in this Agreement. This Agreement is written in English only, which is the controlling language in all respects. Any version in any other language is for accommodation only and is not binding upon the parties. All formal notices given pursuant to this Agreement must be in English. Except as provided in Section 6.1, this Agreement may be amended, modified, and supplemented only by written agreement signed by the parties' authorized personnel hereto.

16.5 Waiver of Breach. The waiver by either party of a breach or violation of any provision of the Agreement shall not operate as, or be construed to be, a waiver of any prior, concurrent or subsequent breach hereof. No waiver or purported waiver will be valid or enforceable unless it is in writing and signed by the party against whom it is sought to be enforced.

16.6 Assignment. No portion of this Agreement or any right or obligation under this Agreement can be transferred or assigned, in whole or in part, whether by operation of law or otherwise, by either party without the prior written consent of the other party, except that Manufacturer may freely transfer and assign its rights and obligations under this Agreement to any of Manufacturer's wholly owned subsidiaries, provided that Manufacturer provides guarantees of the obligations of the wholly owned subsidiaries in form and substance satisfactory to Distributor.

16.7 Force Majeure. If either party fails to perform its obligations hereunder (except for the obligation to pay money) because of fires, floods, earthquakes, riots, civil unrest, war, epidemics, shortages, labor unrest, strikes, accidents, acts of God, weather conditions, or action or inaction of any government body or other proper authority, delays caused beyond its reasonable control, then such failure to perform will not be deemed a default hereunder and will be excused without penalty until such time as such party is capable of performing and will not be liable to the other party for any loss, cost or damages arising out of, or resulting from, such failure to perform.

16.8 Notice. All notices which are required or permitted to be given pursuant to this Agreement shall be in writing and shall be sufficient in all respects if delivered personally, by facsimile, by email, by overnight courier using a nationally recognized courier company, or by registered or certified mail, postage prepaid, addressed to a party as indicated below: Manufacturer: _____; and, Distributor: _____. Notice shall be deemed to have been received upon delivery thereof as to communications which are personally delivered, are sent by facsimile or by email; on the third (3rd) day after mailing as to communications which are sent by overnight courier; and on the seventh (7th) day after mailing as to communications made by mail. The above addresses may be changed by giving written notice of such change in the manner provided above for giving notice.

16.9 Severability. Any provision of this Agreement which is prohibited or unenforceable in any jurisdiction will, as to such jurisdiction, be ineffective to the extent of such prohibition or unenforceability without invalidating the remaining provisions hereof, and any such prohibition or unenforceability in any jurisdiction will not invalidate or render unenforceable such provision or other provision hereof in any other jurisdiction.

16.10 Attorney's Fees. The prevailing party in any arbitration or litigation brought by either party to this Agreement in connection with this Agreement will be entitled to recover from the other party all reasonable costs, attorney's fees, and other expenses incurred by the prevailing party in such arbitration or litigation.

16.11 Third Parties. Nothing herein expressed or implied is intended or will be construed to confer upon or give to any person or entity other than the parties hereto and their successors or permitted assigns, any rights or remedies under or by reason of this Agreement.

16.12 Survival. The provisions of Sections 1, 6.6, 7, 8.2, 9, 10, 11, 12, 13, 14 and 15 of this Agreement will survive any expiration or termination of this Agreement.

16.13 Headings. The headings of the Sections of this Agreement are inserted for convenience of reference only and do not constitute a part hereof or affect in any way the meaning or interpretation of this Agreement.

16.14 Dollar Amount. Any dollar amount in the Agreement is in U.S. dollars.

16.15 Counterparts. This Agreement may be executed in one or more counterparts, each of which shall be deemed an original, but all of which taken together shall constitute one and the same instrument. Each party hereto acknowledges and agrees that the other party may rely on electronic facsimile signatures as conclusive evidence of the valid and binding execution of this Agreement.

IN WITNESS WHEREOF, the parties hereto have executed this Agreement as of the date set forth in the first paragraph hereof.

Dated:

_____

MANUFACTURER:

_____

By:

_____

Name:

_____

Title:

_____

Dated:

_____

DISTRIBUTOR:

_____

By:

_____

Name:

_____

Title:

_____

ATTACHMENT A

LIST OF PRODUCTS AND PRICING

A. Names of Products and Pricing:

(Manufacturer may retain the right to change Products during the Term. Manufacturer may grant the right of approval or first right of refusal to Distributor for such change of Products during the Term.)

B. An initial Order for Products in the amount of $_____ shall be placed within ___ (__) days from the Effective Date of this Agreement.

C. Minimum Dollar Amounts of Products to Be Purchased by Distributor During the Term *(Optional)*:

The minimum purchase of _____ *(name of the Product)* shall be $____.

Any Order placed by Distributor shall be credited against the minimum purchase amount at the time of placing of such Order. Any Order subsequently cancelled by Distributor shall not be given any credit against the minimum purchase amounts.

(Or, the following section can be used.)

C. Minimum Dollar Amounts of Products to Be Purchased by Distributor During the Term *(Optional)*:

For the period from _____ to _____, the minimum purchase of _____ *(name of the Product)* shall be $_____;

For each year subsequent to _____ *(date)*, Distributor shall purchase a minimum dollar amount equal to _____% of the actual amount purchased by Distributor during the immediate preceding year.

Any Order placed by Distributor shall be credited against the minimum purchase amount at the time of placing of such Order. Any Order subsequently cancelled by Distributor shall not be given any credit against the minimum purchase amounts.

D. Manufacturer reserve the right to sell less than the minimum amount of Products if the capacity of its factory is unable to meet the demands of all of its distributors, both domestic and foreign.

APPENDIX G: EXPORT SALES AIDS

1. Sample Responses to Inquiries from Prospective Buyers

Letter #1: Response to buyers not familiar enough with the line to ask about a specific model

Dear _____:

Thank you for your inquiry about our company and products. We appreciate your interest. Our products are now being sold throughout the United States [and in __ countries around the world]. We are very proud of this widespread product acceptance. We are prepared to fill orders from international customers and comply with all reasonable regulatory requirements.

After you have examined our Web site (www.xxxxxxxx.com) [attached descriptive literature], please let us know which model would best meet your requirements. We will prepare a Proforma invoice with a price quote ranging from ex works to CIF, as you require.

Please let us know if you have further questions. We look forward to hearing from you soon.

With kind regards,

* * *

Letter # 2: Response to buyers that ask about a specific model or requirement. This letter requires a quotation on a Proforma invoice

Dear _____:

Thank you for your inquiry about MNC's products. We appreciate your interest. Our products are now being sold throughout the United States [and in __ countries around the world]. We are very proud of this widespread product acceptance. We are prepared to fill orders from international customers and comply with all reasonable regulatory requirements.

We believe that the models selected on the attached Proforma invoices may be the best suited for your requirements. The standard equipment and optional equipment are listed on our Web site (www.xxxxxxxx.com) [the attached specification data sheets for each of these models.].

Please let us know if you require further Proforma invoices or have any questions about our company or products, or concerning delivery, inland freight, insurance, shipping ports, or freight.

With kind regards,

2. Sample Responses to Inquiries from Prospective Agents/Distributors

Letter #3: Response to agents/distributors not familiar with the line and do not ask about a specific model

Dear _____:

Thank you for your inquiry about MNC's products. We appreciate your possible interest in representing MNC in [Country]. Our products are now being sold throughout the United States [and in __ countries around the world]. We are very proud of this widespread product acceptance. We are prepared to fill orders from international customers and comply with all reasonable regulatory requirements.

After you have examined our Web site (www.xxxxxxxx.com) [attached descriptive literature], please let us know which products you feel would offer the most potential in your country if distributed through you. The attached Dealer Confidential Net Price Schedule will provide you with F.O.B. Los Angeles costs on all models, optional equipment, and spare parts. If you wish to be considered as our representative in [Country], please provide information about your organization that would help us assess your qualifications.

Please let us know if you have further questions. We look forward to hearing from you soon.

With kind regards,

* * *

Letter #4: Response to agents/distributors that ask about a specific model or requirement. This letter requires a quotation on a Proforma invoice

Dear _____:

Thank you for your inquiry about MNC's products. We appreciate your possible interest in representing MNC in [Country]. Our products are now being sold throughout the United States [and in __ countries around the world]. We are very proud of this widespread product acceptance. We are prepared to fill orders from international customers and comply with all reasonable regulatory requirements.

We believe that the models selected on the attached Proforma invoices may be of most interest to you. The standard equipment and optional equipment are listed on our Web site (www.xxxxxxxx.com) [the attached specification data sheets for each of these models.]. The attached Dealer Confidential Net Price Schedule will provide you with F.O.B. Los Angeles costs on all models, optional equipment, and spare parts.

If you wish to be considered as our representative in [Country], please let us know why you see a market potential for our products if distributed through you Please also provide information about your organization that would help us assess your qualifications.

We look forward to hearing from you soon.

With kind regards,

3. Export Pricing Template

Ex Works Costs

$ _____ Direct Materials

$ _____ Direct Labor

$ _____ Factory Burden

$ _____ Cost of Goods

$ _____ Selling Expenses (should be less than domestic sales)

$ _____ General Expenses (includes cost of money to borrowers)

$ _____ Administrative Expenses

$ _____ Export Marketing Costs (Web globalization, Social Media)

$ _____ Export Adaptation Costs (product changes, labeling)

$ _____ Profit Margin

$ _____ **Total Ex Works Price**

Additional Exporting Costs

$ _____ Foreign Sales Commission (if applicable)

$ _____ Special Export Packaging Costs (typically 1-1.5% above Ex Works price

$ _____ Special Labeling/Marking (to protect from moisture, theft, rough handling)

$ _____ Inland Freight to Pier (normal domestic common carrier, plus carry insurance)

$ _____ Unloading Charges (include demurrage, if any)

$ _____ Terminal Charges (include wharfage, if any)

$ _____ Export Document Charges (include export license, certificates, etc.)

$ _____ Freight (from factory to specified destination, determined by freight forwarder)

$ _____ Freight Forwarder Fees (must be included)

$ _____ Cargo insurance (if CIF quote)

$ _____ Export credit insurance (if any)

$ _____ Cost of Credit (include credit reports, letter of credit costs, amendments, if any)

$ _____ **Total Additional Exporting Costs**

$ _____ **Quote: Ex Works Price + Total Additional Exporting Costs**

4. Export Offer Template

Products can be offered for export in Web-based trade lead systems or directly by E-mail, Fax or letter to potential buyers. Whatever the medium, provide as much detail as space allows to inform the buyers. The template below prompts for details of most interest to potential buyers.

Product for Export: [Name of product]

HS Code: [six digits]

Product Description: [Describe the products/services for export as specifically as possible (HS Code, dimensions, technical specifications, etc.). Highlight features, uses, benefits or other attributes likely to attract interest.]

Availability: [Indicate available quantities and when product can be delivered.]

Target Respondents: [Indicate whether you seek buyers/end users and/or agents/distributors.]

Target Market(s): [Specify any target market(s), if the product is not for sale worldwide.]

Incentives: [Describe any pricing, credit or other inducements for customers.]

Payment/delivery terms: [Specify any preferred or required terms, such as transport mode, L/C or other payment method; credit terms offered, etc.]

Company Profile: [Provide key facts to highlight your company's capabilities as a reliable and reputable exporter, such as years in business, market coverage, prominent suppliers or customers, etc.]

Bank/Trade References: [Cite organizations that can attest to your bona fides, such as customers or suppliers, a bank, trade association, chamber of commerce, etc.]

Contact Information: [Name, title, address, phone, email, fax, and website of key contact]

5. Template for Responding to a Foreign Request for Quote (RFQ)

Thank you for your interest in our products. For a Request for Quotation, please provide the following information:

- Product(s) and quantity of each
- Include quote for on-site installation and training? Yes/No
- Include quote for a maintenance contract? Yes/No
- Include quote for one-year spare parts kits? Yes/No

All quotations are Ex Works (at factory) unless you specify other INCOTERMS, in which case additional costs for shipping, handling and insurance will be included. Our normal payment terms are: [specify terms, e.g., L/C, D/P, D/A, open account, etc.]

- Comments, if you have any questions or need special terms or conditions)
- Contact information, including name, email, phone, and fax

6. Sample Export Quotation

Here are the fields and information needed to compile an export quotation.

1. From (the seller)
2. To (the buyer)
3. Ship To address
4. Quote number
5. Quote date
6. Delivery date
7. Terms
8. Ship via method
9. INCOTERM
10. Ship From location
11. Ship To location
12. Email address
13. For each item quoted, list the item number, a description of the item, the unit of measure, the quantity, the unit value, and the dollar amount
14. Provide a subtotal of the dollar amounts for all items
15. Add tax
16. Add the freight cost
17. Total the subtotal, tax, and freight cost
18. Authorized signature
19. Any remarks

7. Export Quotation Worksheet

(Costs to be provided by freight forwarder)

I. Export Unit Price

$0.00 a. Export Unit Price

$0.00 b. Multiply by X Number Units

$0.00 EXW [EX Works] Subtotal

II. Financing and Inland Fees (if applicable)

$0.00 a. Financing Fees

$0.00 b. Labeling & Marking Costs

$0.00 c. Export Packing Fees

$0.00 d. Electronic Export Information (EEI) Fee

$0.00 e. Bank Draft Fees

$0.00 f. Certificates of Origin Fees

$0.00 g. Export License Fees

$0.00 h. Freight Forwarder Fees

$0.00 i. Domestic Shipping Insurance Costs

$0.00 j. Inland Freight (Pre-carriage) Costs

$0.00 k. Other (Name)

$0.00 Financing and Inland Fees Subtotal

III. Port Charges

$0.00 a. Unloading (Heavy Lift) Charges

$0.00 b. Terminal Service Fees

$0.00 c. Other (Name)

$0.00 FAS [Free Along Side] Subtotal

$0.00 Loading (Onto Aircraft or Vessel)

$0.00 FOB [Free On Board] Subtotal

$0.00 Port Charges Subtotal

IV. International Air, Sea or Land Freight Charges

$0.00 a. Freight Charge (Main-Carriage)

$0.00 b. Bunker Surcharge

$0.00 c. Port Congestion Surcharge

$0.00 d. Country Landing Charge

$0.00 e. Other

$0.00 Cost and Freight Subtotal

V. International Cargo Insurance

$0.00 International Cargo Insurance Cost

$0.00 Total of Sections I-V

8. International Commercial Terms (Incoterms) 2020

Incoterms are 3-letter acronyms of the International Chamber of Commerce (ICC)[1] that standardize terms for quoting export prices and determining liability for goods if lost or damaged in transit. The ICC updated Incoterms 2010 to Incoterms 2020[2], with a few changes, but mostly the same as Incoterms 2010. They continue to range from Ex Works (EXW)—the seller's least responsibility and risk—to Delivered Duty Paid (DDP)—the most responsibility and risk to the seller. See Incoterms 2020 Rules: Chart of Responsibilities and Transfer of Risk[3] and this free webinar on 2020 Incoterms[4] for more details.

EXW (Ex Works)
The buyer picks up the goods at the seller's premises. The buyer loads and transports the goods to their final destination and assumes liability for any loss of or damage to the goods thereafter...

FCA (Free Carrier Alongside)
The seller delivers the goods to the carrier.

FAS (Free Alongside Ship)
The seller delivers the goods alongside the vessel at the named exit port. The buyer assumes liability and cost for loading onto the vessel and transport to the final destination.

FOB (Free On Board)
The seller delivers and loads the goods on board the vessel at the named exit port. The buyer bears all further costs and liability.

CPT (Carriage Paid to)
The seller delivers the goods to the carrier and contracts for and pays the costs to bring the goods to the named place of destination.

CIP (Carriage and Insurance Paid to)
In addition to CPT conditions, the seller also contracts for minimum

insurance cover against the buyer's risk of loss of or damage in transit. The buyer would need to obtain extra insurance for any added protection.

CFR (Cost and Freight)
The seller pays all costs except cargo insurance to deliver the goods to the final destination. The buyer is liable for any loss or damage to the goods in transit and is expected to obtain cargo insurance.

CIF (Cost, Insurance, Freight)
The seller pays all costs, including cargo insurance, to deliver the goods to the final destination. The buyer may opt to purchase additional cargo insurance for protection beyond the seller's minimum cover policy.

DAT (Delivered at Terminal)
The seller delivers the goods to a named terminal at a named port or place of destination. The seller bears all risks involved up to that point. The buyer pays any duties to release the goods from customs.

DAP (Delivered at Place)
The seller delivers the goods to a named destination. The seller bears all risks up to that point. The buyer pays any duties to release the goods from customs.

DDP (Delivered Duty Paid)
The seller delivers the goods to the buyer's door. The seller is responsible to clear the goods and pay any applicable duties for export as well as for import. The seller bears all the costs and risks involved to bring the goods to the place of destination.

Some general principles apply across all 11 Incoterms. For example, in each of the 11 rules:

- The seller must provide the goods, the commercial invoice, and all other relevant documents specified in the sales contract (e.g., an analysis certificate or other evidence of conformity with the buyer's specifications).

- The buyer must pay the price for the goods stated in the sales contract.
- The seller bears all risks of loss or damage to the goods until they have been delivered to the point specified by the buyer.
- The buyer bears all risks of loss or damage to the goods once the seller has delivered them to the point specified.

APPENDIX H: TRADE FINANCE AIDS

1. Sample Letter of Credit (L/C)

THE MOON BANK
INTERNATIONAL OPERATIONS
5 MOONLIGHT BLVD.,
EXPORT-CITY AND POSTAL CODE
EXPORT-COUNTRY

OUR ADVICE NO.: MB-5432

ISSUING BANK REF. NO. & DATE: SBRE-777, January 26, 2001

TO:

UVW Exports
88 Prosperity Street East, Suite 707
Export-City and Postal Code

Dear Sirs:

We have been requested by [The Sun Bank, Sunlight City, Import-Country] to advise that they have opened with us their [irrevocable] documentary credit number [SB-87654] for account of [DEF Imports, 7 Sunshine Street, Sunlight City, Import-Country] in your favor for the amount of [not exceeding Twenty Five Thousand U.S. Dollars (US$25,000.00)], available by your draft(s) drawn on [us] at [sight] for [full] invoice value, accompanied by the following documents:

1. Signed commercial invoice in five (5) copies indicating the buyer's Purchase Order No. DEF-101 dated January 10, 2001.
2. Packing list in five (5) copies.
3. Full set 3/3 clean on board ocean bill of lading, plus two (2) non-negotiable copies, issued to order of The Sun Bank, Sunlight City, Import-Country, notify the above accountee, marked "freight Prepaid", dated latest March 19, 2001, and showing documentary credit number.
4. Insurance policy in duplicate for 110% CIF value covering Institute Cargo Clauses (A), Institute War and Strike Clauses, evidencing that claims are payable in Import-Country.

Covering: 100 Sets 'ABC' Brand Pneumatic Tools, 1/2" drive, complete with hose and quick couplings, CIF Sunny Port
Shipment from: [Moonbeam Port, Export-Country] to [Sunny Port, Import-Country]
Partial shipment: Prohibited
Transshipment: Permitted

Special conditions

1. All documents indicating the Import License No. IP/123456 dated January 18, 2001.
2. All charges outside the Import-Country are on beneficiary's account.

Documents must be presented for payment within [15] days after the date of shipment.

Draft(s) drawn under this credit must be marked

Drawn under documentary credit No. SB-87654 of The Sun Bank, Sunlight City, Import-Country, dated January 26, 2001

We confirm this credit and hereby undertake that all drafts drawn under and in conformity with the terms of this credit will be duly honored upon delivery of documents as specified, if presented at this office on or before [March 26, 2001]

Very truly yours,

[Authorized Signature]

2. Sample L/C Instructions

1. The letter of Credit shall be IRREVOCABLE.
2. The credit shall be directly advised thru: [Name, address, telex, fax, etc. of exporter's bank]
3. The credit shall be **Confirmed.**
4. The credit shall be "**available with any bank**" and **expire** in country of beneficiary (USA).
5. The credit shall show as the beneficiary: [Name, address, etc. of exporter].
6. The credit shall be payable in **U.S.A. currency** in the amount exactly as the invoice.
7. The credit shall be payable **15 days** from Air Waybill Date.
8. **All Fees/Charges** are for the account of Applicant (importer).
9. Partial shipments **allowed.**
10. The credit shall allow for required transport documents not later than _____ (this date will be determined upon receiving your (importer's) purchase order.)
11. The credit shall allow for a minimum of 21 days after the required transport document date for presentation of documents at the counters of the Bank stated above.
12. The required documents should include:

- Commercial Invoice Totaled Ex-Works Bradford, Massachusetts U.S.A.
- Commercial invoice shall cover the following: _____ (description of merchandise)
- Air Waybill consigned to the Issuing Bank

APPENDIX I: U.S. EXPORT REGULATORY AGENCIES & ENFORCEMENT RESPONSIBILITIES

Here is a list of U.S. export regulatory agencies[1] and their enforcement responsibilities.

Census Bureau: Automated Export System (AES)

Customs & Border Protection (CBP): Automated Commercial Environment (ACE)

Directorate of Defense Trade Controls (DDTC): Export controls —military

Bureau of Industry & Security (BIS): Export controls—non-military

Office of Foreign Assets Control (OFAC): Foreign Assets Control regulations

Food & Drug Administration (FDA): Medical Devices, Drugs, Cosmetics

Animal & Plant Health Inspection Service (APHIS): Animals, animal by-products, plants and unprocessed plant products

Food Safety Inspection Service (FSIS): Meat, poultry and egg products

Agricultural Marketing Service (AMS): Dairy, fresh/processed fruits, vegetables, cotton, poultry, tobacco

Bureau of Alcohol, Tobacco, Firearms & Explosives (ATF): Alcohol and tobacco products

Pipeline & Hazardous Materials Safety Adm. (PHMSA): Hazardous materials

DOJ Fraud Section: Foreign Corrupt Practice Act

Patent & Trademark Office (USPTO): Patents & trademarks

U.S. Copyright Office: Copyrights

Maritime Administration (MARAD): U.S. ocean transport system

APPENDIX J: GLOSSARY OF ONLINE INTERNATIONAL TRADE RESOURCES

20 Epic Fails in Global Branding
https://www.inc.com/geoffrey-james/the-20-worst-brand-translations-of-all-time.html

31 Countries
https://en.wikipedia.org/wiki/Foreign_exchange_controls#Countries_with_current_foreign_exchange_controls

ACE
https://www.cbp.gov/trade/automated

ACE—Getting Started
https://www.cbp.gov/trade/automated/getting-started

AES Proof of Filing Citations
http://www.census.gov/foreign-trade/aes/exporttraining/videos/uscs_videos/Proof_of_filing_citations/index.html

AES Response Messages

http://www.census.gov/foreign-trade/aes/exporttraining/videos/uscs_videos/Response_messages_using_AES/index.html

AES User Guide
https://www.census.gov/foreign-trade/aes/aesdirect/AESDirect-User-Guide.pdf

AESDirect
https://www.census.gov/foreign-trade/aes/aesdirect/transitiontoace.html

AESDirect—The Shipment Manager
http://www.census.gov/foreign-trade/aes/exporttraining/videos/uscs_videos/shipment_manager/index.html

African Development Bank Business Opportunities
http://www.afdb.org/

Air Waybill
https://blanker.org/air-waybill

Air Waybill Sample
https://www.ups.com/aircargo/using/services/supplies/airwaybill.html

Alibaba
http://www.alibaba.com/

American Egyptian Cooperation Foundation
https://www.guidestar.org/profile/54-1402264

Angel Investors
https://www.thebalancesmb.com/angel-investor-2947066

Anti-Boycott Regulations
https://www.bis.doc.gov/index.php/enforcement/oac

Asian Development Bank Business Opportunities
http://www.adb.org/Business/Opportunities/

AUMA Trade Show Directory
https://www.auma.de/en/exhibit/find-your-exhibitions?typ=erw

Automated Export System
https://www.cbp.gov/trade/aes/introduction

Bank Loans
https://blog.yelp.com/2019/02/12-types-small-business-loans-funding

Bills of Lading
https://www.shippingsolutions.com/download-bill-of-lading-forms

Body Language And Gestures Across The World
https://translit.ie/blog/body-language-gestures-across-world/

Brett Tarnet Insurance Services
https://tarnetinsurance.com/

Canadian Customs Tariff
http://www.cbsa-asfc.gc.ca/trade-commerce/tariff-tarif/2013/menu-eng.html

Cash in Advance
https://2016.export.gov/tradefinanceguide/eg_main_043222.asp

CE (Conformité Européenne) Mark
https://europa.eu/youreurope/business/product/ce-mark/index_en.htm

Certificate of Free Sale
https://www.fda.gov/regulatory-information/search-fda-guidance-documents/fda-export-certificates

Certificate of Origin

https://www.shippingsolutions.com/download-certificate-of-origin-forms

Certificate of Origin form

https://www.cbp.gov/document/guidance/certification-origin-template

Certificates of Free Sale

https://www.fda.gov/RegulatoryInformation/Guidances/ucm125789.htm

Chambers of Commerce

https://www.chamber-commerce.net/

Coface Analyze my Customers and Prospects

https://www.coface-usa.com/Our-Offer/Analyze-my-Customers-and-Prospects

Coface Debtor Risk Assessments

https://www.coface-usa.com/Our-Offer/Analyze-my-Customers-and-Prospects/Debtor-Risk-Assessments

Colors Across Cultures

https://www.globalme.net/blog/colours-across-cultures

Commerce Control List

https://www.bis.doc.gov/index.php/regulations/commerce-control-list-ccl

Commercial Invoices

https://en.wikipedia.org/wiki/Commercial_invoice

Consular Invoice

https://maxfreights.com/what-is-a-consular-invoice/

Container Shipping
http://www.containershipping.com/

Corruption Perceptions Index
https://www.transparency.org/whatwedo/publication/corruption-perceptions-index

Cosmetics
https://www.fda.gov/Cosmetics/default.htm

Cost & Freight
https://www.incotermsexplained.com/the-incoterms-rules/the-eleven-rules-in-brief/cost-freight/

Cost Insurance & Freight (CIF)
https://www.incotermsexplained.com/the-incoterms-rules/the-eleven-rules-in-brief/cost-insurance-freight/

Country Guides
https://www.bsicorp.net/articles/country-guides

Country Intercultural Insights
http://www.intercultures.ca/cil-cai/countryinsights-apercuspays-eng.asp

Crowdfunding
https://www.crowdfunding.com/

D&B Hoovers
https://www.dnb.com/

Dangerous Goods Packaging
https://www.faa.gov/hazmat/safecargo/how_to_ship/package_for_shipping/

Datamyne
https://www.datamyne.com/

Denied Entities List
https://www.bis.doc.gov/index.php/policy-guidance/lists-of-parties-of-concern/entity-list

Denied Persons List
https://www.bis.doc.gov/index.php/policy-guidance/lists-of-parties-of-concern/denied-persons-list

Directory of International Commercial Banks in U.S.
https://www.federalreserve.gov/releases/lbr/current/

District Export Council
https://www.usaexporter.org/

Dock Receipt Sample
https://www.pdffiller.com/jsfiller-desk15/?projectId=484987085#afa94e142dc972ca331b9d9e29dd3f58

Documentary Collections
https://www.shippingsolutions.com/blog/methods-of-payment-in-international-trade-documentary-collections

Documents Against Acceptance
https://www.wisegeek.com/what-are-documents-against-acceptance.htm

Documents Against Payment
https://www.wisegeek.com/what-are-documents-against-payment.htm

Drugs
https://www.fda.gov/Drugs/default.htm

Dun & Bradstreet (D&B) Credit Evaluator Plus
https://businesscredit.dnb.com/monitor-other-company-business-credit/

EC Directives
https://en.wikipedia.org/wiki/Directive_(European_Union)

Economic Development Agencies
https://www.eda.gov/resources/

EEI filing Instructions
https://aesdirect.census.gov/download/userguide/AESDirectSampleShipment.pdf

Electronic Export Information
https://www.census.gov/foreign-trade/regulations/forms/index.html#sed

Elimination of the SSN in the AES
http://www.census.gov/foreign-trade/data/video003.html

Equifax International Credit Reports
https://www.equifax.com/pdfs/corp/CS_108_International_Credit_Reports_0204.pdf

EU Tariff Lookup
http://exporthelp.europa.eu/thdapp/taric/TaricServlet?languageId=EN&CFID=4177607&CFTOKEN=15605945&jsessionid=6430f1f6fda46d362b4b

EU/Market Access Sectoral and Trade Barriers Database
http://madb.europa.eu/madb/barriers_select.htm

EU/Market Access Sectoral and Trade Barriers Database
http://madb.europa.eu/madb/barriers_select.htm

Euromonitor
https://www.marketresearch.com/Euromonitor-International-v746/

European Bank's Procurement Opportunities
http://www.ebrd.com/pages/project.shtml

Exim/Export Credit Insurance
https://www.exim.gov/what-we-do/export-credit-insurance

Exim/Export Credit Insurance
My Book

Exim/Export Credit Insurance
https://www.exim.gov/what-we-do/protect-against-buyer-nonpayment

Exim/Export Credit Insurance Policy
https://www.exim.gov/what-we-do/protect-against-buyer-nonpayment

Exim/Export Working Capital Guaranty Program
My Book

Exim/Export Working Capital Guaranty Program
https://www.exim.gov/what-we-do/working-capital

Exim/Medium–and Long-Term Fnancing for Freign Buyers
https://www.exim.gov/what-we-do/finance-a-foreign-buyer-purchase

Exim/U.S. Export-Import Bank
https://www.exim.gov/

Exim/Video Gallery
https://www.exim.gov/learning-resources/video-gallery/how-to

Exim/Webinars
https://www.exim.gov/learning-resources/video-gallery/196

Experian International Business Credit Reports
https://sbcr.experian.com/main.aspx

Export Certificates
http://www.fda.gov/Food/GuidanceRegulation/ImportsExports/
Exporting/ucm2006911.htm

Export Control Classification Number
https://www.bis.doc.gov/index.php/licensing/commerce-control-
list-classification/export-control-classification-number-eccn

Export Packing List Sample
https://www.pdffiller.com/jsfiller-desk12/?projectId=
484984095#24018b5a5a5f5dcd38223cc4e1f3912e

Export Packing Lists
https://www.dripcapital.com/resources/blog/export-packing-list

Export Pricing Strategy
https://www.trade.gov/pricing-strategy

Export Yellow Pages
http://www.exportyellowpages.com/

Export-Import Bank
https://www.exim.gov/

ExportUSA
http://thinkglobal.com/exusa/exusa#.VMfurGB0zX4

ExWorks—EXW
https://www.incotermsexplained.com/the-incoterms-rules/the-
eleven-rules-in-brief/ex-works/

Facebook Ads Manager
https://www.facebook.com/business/tools/ads-manager

Factoring
https://www.mbaknol.com/business-finance/factoring-concept-in-export-finance/

FAS Web Portal
https://www.fas.usda.gov/

FAS.gov
https://www.fas.usda.gov/

FAS/50% CostShare Program
https://www.susta.org/whatwedo/costshare/

FAS/Agricultural Trade Promotion Program
https://www.fas.usda.gov/programs/agricultural-trade-promotion-program-atp

FAS/Commodities and Products
https://www.fas.usda.gov/commodities

FAS/Countries and Regions
https://www.fas.usda.gov/regions

FAS/Data and Analysis
https://www.fas.usda.gov/data

FAS/Emerging Markets Program
https://www.fas.usda.gov/programs/emerging-markets-program-emp

FAS/Export Credit Guarantee Program
https://www.fas.usda.gov/programs/export-credit-guarantee-program-gsm-102

FAS/Foreign Market Development (FMD) Program
https://www.fas.usda.gov/programs/foreign-market-development-program-fmd

FAS/FundMatch Program
https://www.wusata.org/whatwedo/fundmatchprogram/

FAS/Market Research
https://www.fas.usda.gov/data

FAS/Southern U.S. Trade Association
https://www.susta.org/whatwedo/overview/

FAS/Trade Programs
https://www.fas.usda.gov/programs

FAS/Western U.S. Trade Association
https://www.fas.usda.gov/programs/foreign-market-development-program-fmd

FCIB Worldwide Credit Reports
https://fcibglobal.com/credit-country-reports/worldwide-credit-reports.html

FDA/Compliance and Enforcement
https://www.fda.gov/Food/ComplianceEnforcement/default.htm

FDA/Food & Drug Administration
https://www.fda.gov/

Filing a Shipment in AESDirect
http://www.census.gov/foreign-trade/aes/exporttraining/videos/uscs_videos/Filing_a_shipment_with_AES/index.html

FITA
http://fita.org/

FITA Comprehensive Directory of Associations
http://fita.org/webindex/browse.cgi/
International_Transportation_and_Logistics/Transportation_Associati
onsOrganizations

Food and Drink Prohibitions
https://en.wikipedia.org/wiki/Food_and_drink_prohibitions

Foreign Agricultural Service
https://www.fas.usda.gov/

Foreign Assets Control Regulations
https://www.gpo.gov/fdsys/granule/CFR-2004-title31-vol2/CFR-
2004-title31-vol2-part500/content-detail.html

Foreign Corrupt Practices Act (FCPA)
https://www.justice.gov/criminal-fraud/foreign-corrupt-practices-act

Foreign trade statistics
http://www.tradecomplianceinstitute.org/p_trade_info_db_links.
php?SubCatID=18&Cat=Trade%20&%20Economic%20Data/Policy&
SubCat=Foreign%20Trade%20Data

Free Alongside Ship
https://www.incotermsexplained.com/the-incoterms-rules/the-
eleven-rules-in-brief/free-alongside-ship/

Free on Board
https://www.incotermsexplained.com/the-incoterms-rules/the-
eleven-rules-in-brief/free-board/

Free Trade Agreements
https://ustr.gov/trade-agreements/free-trade-agreements

Freight Forwarder
https://www.forwarders.com/index.html

Freight Forwarders
https://ncbfaa.org/

Freight Forwarders
https://graduateway.com/role-and-function-of-freight-forwarders/

Freight Forwarders
https://en.wikipedia.org/wiki/Freight_forwarder

FreightWorld
http://www.freightworld.com/

FTA Tariff Search Tool by Country
https://beta.trade.gov/fta/tariff-rates-search

General Average
https://www.marineinsight.com/maritime-law/the-role-of-general-average-in-the-maritime-industry/

Getting to Global
https://gettingtoglobal.org/

globalEDGE
http://globaledge.msu.edu/

globalEdge/Diagnostic Tools
https://globaledge.msu.edu/tools-and-data/diagnostic-tools

globalEdge/Export Tutorials
https://globaledge.msu.edu/reference-desk/export-tutorials

globalEDGE/Global Resources
https://globaledge.msu.edu/global-resources

globalEdge/Industry-and Country Information
https://globaledge.msu.edu/global-insights

Google Ads
https://ads.google.com/home/

Google/Market Finder
https://www.thinkwithgoogle.com/intl/en-gb/tools/market-finder/

Graydon's International Credit Reports
https://www.graydon.nl/en/credit-management/clientacceptance/
international-credit-report

Guide to Website Internationalization
https://thenextweb.com/dd/2011/05/20/web-design-with-the-
world-in-mind-a-guide-to-website-internationalization/

Harmonized System
https://www.foreign-trade.com/reference/hscode.htm

Harmonized System (HS) Code.
https://www.trade.gov/harmonized-system-hs-codes

Harmonized Tariff Schedule of the United States (HTSUSA) Codes
https://www.usitc.gov/harmonized_tariff_information

Hazardous Materials Regulations
https://www.phmsa.dot.gov/approvals-and-permits/hazmat/
hazardous-materials-approvals-and-permits-overview

High Context Cultures
https://culturematters.com/what-is-high-context-culture/

Incoterms 2020
https://incodocs.com/blog/incoterms-2020-explained-the-complete-
guide/

Inter-American Development Bank Projects
http://www.iadb.org/projects/index.cfm?language=english

International Air Transport Association
https://www.iata.org/

International Commercial Term
hhttps://globalnegotiator.com/files/incoterms-2020-book.pdf

International Credit Reporting Agencies
http://fita.org/webindex/browse.cgi/
International_Finance_Letters_of_Credit_and_Investment/
Credit_Reporting_Services_and_Debt_Recovery/Credit_Reporting_Se
rvices

International Insurance Carrier
https://www.internationalinsurance.com/companies.php

International Maritime Organization
http://www.imo.org/EN/Pages/Default.aspx

International Monetary Fund
https://www.imf.org/external/index.htm

International Plant Protection Convention
https://www.ippc.int/en/

International Standards for Phytosanitary Measures
https://www.ippc.int/en/core-activities/standards-setting/ispms/

International Trade Administration
https://www.trade.gov/

Internet World Stats
https://www.internetworldstats.com/stats.htm

ITA/BIS/Export Administration Regulations
https://www.bis.doc.gov/index.php/regulations/export-
administration-regulations-ear

ITA/Bureau of Industry and Security
https://www.bis.doc.gov/

ITA/Country Commercial Guides
https://www.trade.gov/ccg-landing-page

ITA/Customized Market Research
https://www.trade.gov/customized-market-research

ITA/DECs
https://www.usaexporter.org/local-dec-locator/

ITA/Directory of Overseas Commercial Offices
https://2016.export.gov/worldwide_us/index.asp

ITA/Directory of U.S. Commercial Offices
https://www.trade.gov/let-our-experts-help-0

ITA/eCommerce Innovation Lab
https://www.trade.gov/ecommerce

ITA/Export Administration Regulations
https://www.bis.doc.gov/index.php/regulations/export-administration-regulations-ear

ITA/Exporter Assessments
https://www.trade.gov/exporter-assessments

ITA/Foreign Commercial Service (FCS)
https://www.afsa.org/foreign-commercial-service

ITA/Gold Key Matching Service
https://www.trade.gov/gold-key-service

ITA/Gold Key Service
https://www.export.gov/Gold-Key-Service

ITA/International Company Profile
https://www.trade.gov/international-company-profile

ITA/International Partner Agreements
https://www.trade.gov/negotiating-agreement-foreign-representative

ITA/International Partner Search (IPS)
https://www.export.gov/International-Partner-Search

ITA/Manufactures and Services Research
https://legacy.trade.gov/industry/

ITA/Office of Anti-Boycott Compliance
https://www.bis.doc.gov/index.php/enforcement/oac

ITA/Pricing Strategy
https://www.trade.gov/pricing-strategy

ITA/Protect Your Intellectual Property
https://www.trade.gov/protect-intellectual-property

ITA/Sample Export Plan
https://www.trade.gov/sample-export-plan

ITA/Search Trade Events
https://www.trade.gov/trade-events-search#/

ITA/Top Market Series
https://www.trade.gov/topmarkets/

ITA/Trade Event Partnership Program
https://www.trade.gov/tepp-faqs

ITA/Trade Finance Guide
https://grow.exim.gov/hs-fs/hub/421983/file-2055772500-pdf/
Guides/trade-guide.pdf

ITA/Trade Missions
https://www.trade.gov/trade-missions

ITA/Trade Missions Search
https://www.trade.gov/trade-events-search#/

ITA/Trade Show Directory
https://www.trade.gov/trade-events-search#/

ITA/Trade Shows
https://www.trade.gov/trade-shows

ITA/Trade Shows and Trade Missions Programs
https://www.trade.gov/attend-event

ITA/Trade Stats Express
https://tse.export.gov/

ITA/Trade.gov
https://www.trade.gov/

ITA/U.S. Export Assistance Center
https://www.trade.gov/us-commercial-service-office-map

ITA/Upcoming DOC Webinars
https://www.trade.gov/trade-events-search#/search?
start_date_range%5Bfrom%5D=2019-12-01&start_date_range%5Bto%5D=2024-03-31&event_types=Seminar-Webinar

ITCI Market Research Portal
http://www.tradecomplianceinstitute.org/p_trade_info_database.php

ITCI Trade Information Database
http://www.tradecomplianceinstitute.org/p_trade_info_database.php

ITCI/Directories of Foreign Manufacturers and Importers
http://www.tradecomplianceinstitute.org/p_trade_info_db_links.
php?SubCatID=30&Cat=Trade%20Contacts%20&%20Leads&SubCat=
Foreign%20Manufacturers%20&%20Importers

ITCI/Directories of Manufacturers
http://www.tradecomplianceinstitute.org/p_trade_info_db_links.
php?SubCatID=29&Cat=Trade%20Contacts%20&%20Leads&SubCat=
U.S.%20Producers%20&%20Exporters

ITCI/Export FAQ
http://www.tradecomplianceinstitute.org/x_plfls/Export%20FAQs%
20by%20Maurice%20Kogon%202014%20092114.pdf

ITCI/Export Guides
http://www.tradecomplianceinstitute.org/p_trade_info_db_links.
php?SubCatID=2&Cat=Trade%20Readiness%20Tools&SubCat=
Export%20Guides

ITCI/Export Readiness Assessment System
http://www.tradecomplianceinstitute.org/ERAS/

ITCI/Export Start-Up Kit
http://www.
tradecomplianceinstitute.org/p_export_import_basics.php

ITCI/Exporting Basics
http://www.tradecomplianceinstitute.org/x_plfls/Exporting%
20Basics%20Final%20With%20Pegination%20for%
20Wafer%20Drive.pdf

ITCI/Foreign Trade Laws & Regulations
http://www.
tradecomplianceinstitute.org/p_trade_info_db_links.php?

ITCI/Free Export Guides
http://www.tradecomplianceinstitute.org/p_trade_info_db_links.
php?SubCatID=2&Cat=Trade%20Readiness%20Tools&SubCat=
Export%20Guides

ITCI/Hot Trade Leads
http://www.tradecomplianceinstitute.org/p_trade_info_db_links.
php?SubCatID=31&Cat=Trade%20Contacts%20&%20Leads&SubCat=
Hot%20Trade%20Leads

ITCI/Intercultural Research
http://www.tradecomplianceinstitute.org/p_trade_info_db_links.
php?SubCatID=27&Cat=Foreign%20Market%20Research&SubCat=
Intercultural%20Research

ITCI/International Legal Resources
http://www.tradecomplianceinstitute.org/p_trade_info_db_links.
php?SubCatID=37&Cat=Trade/Investment%20Regulations&SubCat=
International%20Legal%20Resources

ITCI/International Trade Compliance Institute Website
http://www.tradecomplianceinstitute.org/

ITCI/Other U.S. Export Laws & Regulations
http://www.tradecomplianceinstitute.org/p_trade_info_db_links.
php?SubCatID=34&Cat=Trade/Investment%20Regulations&SubCat=
Other%20U.S.%20Export%20Laws%20&%20Regulations

ITCI/TID Categories and Subjects Covered
http://www.tradecomplianceinstitute.org/p_trade_info_database.php

ITCI/Trade Information Database
http://www.tradecomplianceinstitute.org/p_trade_info_database.php

ITCI/U.S. National Security Export Controls (EAR, ITAR, FACR)
http://www.tradecomplianceinstitute.org/p_trade_info_db_links.
php?SubCatID=93&Cat=Trade/Investment%20Regulations&SubCat=
U.S.%20National%20Security%20Export%20Controls%20(EAR,%20I-
TAR,%20FACR)

ITCI/U.S. Regulatory and Enforcement Agencies
http://www.tradecomplianceinstitute.org/p_trade_info_db_links.
php?SubCatID=90&Cat=Trade%20Resources%20Directory&SubCat=
U.S.%20Government%20Trade%20Regulatory%20Organizations

ITCI/Web-Based Export Tutorials
http://www.tradecomplianceinstitute.org/p_trade_info_db_links.
php?SubCatID=10&Cat=Trade%20Readiness%20Tools&SubCat=
Trade%20Tutorials%20-%20Webinars,%20Courses,%20Videos

ITCI/Web-Based Free Export Guides
http://www.tradecomplianceinstitute.org/p_trade_info_db_links.
php?SubCatID=2&Cat=Trade%20Readiness%20Tools&SubCat=
Export%20Guides

ITCI/Webinar and Videos
http://www.tradecomplianceinstitute.org/p_trade_info_db_links.
php?SubCatID=10&Cat=Trade%20Readiness%20Tools&SubCat=
Trade%20Tutorials%20-%20Webinars,%20Courses,%20Videos

ITCI/World Economic and Demographic Data
http://www.tradecomplianceinstitute.org/p_trade_info_db_links.
php?SubCatID=19&Cat=Trade%20&%20Economic%20Data/Policy&
SubCat=World%20Economic%20&%20Demographic%20Data

Japan Import Tariffs
http://www.customs.go.jp/english/tariff/index.htm

Keys to Success
https://www.bsicorp.net/articles/keys-to-success

Kogon/2011 Congressional Testimony on Exporting
https://www.youtube.com/watch?v=P_YNaxEGMM

Kompass
https://us.kompass.com/

Kwintessential Global Guide to Etiquette
https://www.kwintessential.co.uk/resources-types/guides

Letter of Credit
https://globaltradefunding.com/trade-finance-solutions/export-financing/export-letter-of-credit/#:~:text=%20Export%20Letters%20of%20Credit%20Key%20Features%20,for%20the%20transaction%20on%20which%20it...%20More%20

Letters of Credit
https://www.thebalance.com/types-of-letters-of-credit-315040

LinkedIn Leads
https://linkedupsales.com/

Los Angeles Customs Bureau and Freight Forwarders Association
https://www.lacbffa.org/cpages/about

Marine Insurance
https://www.marineinsight.com/know-more/what-is-marine-insurance/

Marking and Labeling Regulations
https://www.trade.gov/trade-search?q=labeling

USMCA Certificate of Origin
https://www.usmcacertificate.com/wp-content/uploads/2020/05/USMCA-Certificate-of-Origin-Form-Sample-May-8-2020.pdf

Medical Devices
https://www.fda.gov/MedicalDevices/default.htm

Meridian Export Insurance
http://www.meridianfinance.com/insurance/

Microloans
https://www.fundera.com/business-loans/guides/microloans

Milken/New-to-Export (NTE) 101-LA
https://milkeninstitute.org/reports/new-export-101-strengthening-capacity-us-regional-economies-export-abroad

Munitions List
https://www.ecfr.gov/cgi-bin/retrieveECFR?gp=&SID=70e390c181ea17f847fa696c47e3140a&mc=true&r=PART&n=pt22.1.121

National Customs Bureau and Freight Forwarders Association
https://ncbfaa.org/

Negotiating International Partner Agreements
https://www.trade.gov/negotiating-agreement-foreign-representative

NIST/ExporTech Program
https://www.nist.gov/exportech

NIST/MEP/ Product Design and Development
https://www.nist.gov/mep/product-design-and-development

NIST/MEPs
https://www.nist.gov/mep/centers

North American Development Bank Information
http://www.nadbank.org/projects/procurementinfo.html

North American Industry Classification System (NAICS) Codes
https://www.census.gov/eos/www/naics/
2017NAICS/2017_NAICS_Manual.pdf

Ocean B/L Sample
https://www.shippingsolutions.com/ocean-bill-of-lading

Ocean Bill of Lading
https://www.shippingsolutions.com/download-bill-of-lading-
forms#ocean

Open Account
https://globaltradefunding.com/trade-finance-solutions/import-
financing/open-accounts/

Panjiva
https://panjiva.com/

Passport to Trade—Business Etiquette—31 Countries
https://businessculture.org/business-culture/

Phytosanitary Certificates
https://www.aphis.usda.gov/aphis/ourfocus/planthealth/
sa_export/sa_forms/ct_export_certificates_forms

Phytosanitary Certificates
http://www.fao.org/docrep/004/y3241e/y3241e06.htm

PIERS
https://ihsmarkit.com/products/piers.html

Pre-Shipment Inspection (PSI) Certificate
http://www.omicnet.com/omicnet/pdf/psiguide.pdf

Proforma Invoices
https://www.shippingsolutions.com/proforma-invoice-english

Radiation-Emitting Products
https://www.fda.gov/Radiation-EmittingProducts/default.htm

Registering for AESDirect
http://www.census.gov/foreign-trade/aes/exporttraining/videos/uscs_videos/Registering_for_AES_direct/index.html

SBA investment Loans
https://www.sba.gov/funding-programs/investment-capital

SBA/Business Plan Templates
https://www.sba.gov/business-guide/plan-your-business/write-your-business-plan

SBA/Export Express
https://www.sba.gov/category/type-loan/export-express

SBA/Export Working Capital Guaranty Program
https://www.sba.gov/sites/default/files/articles/oit_export_cap_prgm_business_0.pdf

SBA/Office of International Trade
https://www.sba.gov/offices/headquarters/oit

SBA/SBDCs
https://www.sba.gov/local-assistance/find/?q=sbdc&pageNumber=1

SBA/Small Business Administration
https://www.sba.gov/

SBA/Small Business Development Centers
https://www.sba.gov/offices/headquarters/osbdc/resources/11409

SBA/State Trade Expansion Program (STEP)
https://www.sba.gov/funding-programs/grants/state-trade-expansion-program-step

SBA/State Trade Expansion Program (STEP)—Application
https://www.sba.gov/document/support--state-trade-expansion-program-step-grant-application-instructions

SBA/U.S. Small Business Administration
https://www.sba.gov/category/navigation-structure/loans-grants/small-business-loans/sba-loan-programs/7a-loan-program/sb

Schedule B Export Codes
https://www.census.gov/foreign-trade/schedules/b/index.html#search

Search Engine Optimization
https://en.wikipedia.org/wiki/Search_engine_optimization

Simplified Network Application Process Redesign (SNAP-R)
https://www.bis.doc.gov/index.php/licensing/simplified-network-application-process-redesign-snap-r

Small Business Administration
https://www.sba.gov/

Spam
https://en.wikipedia.org/wiki/Email_spam

Standard International Trade Classification (SITC) Codes
https://unstats.un.org/unsd/classifications/Econ/Download/In%20Text/CPCprov_english.pdf

State Trade Development Offices
https://www.sidoamerica.org/

State/Directorate of Defense Trade Controls
https://www.pmddtc.state.gov/ddtc_public

State/International Traffic in Arms Regulations
https://www.pmddtc.state.gov/regulations_laws/itar.html/?id=
ddtc_kb_article_page&sys_id=%2024d528fddbfc930044f9ff621f961987

State/National Trade Estimate Reports on Foreign Trade Barriers
https://ustr.gov/sites/default/files/files/Press/Reports/2018%
20National%20Trade%20Estimate%20Report.pdf

Straight B/L
http://export.gov/static/form_12_2_Latest_eg_main_044741.pdf

Tariff Engineering
http://www.barnesrichardson.com/4E8FDC/assets/files/News/
tariff-engineering.pdf

Tariffs
https://theconversation.com/what-is-a-tariff-an-economist-explains-
93392?
gclid=EAIaIQobChMInpDtgem54gIVjMpkCh2EtwsdEAAYASAAEgK
O8_D_BwE

TDA/Project Preparation Assistance Program
https://ustda.gov/about/

TDA/Reverse Trade Mission Program
https://ustda.gov/about/

ThinkGlobal/ExportUSA
https://www.think.global/#.VLsY4GB0zX4

Trade and Development Agency
https://www.ustda.gov/

Trade Development Agency (TDA)
Feasibility Studies & Projects
http://www.tda.gov/library/search_criteria.cfm

Trade Development Agency (TDA) Pipeline
http://www.tda.gov/pipeline/index.html

Transportation/Pipeline and Hazardous Materials Safety Admin
https://www.phmsa.dot.gov/regulations-and-compliance

Treasury/Office of Foreign Assets Control
https://www.treasury.gov/about/organizational-structure/offices/Pages/Office-of-Foreign-Assets-Control.aspx

U.S. Commercial Banks
https://www.usbanklocations.com/

U.S. Export Assistance Centers
https://www.trade.gov/us-commercial-service-office-map

U.S. Export Import Bank
https://www.exim.gov/

U.S. Flag Carriers
https://www.maritime.dot.gov/sites/marad.dot.gov/files/docs/ports/cargo-preference/2841/us-flag-contact-list_0.pdf

U.S. International Trade Lawyers
https://www.hg.org/law-firms/usa-international-law.html

U.S. Trade Statistics
http://www.tradecomplianceinstitute.org/p_trade_info_db_links.php?SubCatID=17&Cat=Trade%20&%20Economic%20Data/Policy&SubCat=U.S.%20Trade%20Data

U.S.-Arab Chamber of Commerce
http://www.nusacc.org/

U.S.-Saudi Business Council
https://us-sabc.org/services-2/

UL Standards
https://ulstandards.ul.com/about/understanding-standards/
standards-faq/

UN COMTRADE
https://comtrade.un.org/data

UN Regional Commissions
http://www.regionalcommissions.org/

UN/COMTRADE
https://comtrade.un.org/

UN/Foreign Import Statistics by Product and Country
https://www.intracen.org/itc/market-info-tools/trade-statistics/

UN/International Trade Centre Trade Map
https://www.trademap.org/

UN/International Trade Centre Website
https://www.intracen.org/itc/market-info-tools/trade-statistics/

U.S. Airport Information
https://www.globalair.com/airport/

U.S. Commercial Service (USCS)
https://www.trade.gov/let-our-experts-help-0

USDA/Animal and Plant Health Inspection Service
https://www.aphis.usda.gov/aphis/ourfocus/importexport

USDA/Federal Grain Inspection Service (FGIS)
https://www.ams.usda.gov/about-ams/programs-offices/federal-grain-inspection-service

USDA/Food Safety Inspection Service (FSIS)
https://www.fsis.usda.gov/wps/portal/fsis/home

USITC Trade DataWeb
https://dataweb.usitc.gov/

USITC/DataWeb
https://dataweb.usitc.gov/

Vaccines, Blood & Biologics
https://www.fda.gov/BiologicsBloodVaccines/default.htm

Venture Capital
https://nvca.org/

Website Localization
https://ibt.onl/services/website-localization

World Bank
https://www.worldbank.org/

World Bank International Business Opportunities
http://www.worldbank.org/html/opr/procure/bopage.html

World Freight Ship Companies
https://en.wikipedia.org/wiki/List_of_freight_ship_companies

World Trade Centers
https://www.wtca.org/

WTO Tariff Analysis Online
https://tao.wto.org/welcome.aspx?ReturnUrl=%2f%3fui%3d1&ui=1

WTO Tariff Schedules

http://tariffdata.wto.org/ReportersAndProducts.aspx

YouTube Ads

https://youtube.com/ads/

INDEX TO LINKED RESOURCES

Introduction

1. **Kogon/2011 Congressional Testimony on Exporting:** https://www.youtube.com/watch?v=P_YNaxEGMM
2. **ITCI/Exporting Basics:** http://www.tradecomplianceinstitute.org/x_plfls/Exporting%20Basics%20Final%20With%20Pegination%20for%20Wafer%20Drive.pdf
3. **ITCI/Export FAQ:** http://www.tradecomplianceinstitute.org/x_plfls/Export%20FAQs%20by%20Maurice%20Kogon%202014%20092114.pdf
4. **ITCI/Export Readiness Assessment System:** http://www.tradecomplianceinstitute.org/ERAS/

About the Author

1. **ITCI/Trade Information Database:** http://www.tradecomplianceinstitute.org/p_trade_info_database.php
2. **ITCI/International Trade Compliance Institute Website:** http://www.tradecomplianceinstitute.org/
3. **Milken/New-to-Export (NTE) 101-LA:** https://

milkeninstitute.org/reports/new-export-101-strengthening-capacity-us-regional-economies-export-abroad

4. **ITCI/Exporting Basics:** http://www.tradecomplianceinstitute. org/x_plfls/Exporting%20Basics%20Final%20With% 20Pegination%20for%20Wafer%20Drive.pdf

5. **ITCI/Export FAQ:** http://www.tradecomplianceinstitute.org/ x_plfls/Exporting%20Basics%20Final%20With%20Pegination% 20for%20Wafer%20Drive.pdf

6. **ITCI/Export Readiness Assessment System:** http://www. tradecomplianceinstitute.org/ERAS/

Chapter 1

1. **SBA/U.S. Small Business Administration:** https://www.sba. gov/category/navigation-structure/loans-grants/small-business-loans/sba-loan-programs/7a-loan-program/sb

2. **Exim/U.S. Export-Import Bank:** https://www.exim.gov/

3. **SBA/U.S. Small Business Administration:** https://www.sba. gov/category/navigation-structure/loans-grants/small-business-loans/sba-loan-programs/7a-loan-program/sb

4. **Exim/U.S. Export-Import Bank:** https://www.exim.gov/

5. **ITCI/Export Guides:** http://www.tradecomplianceinstitute. org/p_trade_info_db_links.php?SubCatID=2&Cat=Trade% 20Readiness%20Tools&SubCat=Export%20Guides

6. **ITCI/Webinar and Videos:** http://www. tradecomplianceinstitute.org/p_trade_info_db_links.php? SubCatID=10&Cat=Trade%20Readiness%20Tools&SubCat= Trade%20Tutorials%20-%20Webinars,%20Courses,%20Videos

7. **ITCI/Trade Information Database:** http://www. tradecomplianceinstitute.org/p_trade_info_database.php

8. **ITA/Trade.gov:** https://www.trade.gov/

9. **Search Engine Optimization:** https://en.wikipedia.org/ wiki/Search_engine_optimization

10. **Export Yellow Pages:** http://www.exportyellowpages.com/

11. **Letter of Credit:** https://globaltradefunding.com/trade-finance-solutions/export-financing/export-letter-of-credit/

12. **Exim/Export Credit Insurance:** https://www.exim.gov/what-we-do/export-credit-insurance
13. **ITA/International Company Profile:** https://www.trade.gov/international-company-profile
14. **ITCI/Foreign Trade Laws & Regulations:** http://www.tradecomplianceinstitute.org/p_trade_info_db_links.php?
15. **ITCI/Trade Information Database:** http://www.tradecomplianceinstitute.org/p_trade_info_database.php

Chapter 2

1. **ITCI/Export Readiness Assessment:** http://www.
tradecomplianceinstitute.org/p_trade_info_db_links.php?
SubCatID=1&Cat=Trade%20Readiness%20Tools&SubCat=
Export%20Readiness%20Assessment
2. **ITCI/Free Export Guides:** http://www.
tradecomplianceinstitute.org/p_trade_info_db_links.php?
SubCatID=2&Cat=Trade%20Readiness%20Tools&SubCat=
Export%20Guides
3. **ITCI/Trade Information Database:** http://www.
tradecomplianceinstitute.org/p_trade_info_database.php
4. **ITA/Trade.gov:** https://www.trade.gov/
5. **globalEDGE:** http://globaledge.msu.edu/
6. **USITC Dataweb:** https://dataweb.usitc.gov/
7. **UN/Intracen:** https://www.intracen.org/itc/market-info-
tools/trade-statistics/
8. **ITA/Country Commercial Guides:** https://www.trade.gov/
ccg-landing-page
9. **ITA/Top Market Series:** https://www.trade.gov/topmarkets/
10. **Export Yellow Pages:** http://www.exportyellowpages.com/
11. **ThinkGlobal/ExportUSA:** https://www.think.
global/#.VLsY4GB0zX4
12. **ITA/U.S. Export Assistance Center:** https://www.trade.gov/
us-commercial-service-office-map
13. **Exim/U.S. Export-Import Bank:** https://www.exim.gov
14. **Incoterms 2020:** https://incodocs.com/blog/incoterms-2020-
explained-the-complete-guide/

Chapter 3

1. **SBA/SBDCs:** https://www.sba.gov/local-assistance/find/?q=sbdc&pageNumber=1
2. **SBA/SCORE:** https://www.sba.gov/local-assistance/find/?q=score&pageNumber=1
3. **NIST/MEPs:** https://www.nist.gov/mep/centers
4. **SBA/Business Plan Templates:** https://www.sba.gov/business-guide/plan-your-business/write-your-business-plan
5. **NIST/MEP/ Product Design and Development:** https://www.nist.gov/mep/product-design-and-development
6. **SBA investment Loans:** https://www.sba.gov/funding-programs/investment-capital
7. **Bank Loans:** https://blog.yelp.com/2019/02/12-types-small-business-loans-funding
8. **Microloans:** https://www.fundera.com/business-loans/guides/microloans
9. **Crowdfunding:** https://www.crowdfunding.com/
10. **Angel Investors:** https://www.thebalancesmb.com/angel-investor-2947066
11. **Venture Capital:** https://nvca.org/
12. **ITCI/Export Readiness Assessment System:** http://www.tradecomplianceinstitute.org/ERAS/
13. **ITA/Exporter Assessments:** https://www.trade.gov/exporter-assessments
14. **ITA/U.S. Export Assistance Center:** https://www.trade.gov/us-commercial-service-office-map
15. **ITA/DECs:** https://www.usaexporter.org/local-dec-locator/
16. **State Trade Development Offices:** https://www.sidoamerica.org/
17. **Freight Forwarders:** https://ncbfaa.org/
18. **U.S. Commercial Banks:** https://www.usbanklocations.com/
19. **U.S. International Trade Lawyers:** https://www.hg.org/law-firms/usa-international-law.html
20. **ITCI/Web-Based Free Export Guides:** http://www.tradecomplianceinstitute.org/p_trade_info_db_links.php?

SubCatID=2&Cat=Trade%20Readiness%20Tools&SubCat=
Export%20Guides

21. **ITCI/Web-Based Export Tutorials:** http://www.
tradecomplianceinstitute.org/p_trade_info_db_links.php?
SubCatID=10&Cat=Trade%20Readiness%20Tools&SubCat=
Trade%20Tutorials%20-%20Webinars,%20Courses,%20Videos

22. **ITA/Upcoming DOC Webinars:** https://www.trade.gov/
trade-events-search#/search?start_date_range%5Bfrom%5D=
2019-12-01&start_date_range%5Bto%5D=2024-03-31&
event_types=Seminar-Webinar

23. **ITA/eCommerce Innovation Lab:** https://www.
trade.gov/ecommerce

24. **Getting to Global:** https://gettingtoglobal.org/

25. **State Trade Expansion Program:** https://www.sba.gov/
funding-programs/grants/state-trade-expansion-program-
step

26. **USITC/Dataweb:** https://dataweb.usitc.gov/

27. **ITA/Trade Stats Express:** https://tse.export.gov/

28. **UN/Foreign Import Statistics by Product and Country:**
https://www.intracen.org/itc/market-info-tools/trade-
statistics/

29. **ITA/Top Market Series:** https://www.trade.gov/topmarkets/

30. **Google/Market Finder:** https://www.thinkwithgoogle.com/
intl/en-gb/tools/market-finder/

31. **ITA/Sample Export Plan:** https://www.trade.gov/
sample-export-plan

32. **ITA/Country Commercial Guides:** https://www.trade.gov/
ccg-landing-page

33. **NIST/ExporTech Program:** https://www.nist.gov/exportech

34. **ITA/Search Trade Events:** https://www.trade.gov/trade-
events-search#/

35. **ITA/Trade Shows and Trade Missions Programs:** https://
www.trade.gov/attend-event

36. **Getting to Global:** https://gettingtoglobal.org/

37. **Export Pricing Strategy:** https://www.trade.gov/pricing-
strategy

38. **ITA/International Partner Search (IPS):** https://www.export.gov/International-Partner-Search
39. **ITA/Gold Key Service:** https://www.export.gov/Gold-Key-Service
40. **ITA/International Company Profile (ICP):** https://www.export.gov/International-Company-Profile
41. **ITA/International Partner Agreements:** https://www.trade.gov/negotiating-agreement-foreign-representative
42. **ITA/Pricing Strategy:** https://www.trade.gov/pricing-strategy
43. **Incoterms 2020:** https://globalnegotiator.com/files/incoterms-2020-book.pdf
44. **SBA/Export Working Capital Guaranty Program:** https://www.sba.gov/sites/default/files/articles/oit_export_cap_prgm_business_0.pdf
45. **Exim/Export Working Capital Guaranty Program:** https://www.exim.gov/what-we-do/working-capital
46. **ITA/Trade Finance Guide:** https://grow.exim.gov/hs-fs/hub/421983/file-2055772500-pdf/Guides/trade-guide.pdf
47. **Exim/Export Credit Insurance:** https://www.exim.gov/what-we-do/export-credit-insurance
48. **Meridian Export Insurance:** http://www.meridianfinance.com/insurance/
49. **Brett Tarnet Insurance Services:** https://tarnetinsurance.com/
50. **ITA/Protect Your Intellectual Property:** https://www.trade.gov/protect-intellectual-property
51. **ITA/BIS/Export Administration Regulations:** https://www.bis.doc.gov/index.php/regulations/export-administration-regulations-ear
52. **State/International Traffic in Arms Regulations:** https://www.pmddtc.state.gov/regulations_laws/itar.html/?id=ddtc_kb_article_page&sys_id=%2024d528fddbfc930044f9ff621f961987

Chapter 4

1. **ITCI/Export Readiness Assessment:** http://www.
   tradecomplianceinstitute.org/p_trade_info_db_links.php?
   SubCatID=1&Cat=Trade%20Readiness%20Tools&SubCat=
   Export%20Readiness%20Assessment
2. **Schedule B:** https://www.census.gov/foreign-trade/
   schedules/b/index.html#search
3. **Harmonized System:** https://www.foreign-trade.com/
   reference/hscode.htm
4. **USITC Trade DataWeb:** https://dataweb.usitc.gov/
5. **UN/International Trade Centre Website:** https://www.
   intracen.org/itc/market-info-tools/trade-statistics/
6. **ITCI/Export Readiness Assessment:** http://www.
   tradecomplianceinstitute.org/p_trade_info_db_links.php?
   SubCatID=1&Cat=Trade%20Readiness%20Tools&SubCat=
   Export%20Readiness%20Assessment
7. **Economic Development Agencies:** https://www.
   eda.gov/resources/
8. **World Trade Centers:** https://www.wtca.org/
9. **Chambers of Commerce:** https://www.chamber-
   commerce.net/
10. **State Trade Development Offices:** https://www.
    sidoamerica.org/
11. **SBA/State Trade Expansion Program:** https://www.sba.gov/
    funding-programs/grants/state-trade-expansion-program-step
12. **International Trade Administration:** https://www.trade.gov/
13. **Foreign Agricultural Service:** https://www.fas.usda.gov/
14. **Small Business Administration:** https://www.sba.gov/
15. **Export-Import Bank:** https://www.exim.gov/
16. **Trade and Development Agency:** https://www.ustda.gov/
17. **U.S. Commercial Service (USCS):** https://www.trade.gov/let-
    our-experts-help-0
18. **ITA/U.S. Export Assistance Center:** https://www.trade.gov/
    us-commercial-service-office-map

19. **ITA/Trade Missions:** https://www.trade.gov/trade-missions
20. **ITA/Trade Shows:** https://www.trade.gov/trade-shows
21. **ITA/International Partner Search:** https://www.trade.gov/international-partner-search
22. **ITA/Gold Key Matching Service:** https://www.trade.gov/gold-key-service
23. **ITA/International Company Profile (ICP):** https://www.export.gov/International-Company-Profile
24. **ITA/Foreign Commercial Service (FCS):** https://www.afsa.org/foreign-commercial-service
25. **ITA/Directory of U.S. Commercial Offices:** https://www.trade.gov/let-our-experts-help-0
26. **ITA/Directory of Overseas Commercial Offices:** https://2016.export.gov/worldwide_us/index.asp
27. **FAS Web Portal:** https://www.fas.usda.gov/
28. **FAS/Market Research:** https://www.fas.usda.gov/data
29. **FAS/Agricultural Trade Promotion Program:** https://www.fas.usda.gov/programs/agricultural-trade-promotion-program-atp
30. **FAS/Emerging Markets Program:** https://www.fas.usda.gov/programs/emerging-markets-program-emp
31. **FAS/Export Credit Guarantee Program:** https://www.fas.usda.gov/programs/export-credit-guarantee-program-gsm-102
32. **FAS/Foreign Market Development (FMD) Program:** https://www.fas.usda.gov/programs/foreign-market-development-program-fmd
33. **SBA/Office of International Trade:** https://www.sba.gov/offices/headquarters/oit
34. **SBA/Small Business Development Centers:** https://www.sba.gov/offices/headquarters/osbdc/resources/11409
35. **SBA/SCORE:** https://www.sba.gov/local-assistance/find/?q=score&pageNumber=1
36. **TDA/Project Preparation Assistance Program:** https://ustda.gov/about/

37. **TDA/Reverse Trade Mission Program:** https://ustda.gov/about/
38. **ITCI/Trade Information Database:** http://www.tradecomplianceinstitute.org/p_trade_info_database.php
39. **ITA/Trade.gov:** https://www.trade.gov/learn-how-export
40. **FAS.gov:** https://www.fas.usda.gov/
41. **globalEDGE:** https://globaledge.msu.edu/
42. **ITCI/Export Start-Up Kit:** http://www.tradecomplianceinstitute.org/p_export_import_basics.php
43. **ITCI/Trade Information Database:** http://www.tradecomplianceinstitute.org/p_trade_info_database.php
44. **ITCI/TID Categories and Subjects Covered:** http://www.tradecomplianceinstitute.org/p_trade_info_database.php
45. **FAS/Commodities and Products:** https://www.fas.usda.gov/commodities
46. **FAS/Countries and Regions:** https://www.fas.usda.gov/regions
47. **FAS/Data and Analysis:** https://www.fas.usda.gov/data
48. **FAS/Trade Programs:** https://www.fas.usda.gov/programs
49. **globalEDGE:** https://globaledge.msu.edu/
50. **globalEDGE/Global Resources:** https://globaledge.msu.edu/global-resources
51. **globalEdge/Export Tutorials:** https://globaledge.msu.edu/reference-desk/export-tutorials
52. **globalEdge/Diagnostic Tools:** https://globaledge.msu.edu/tools-and-data/diagnostic-tools
53. **globalEdge/Industry-and Country Information:** https://globaledge.msu.edu/global-insights
54. **UN Regional Commissions:** http://www.regionalcommissions.org/
55. **UN/COMTRADE:** https://comtrade.un.org/
56. **World Bank:** https://www.worldbank.org/
57. **International Monetary Fund:** https://www.imf.org/external/index.htm
58. **Euromonitor:** https://www.marketresearch.com/Euromonitor-International-v746/

59. **Internet World Stats:** https://www.internetworldstats.com/stats.htm
60. **Kompass:** https://us.kompass.com/
61. **D&B Hoovers:** https://www.dnb.com/
62. **PIERS:** https://ihsmarkit.com/products/piers.html
63. **Datamyne:** https://www.datamyne.com/
64. **Panjiva:** https://panjiva.com/
65. **U.S. Export Import Bank:** https://www.exim.gov/
66. **SBA/Small Business Administration:** https://www.sba.gov/
67. **SBA/State Trade Expansion Programs:** https://www.sba.gov/funding-programs/grants/state-trade-expansion-program-step
68. **Exim/Export Working Capital Guaranty Program:** https://www.exim.gov/what-we-do/working-capital
69. **Exim/Medium–and Long-Term Financing for Foreign Buyers:** https://www.exim.gov/what-we-do/finance-a-foreign-buyer-purchase
70. **Exim/Export Credit Insurance:** https://www.exim.gov/what-we-do/export-credit-insurance
71. **Exim/Video Gallery:** https://www.exim.gov/learning-resources/video-gallery/how-to
72. **Exim/Webinars:** https://www.exim.gov/learning-resources/video-gallery/196
73. **SBA/Export Working Capital Guaranty Program:** https://www.sba.gov/content/financing-your-small-business-exports-foreign-investments-or-projects-0
74. **SBA/Export Express:** https://www.sba.gov/category/type-loan/export-express
75. **SBA/State Trade Expansion Program (STEP):** https://www.sba.gov/document/support--state-trade-expansion-program-step-grant-application-instructions
76. **FAS/Export Credit Guarantee Program:** https://www.fas.usda.gov/programs/export-credit-guarantee-program-gsm-102
77. **FAS/Foreign Market Development (FMD) Program:** https://

www.fas.usda.gov/programs/foreign-market-development-program-fmd

78. **FAS/Western U.S. Trade Association:** https://www.fas.usda.gov/programs/foreign-market-development-program-fmd

79. **FAS/Southern U.S. Trade Association:** https://www.susta.org/whatwedo/overview/

80. **FAS/FundMatch Program:** https://www.wusata.org/whatwedo/fundmatchprogram/

81. **FAS/50% CostShare Program:** https://www.susta.org/whatwedo/costshare/

82. **Directory of International Commercial Banks in U.S.:** https://www.federalreserve.gov/releases/lbr/current/

83. **National Customs Brokers & Freight Forwarders Association:** https://www.ncbfaa.org/Scripts/4Disapi.dll/4DCGI/index.html

84. **District Export Council:** https://www.usaexporter.org/

Chapter 5

1. **ITCI Trade Information Database:** http://www.tradecomplianceinstitute.org/p_trade_info_database.php

2. **USITC/DataWeb:** https://dataweb.usitc.gov/

3. **ITA/Trade Stats Express:** http://tse.export.gov/tse/tsehome.aspx

4. **UN COMTRADE:** https://comtrade.un.org/data

5. **UN/International Trade Centre Trade Map:** https://www.trademap.org/

6. **ITA/Country Commercial Guides:** https://www.trade.gov/ccg-landing-page

7. **ITA/Top Market Series:** https://www.trade.gov/topmarkets/

8. **ITCI/World Economic and Demographic Data:** http://www.tradecomplianceinstitute.org/p_trade_info_db_links.php?SubCatID=19&Cat=Trade%20&%20Economic%20Data/Policy&SubCat=World%20Economic%20&%20Demographic%20Data

9. **ITCI/Trade Information Database:** http://www.
tradecomplianceinstitute.org/p_trade_info_database.php

10. **U.S. Trade Statistics:** http://www.tradecomplianceinstitute.org/
p_trade_info_db_links.php?SubCatID=17&Cat=Trade%20&%
20Economic%20Data/Policy&SubCat=U.S.%20Trade%20Data

11. **USITC/DataWeb:** https://dataweb.usitc.gov/

12. **ITA/Trade Stats Express:** http://tse.export.
gov/tse/tsehome.aspx

13. **Foreign trade statistics:** http://www.tradecomplianceinstitute.
org/p_trade_info_db_links.php?SubCatID=18&Cat=Trade%
20&%20Economic%20Data/Policy&SubCat=Foreign%
20Trade%20Data

14. **UN COMTRADE:** https://comtrade.un.org/data

15. **UN/International Trade Centre:** https://www.trademap.org/

16. **ITA/Country Commercial Guides:** https://www.trade.gov/
ccg-landing-page

17. **ITA/Manufactures and Services Research:** https://legacy.
trade.gov/industry/

18. **ITA/Customized Market Research:** https://www.trade.gov/
customized-market-research

19. **ITA/Top Market Series:** https://www.trade.gov/topmarkets/

20. **ITA/Country Commercial Guides:** https://www.trade.gov/
ccg-landing-page

21. **ITA/Top Market Series:** https://legacy.trade.gov/topmarkets/

22. **ITA/Customized Market Research:** https://www.trade.gov/
customized-market-research

23. **Food and Drink Prohibitions:** https://en.wikipedia.org/
wiki/Food_and_drink_prohibitions

24. **Colors Across Cultures:** https://www.globalme.net/blog/
colours-across-cultures

25. **20 Epic Fails in Global Branding:** https://www.inc.com/
geoffrey-james/the-20-worst-brand-translations-of-all-
time.html

26. **High Context Cultures:** https://culturematters.com/what-is-
high-context-culture/

27. **Body Language And Gestures Across The World:** https://translit.ie/blog/body-language-gestures-across-world/
28. **Foreign Corrupt Practices Act:** https://www.justice.gov/criminal-fraud/foreign-corrupt-practices-act
29. **ITCI/Intercultural Research:** http://www.tradecomplianceinstitute.org/p_trade_info_db_links.php?SubCatID=27&Cat=Foreign%20Market%20Research&SubCat=Intercultural%20Research
30. **ITCI/Trade Information Database:** http://www.tradecomplianceinstitute.org/p_trade_info_database.php
31. **ITA/Top Market Series:** https://www.trade.gov/topmarkets/
32. **ITA/Country Commercial Guides:** https://www.trade.gov/ccg-landing-page
33. **Kwintessential Global Guide to Etiquette:** https://www.kwintessential.co.uk/resources-types/guides
34. **Passport to Trade—Business Etiquette—31 Countries:** https://businessculture.org/business-culture/
35. **Country Intercultural Insights:** http://www.intercultures.ca/cil-cai/countryinsights-apercuspays-eng.asp
36. **Country Guides:** https://www.bsicorp.net/articles/country-guides
37. **Keys to Success:** https://www.bsicorp.net/articles/keys-to-success
38. **State/National Trade Estimate Reports on Foreign Trade Barriers:** https://ustr.gov/sites/default/files/files/Press/Reports/2018%20National%20Trade%20Estimate%20Report.pdf
39. **ITA/Country Commercial Guides:** https://www.trade.gov/ccg-landing-page
40. **ITA/Top Market Series:** https://www.trade.gov/topmarkets/
41. **EU/Market Access Sectoral and Trade Barriers Database:** http://madb.europa.eu/madb/barriers_select.htm
42. **Search Engine Optimization:** https://en.wikipedia.org/wiki/Search_engine_optimization
43. **Guide to Website Internationalization:** https://thenextweb.

com/dd/2011/05/20/web-design-with-the-world-in-mind-a-guide-to-website-internationalization/

44. **Website Localization:** https://ibt.onl/services/website-localization

45. **Guide to Website Internationalization:** https://thenextweb.com/dd/2011/05/20/web-design-with-the-world-in-mind-a-guide-to-website-internationalization/

46. **Google Ads:** https://ads.google.com/home/

47. **YouTube Ads:** https://youtube.com/ads/

48. **Facebook Ads Manager:** https://www.facebook.com/business/tools/ads-manager

49. **LinkedIn Leads:** https://linkedupsales.com/

50. **Spam:** https://en.wikipedia.org/wiki/Email_spam

51. **ITCI/Directories of Manufacturers:** http://www.tradecomplianceinstitute.org/p_trade_info_db_links.php?SubCatID=29&Cat=Trade%20Contacts%20&%20Leads&SubCat=U.S.%20Producers%20&%20Exporters

52. **Export Yellow Pages:** http://www.exportyellowpages.com/

53. **ExportUSA:** http://thinkglobal.com/exusa/exusa#.VMfurGB0zX4

54. **Alibaba:** http://www.alibaba.com/

55. **ITA/Gold Key:** https://www.trade.gov/gold-key-service

56. **AUMA Trade Show Directory:** https://www.auma.de/en/exhibit/find-your-exhibitions?typ=erw

57. **ITA/Trade Show Directory:** https://www.trade.gov/trade-events-search#/

58. **ITA/Trade Event Partnership Program:** https://www.trade.gov/tepp-faqs

59. **ITA/Trade Missions:** https://www.trade.gov/trade-events-search#/

60. **ITCI/Trade Information Database:** http://www.tradecomplianceinstitute.org/p_trade_info_database.php

61. **ITCI/Hot Trade Leads:** http://www.tradecomplianceinstitute.org/p_trade_info_db_links.php?SubCatID=31&Cat=Trade%20Contacts%20&%20Leads&SubCat=Hot%20Trade%20Leads

62. **World Bank International Business Opportunities:** http://www.worldbank.org/html/opr/procure/bopage.html

63. **African Development Bank Business Opportunities:** http://www.afdb.org/

64. **Asian Development Bank Business Opportunities:** http://www.adb.org/Business/Opportunities/

65. **European Bank's Procurement Opportunities:** http://www.ebrd.com/pages/project.shtml

66. **Inter-American Development Bank Projects:** http://www.iadb.org/projects/index.cfm?language=english

67. **North American Development Bank Information:** http://www.nadbank.org/projects/procurementinfo.html

68. **Trade Development Agency (TDA) Pipeline:** http://www.tda.gov/pipeline/index.html

69. **Trade Development Agency (TDA) Feasibility Studies & Projects:** http://www.tda.gov/library/search_criteria.cfm

70. **ITCI/Directories of Foreign Manufacturers and Importers:** http://www.tradecomplianceinstitute.org/p_trade_info_db_links.php?SubCatID=30&Cat=Trade%20Contacts%20&%20Leads&SubCat=Foreign%20Manufacturers%20&%20Importers

71. **ITA/International Partner Search:** https://www.trade.gov/international-partner-search

72. **ITA/Gold Key Matching:** https://www.trade.gov/gold-key-service

73. **ITA/International Company Profile:** https://www.trade.gov/international-company-profile

74. **International Credit Reporting Agencies:** http://fita.org/webindex/browse.cgi/International_Finance_Letters_of_Credit_and_Investment/Credit_Reporting_Services_and_Debt_Recovery/Credit_Reporting_Services

75. **Negotiating International Partner Agreements:** https://www.trade.gov/negotiating-agreement-foreign-representative

Chapter 6

1. **International Credit Reporting Agencies:** http://fita.org/webindex/browse.cgi/International_Finance_Letters_of_Credit_and_Investment/Credit_Reporting_Services_and_Debt_Recovery/Credit_Reporting_Services
2. **Equifax International Credit Reports:** https://www.equifax.com/pdfs/corp/CS_108_International_Credit_Reports_0204.pdf
3. **Experian International Business Credit Reports:** https://sbcr.experian.com/main.aspx
4. **FCIB Worldwide Credit Reports:** https://fcibglobal.com/credit-country-reports/worldwide-credit-reports.html
5. **Coface Analyze my Customers and Prospects:** https://www.coface-usa.com/Our-Offer/Analyze-my-Customers-and-Prospects
6. **Coface Debtor Risk Assessments:** https://www.coface-usa.com/Our-Offer/Analyze-my-Customers-and-Prospects/Debtor-Risk-Assessments
7. **Dun & Bradstreet (D&B) Credit Evaluator Plus:** https://businesscredit.dnb.com/monitor-other-company-business-credit/
8. **Graydon's International Credit Reports:** https://www.graydon.nl/en/credit-management/clientacceptance/international-credit-report
9. **ITA/International Company Profile:** https://www.trade.gov/international-company-profile
10. **International Commercial Term:** https://globalnegotiator.com/files/incoterms-2020-book.pdf
11. **Proforma Invoice:** https://www.shippingsolutions.com/proforma-invoice-english
12. **Cash in Advance:** https://2016.export.gov/tradefinanceguide/eg_main_043222.asp
13. **Factoring:** https://www.mbaknol.com/business-finance/factoring-concept-in-export-finance/

14. **Letters of Credit:** https://www.thebalance.com/types-of-letters-of-credit-315040
15. **Documentary Collections:** https://www.shippingsolutions.com/blog/methods-of-payment-in-international-trade-documentary-collections
16. **Documents Against Payment:** https://www.wisegeek.com/what-are-documents-against-payment.htm
17. **Documents Against Acceptance:** https://www.wisegeek.com/what-are-documents-against-acceptance.htm
18. **Exim/Export Credit Insurance:** https://www.exim.gov/what-we-do/protect-against-buyer-nonpayment
19. **Open Account:** https://globaltradefunding.com/trade-finance-solutions/import-financing/open-accounts/
20. **Exim/Export Credit Insurance Policy:** https://www.exim.gov/what-we-do/protect-against-buyer-nonpayment

Chapter 7

1. **Export Control Classification Number:** https://www.bis.doc.gov/index.php/licensing/commerce-control-list-classification/export-control-classification-number-eccn
2. **ITA/Bureau of Industry and Security:** https://www.bis.doc.gov/
3. **State/Directorate of Defense Trade Controls:** https://www.pmddtc.state.gov/ddtc_public
4. **State/International Traffic in Arms Regulations:** https://www.pmddtc.state.gov/ddtc_public?id=ddtc_kb_article_page&sys_id=24d528fddbfc930044f9ff621f961987
5. **Munitions List:** https://www.ecfr.gov/cgi-bin/retrieveECFR?gp=&SID=70e390c181ea17f847fa696c47e3140a&mc=true&r=PART&n=pt22.1.121
6. **ITA/Export Administration Regulations:** https://www.bis.doc.gov/index.php/regulations/export-administration-regulations-ear

7. **Commerce Control List:** https://www.bis.doc.gov/index. php/regulations/commerce-control-list-ccl
8. **Automated Export System:** https://www.cbp.gov/ trade/aes/introduction
9. **Denied Persons List:** https://www.bis.doc.gov/index.php/ policy-guidance/lists-of-parties-of-concern/denied-persons-list
10. **Denied Entities List:** https://www.bis.doc.gov/index.php/ policy-guidance/lists-of-parties-of-concern/entity-list
11. **Treasury/Office of Foreign Assets Control:** https://www. treasury.gov/about/organizational-structure/offices/Pages/ Office-of-Foreign-Assets-Control.aspx
12. **Foreign Assets Control Regulations:** https://www.gpo.gov/ fdsys/granule/CFR-2004-title31-vol2/CFR-2004-title31-vol2-part500/content-detail.html
13. **Phytosanitary Certificate:** http://www.aphis.usda.gov/ import_export/plants/plant_exports/downloads/ppq572.pdf
14. **Export Certificates:** http://www.fda.gov/Food/ GuidanceRegulation/ImportsExports/Exporting/ ucm2006911.htm
15. **Transportation/Pipeline and Hazardous Materials Safety Admin:** https://www.phmsa.dot.gov/regulations-and-compliance
16. **Hazardous Materials Regulations:** https://www.phmsa.dot. gov/approvals-and-permits/hazmat/hazardous-materials-approvals-and-permits-overview
17. **USDA/Animal and Plant Health Inspection Service:** https:// www.aphis.usda.gov/aphis/ourfocus/importexport
18. **Phytosanitary Certificates:** http://www.fao.org/docrep/004/ y3241e/y3241e06.htm
19. **USDA/Federal Grain Inspection Service (FGIS):** https:// www.ams.usda.gov/about-ams/programs-offices/federal-grain-inspection-service
20. **USDA/Food Safety Inspection Service (FSIS):** https://www. fsis.usda.gov/wps/portal/fsis/home
21. **FDA/Food & Drug Administration:** https://www.fda.gov/

22. **FDA/Compliance and Enforcement:** https://www.fda.gov/Food/ComplianceEnforcement/default.htm

23. **Medical Devices:** https://www.fda.gov/MedicalDevices/default.htm

24. **Radiation-Emitting Products:** https://www.fda.gov/Radiation-EmittingProducts/default.htm

25. **Drugs:** https://www.fda.gov/Drugs/default.htm

26. **Vaccines, Blood & Biologics:** https://www.fda.gov/BiologicsBloodVaccines/default.htm

27. **Cosmetics:** https://www.fda.gov/Cosmetics/default.htm

28. **Certificates of Free Sale:** https://www.fda.gov/RegulatoryInformation/Guidances/ucm125789.htm

29. **Foreign Corrupt Practices Act (FCPA):** https://www.justice.gov/criminal-fraud/foreign-corrupt-practices-act

30. **Anti-Boycott Regulations:** https://www.bis.doc.gov/index.php/enforcement/oac

31. **ITA/Office of Anti-Boycott Compliance:** https://www.bis.doc.gov/index.php/enforcement/oac

32. **Freight Forwarders:** https://en.wikipedia.org/wiki/Freight_forwarder

33. **U.S. Export Assistance Centers:** https://www.trade.gov/us-commercial-service-office-map

34. **ITCI/U.S. National Security Export Controls (EAR, ITAR, FACR):** http://www.tradecomplianceinstitute.org/p_trade_info_db_links.php?SubCatID=93&Cat=Trade/Investment%20Regulations&SubCat=U.S.%20National%20Security%20Export%20Controls%20(EAR,%20ITAR,%20FACR)

35. **ITCI/Other U.S. Export Laws & Regulations:** http://www.tradecomplianceinstitute.org/p_trade_info_db_links.php?SubCatID=34&Cat=Trade/Investment%20Regulations&SubCat=Other%20U.S.%20Export%20Laws%20&%20Regulations

36. **Tariffs:** https://theconversation.com/what-is-a-tariff-an-economist-explains-93392?gclid=EAIaIQobChMInpDtgem54gIVjMpkCh2EtwsdEAAYAS

AAEgKO8_D_BwE

37. **Harmonized System (HS) Code:** https://www.trade.gov/harmonized-system-hs-codes

38. **Free Trade Agreements:** https://ustr.gov/trade-agreements/free-trade-agreements

39. **Tariff Engineering:** http://www.barnesrichardson.com/4E8FDC/assets/files/News/tariff-engineering.pdf

40. **WTO Tariff Schedules:** http://tariffdata.wto.org/ReportersAndProducts.aspx

41. **WTO Tariff Analysis Online:** https://tao.wto.org/welcome.aspx?ReturnUrl=%2f%3fui%3d1&ui=1

42. **FTA Tariff Search Tool by Country:** https://beta.trade.gov/fta/tariff-rates-search

43. **Japan Import Tariffs:** http://www.customs.go.jp/english/tariff/index.htm

44. **Canadian Customs Tariff:** http://www.cbsa-asfc.gc.ca/trade-commerce/tariff-tarif/2013/menu-eng.html

45. **EU Tariff Lookup:** http://exporthelp.europa.eu/thdapp/taric/TaricServlet?languageId=EN&CFID=4177607&CFTOKEN=15605945&jsessionid=6430f1f6fda46d362b4b

46. **UL Standards:** https://ulstandards.ul.com/about/understanding-standards/standards-faq/

47. **CE (Conformité Européenne) Mark:** https://europa.eu/youreurope/business/product/ce-mark/index_en.htm

48. **EC Directives:** https://en.wikipedia.org/wiki/Directive_(European_Union)

49. **31 Countries:** https://en.wikipedia.org/wiki/Foreign_exchange_controls#Countries_with_current_foreign_exchange_controls

50. **Corruption Perceptions Index:** https://www.transparency.org/whatwedo/publication/corruption-perceptions-index

51. **Foreign Corrupt Practices Act:** https://www.justice.gov/criminal-fraud/foreign-corrupt-practices-act

52. **ITA/Country Commercial Guides:** https://www.trade.gov/ccg-landing-page

53. **State/National Trade Estimate Reports on Foreign Trade**

Barriers: https://ustr.gov/sites/default/files/files/Press/Reports/2018%20National%20Trade%20Estimate%20Report.pdf

54. **EU/Market Access Sectoral and Trade Barriers Database:** http://madb.europa.eu/madb/barriers_select.htm

55. **ITCI/International Legal Resources:** http://www.tradecomplianceinstitute.org/p_trade_info_db_links.php?SubCatID=37&Cat=Trade/Investment%20Regulations&SubCat=International%20Legal%20Resources

56. **ACE:** https://www.cbp.gov/trade/automated

57. **ACE—Getting Started:** https://www.cbp.gov/trade/automated/getting-started

58. **AESDirect:** https://www.census.gov/foreign-trade/aes/aesdirect/transitiontoace.html

59. **Electronic Export Information:** https://www.census.gov/foreign-trade/regulations/forms/index.html#sed

60. **AES User Guide:** https://www.census.gov/foreign-trade/aes/aesdirect/AESDirect-User-Guide.pdf

61. **EEI filing Instructions:** https://aesdirect.census.gov/download/userguide/AESDirectSampleShipment.pdf

62. **Registering for AESDirect:** http://www.census.gov/foreign-trade/aes/exporttraining/videos/uscs_videos/Registering_for_AES_direct/index.html

63. **Filing a Shipment in AESDirect:** http://www.census.gov/foreign-trade/aes/exporttraining/videos/uscs_videos/Filing_a_shipment_with_AES/index.html

64. **AES Response Messages:** http://www.census.gov/foreign-trade/aes/exporttraining/videos/uscs_videos/Response_messages_using_AES/index.html

65. **AES Proof of Filing Citations:** http://www.census.gov/foreign-trade/aes/exporttraining/videos/uscs_videos/Proof_of_filing_citations/index.html

66. **AESDirect—The Shipment Manager:** http://www.census.gov/foreign-trade/aes/exporttraining/videos/uscs_videos/shipment_manager/index.html

67. **Elimination of the SSN in the AES:** http://www.census.gov/foreign-trade/data/video003.html
68. **Simplified Network Application Process Redesign (SNAP-R):** https://www.bis.doc.gov/index.php/licensing/simplified-network-application-process-redesign-snap-r
69. **Consular Invoice:** https://maxfreights.com/what-is-a-consular-invoice/
70. **Phytosanitary Certificates:** https://www.aphis.usda.gov/aphis/ourfocus/planthealth/sa_export/sa_forms/ct_export_certificates_forms
71. **Certificate of Free Sale:** https://www.fda.gov/regulatory-information/search-fda-guidance-documents/fda-export-certificates
72. **Pre-Shipment Inspection (PSI) Certificate:** http://www.omicnet.com/omicnet/pdf/psiguide.pdf
73. **Certificate of Origin:** https://www.shippingsolutions.com/download-certificate-of-origin-forms
74. **Certificate of Origin Form:** https://www.cbp.gov/document/guidance/certification-origin-template
75. **U.S.-Arab Chamber of Commerce:** http://www.nusacc.org/
76. **American Egyptian Cooperation Foundation:** https://www.guidestar.org/profile/54-1402264
77. **U.S.-Saudi Business Council:** https://us-sabc.org/services-2/
78. **USMCA Certificate of Origin:** https://www.usmcacertificate.com/wp-content/uploads/2020/05/USMCA-Certificate-of-Origin-Form-Sample-May-8-2020.pdf
79. **Free Trade Agreements:** https://ustr.gov/trade-agreements/free-trade-agreements
80. **Proforma Invoices:** https://www.shippingsolutions.com/proforma-invoice-english
81. **Commercial Invoices:** https://en.wikipedia.org/wiki/Commercial_invoice
82. **Export Packing Lists:** https://www.dripcapital.com/resources/blog/export-packing-list
83. **Export Packing List Sample:** https://www.pdffiller.com/

jsfiller-desk12/?projectId=
484984095#24018b5a5a5f5dcd38223cc4e1f3912e

84. **Dock Receipt Sample:** https://www.pdffiller.com/jsfiller-
desk15/?projectId=
484987085#afa94e142dc972ca331b9d9e29dd3f58

85. **Bills of Lading:** https://www.shippingsolutions.com/
download-bill-of-lading-forms

86. **Ocean Bill of Lading:** https://www.shippingsolutions.com/
download-bill-of-lading-forms#ocean

87. **Ocean B/L Sample:** https://www.shippingsolutions.com/
ocean-bill-of-lading

88. **Straight B/L:** http://export.gov/static/
form_12_2_Latest_eg_main_044741.pdf

89. **Air Waybill:** https://blanker.org/air-waybill

90. **Air Waybill Sample:** https://www.ups.com/aircargo/using/
services/supplies/airwaybill.html

91. **International Air Transport Association:** https://www.
iata.org/

92. **International Maritime Organization:** http://www.imo.org/
EN/Pages/Default.aspx

Chapter 8

1. **Freight Forwarders:** https://graduateway.com/role-and-
function-of-freight-forwarders/

2. **International Plant Protection Convention:** https://www.
ippc.int/en/

3. **International Standards for Phytosanitary Measures:** https://
www.ippc.int/en/core-activities/standards-setting/ispms/

4. **Dangerous Goods Packaging:** https://www.faa.gov/hazmat/
safecargo/how_to_ship/package_for_shipping/

5. **Marking and Labeling Regulations:** https://www.trade.gov/
trade-search?q=labeling

Chapter 9

1. **Marine Insurance:** https://www.marineinsight.com/know-more/what-is-marine-insurance/
2. **ExWorks—EXW:** https://www.incotermsexplained.com/the-incoterms-rules/the-eleven-rules-in-brief/ex-works/
3. **Cost Insurance & Freight (CIF):** https://www.incotermsexplained.com/the-incoterms-rules/the-eleven-rules-in-brief/cost-insurance-freight/
4. **General Average:** https://www.marineinsight.com/maritime-law/the-role-of-general-average-in-the-maritime-industry/
5. **International Insurance Carrier:** https://www.internationalinsurance.com/companies.php
6. **Freight Forwarder:** https://www.forwarders.com/index.html
7. **Free Alongside Ship:** https://www.incotermsexplained.com/the-incoterms-rules/the-eleven-rules-in-brief/free-alongside-ship/
8. **Free on Board:** https://www.incotermsexplained.com/the-incoterms-rules/the-eleven-rules-in-brief/free-board/
9. **Cost & Freight:** https://www.incotermsexplained.com/the-incoterms-rules/the-eleven-rules-in-brief/cost-freight/
10. **National Customs Bureau and Freight Forwarders Association:** https://ncbfaa.org/
11. **Los Angeles Customs Bureau and Freight Forwarders Association:** https://www.lacbffa.org/cpages/about
12. **U.S. Airport Information:** https://www.globalair.com/airport/
13. **FreightWorld:** http://www.freightworld.com/
14. **Container Shipping:** http://www.containershipping.com/
15. **U.S. Flag Carriers:** https://www.maritime.dot.gov/sites/marad.dot.gov/files/docs/ports/cargo-preference/2841/us-flag-contact-list_0.pdf
16. **World Freight Ship Companies:** https://en.wikipedia.org/wiki/List_of_freight_ship_companies
17. **FITA:** http://fita.org/
18. **FITA Comprehensive Directory of Associations:** http://fita.

org/webindex/browse.cgi/
International_Transportation_and_Logistics/Transportation_A
ssociationsOrganizations

Appendix B

1. **Schedule B Export Codes:** https://www.census.gov/foreign-trade/schedules/b/index.html#search
2. **Harmonized System (HS) Codes:** https://www.foreign-trade.com/reference/hscode.htm
3. **Harmonized Tariff Schedule of the United States (HTSUSA) Codes:** https://www.usitc.gov/harmonized_tariff_information
4. **Standard International Trade Classification (SITC) Codes:** https://unstats.un.org/unsd/classifications/Econ/Download/In%20Text/CPCprov_english.pdf
5. **North American Industry Classification System (NAICS) Codes:** https://www.census.gov/eos/www/naics/2017NAICS/2017_NAICS_Manual.pdf

Appendix C

1. **ITCI Market Research Portal:** http://www.tradecomplianceinstitute.org/p_trade_info_database.php

Appendix G

1. **International Chamber of Commerce (ICC):** https://iccwbo.org/resources-for-business/incoterms-rules/incoterms-2020/
2. **Incoterms 2020:** https://www.shippingsolutions.com/hubfs/download-assets/Incoterms%C2%AE%2020
3. **Incoterms 2020 Rules: Chart of Responsibilities and Transfer of Risk:** https://www.shippingsolutions.com/incoterms-chart-of-responsibilities
4. **Incoterms 2020 Webinar:** https://www.shippingsolutions.com/incoterms-2020-in-practice

Appendix I

1. **ITCI/U.S. Regulatory and Enforcement Agencies:** http://
   www.tradecomplianceinstitute.org/p_trade_info_db_links.
   php?SubCatID=90&Cat=Trade%20Resources%20Directory&
   SubCat=U.S.%20Government%20Trade%
   20Regulatory%20Organizations

CPSIA information can be obtained
at www.ICGtesting.com
Printed in the USA
LVHW081638140822
725923LV00007B/357